Money, Markets and Capital

Money and payments are familiar to everybody. Economists, however, are often at a loss in assessing the extent to which money matters. As a matter of fact, money is at the origin of the main cleavage in economic theory. Beyond sophisticated models what is at stake is whether money is just an appearance which hides the essence of economic life (value and happiness of people) or, on the contrary, the very substance of economic relations, not limited to exchanges, in which power and sovereignty are ever present.

In a first part, the author shows how fragile and shaky are the attempts made by value theoreticians to integrate money into their analysis. In a second part, he develops a rigorous alternative theory by giving strong logical foundations to a monetary analysis in the spirit of Keynes. Many important economic phenomena left unexplained by academic theory are accounted for (involuntary equilibrium unemployment), a new method in dynamics is resorted to (viability theory) and various economic relations are elucidated which are not reducible to exchange, the only one dealt with by academic theoreticians. This is the case of the wage relationship.

Although written in view of an audience acquainted with economic theory, this book can be read nevertheless by a larger circle since the technicalities have been reduced to what is strictly necessary to understand what is at stake.

Jean Cartelier is Professor Emeritus at Paris Nanterre University. His main fields of interest are general economics, money theory and history of economic thought.

T0384098

Routledge International Studies in Money and Banking

Money, Markets and Capital

The case for a monetary analysis

Jean Cartelier

Routledge
Taylor & Francis Group

LONDON AND NEW YORK

First published 2018
by Routledge

2 Park Square, Milton Park, Abingdon, Oxfordshire OX14 4RN
52 Vanderbilt Avenue, New York, NY 10017

Routledge is an imprint of the Taylor & Francis Group, an informa business

First issued in paperback 2020

British Library Cataloguing-in-Publication Data
A catalogue record for this book is available from the British Library

Library of Congress Cataloging-in-Publication Data
Names: Cartelier, Jean, author.
Title: Money, markets and capital : a case for monetary analysis /
    Jean Cartelier.
Description: Abingdon, Oxon ; New York, NY : Routledge, [2018] |
    Series: Routledge international studies in money and banking |
    Includes bibliographical references and index.
Identifiers: LCCN 2017061082 | ISBN 9780815355779 (hardback) |
    ISBN 9781351129244 (ebook)
Subjects: LCSH: Money—Philosophy. | Monetary policy. |
    Capital market.
Classification: LCC HG221 .C375 2018 | DDC 332.401—dc23
LC record available at https://lccn.loc.gov/2017061082

ISBN: 978-0-8153-5577-9 (hbk)
ISBN: 978-0-367-59117-5 (pbk)

Typeset in Bembo
by Apex CoVantage, LLC

Contents

Figures

Tables

Schemas

Introduction

Money pervades our everyday life.[1] We use it to finance our purchases, taxes and other expenses. We consult our various accounts in euros or dollars to check our economic situation (personal bank accounts, system of payments accounts and so forth). From an economic point of view, we are nothing but nodes in a huge network of inter-related accounts. Corporate and individual enterprises, households, foundations, associations and so on, observe, analyze and manage themselves using more or less sophisticated accounting. Any physical or moral person living in our society is or can be described by their money accounts.

These accounts are not an anecdotal or innocuous description of what individuals or collective entities do. If insolvency or illiquidity show up, then the people concerned are put in danger of being expelled from the economy. Accounts are performative. More than reflecting economic activity, recorded transfers of dollars from an account to another *are* economic activity itself; figures in these accounts are directly or indirectly written down by the current flows of payment taking place between economic agents. Most of these flows transit through banks. It is one of the reasons why banks play a central role in economic activity. They are the "great accountants" and perhaps are more than that, since they have some control over monetary flows. Money, accounting, banks, etc. seem to be the stuff economic activity is made of.

However, when academic theoreticians come to think about "economic reality" they dismiss accounts and monetary quantities. They resort instead to a sophisticated representation where goods or commodities are at the centre of the scene and money, if at all, is nothing but a special commodity called *fiat money*. No nominal unit of account is required. Wealth is expressed in an arbitrary *numéraire* and defined as a scalar product of a real prices vector by a commodity allocation vector. In order to restore a monetary image of economic relations, academic economists introduce fiat money amongst commodities and try to determine its price using the value theory they have adopted for other commodities. This exercise is known as *integration of money into value theory*.

Conceiving money as a commodity (however special) may appear strange in regard of what ordinary economic life suggests. The everyday economic relations that we can observe seem to belong to a complex system in which rules, institutions and commercial laws play an important role. Trying to give an account of such a payment system by resorting to the typical abstractions of value theory (commodity space, preferences, relative values expressed in a *numéraire*) may appear to be pure nonsense. For value theoreticians it is quite the opposite since these abstractions are the only scientific way to get to the essence of economic relations – and economic relations are not what a naive observer may believe them to be. Money hides what economic relations are about. Money has to be discarded at the first step because it is not a relevant expression of wealth. We have to build an appropriate value system based on goods or commodities conceived of as the natural basis on which societies rely. People are commodity producers and consumers; they are interested in real wealth, not in nominal magnitudes. They have preferences for certain commodities and are free of money illusion.

Moreover, according to academic economists, exchange is the basic relation between economic agents. Pure competition – since no agent can exert an influence on what happens in the market – is the benchmark. Desired allocations are realized only when individual actions are mutually compatible at equilibrium prices. The main task of economic theory is to determine these relative prices, and the way prices are determined reveals the essence of economic life: *difficulty of production* in Classical and Ricardo-Sraffian theory, *relative scarcity* in modern Neoclassical theory. In any case, money cannot be understood but as a (special) commodity whose relative price is ruled by the same principle other commodities are subject to.

Wealth is not nominal but real. English Classical economists conceived it as the capacity to produce and to yield profit. Modern academics are concerned with social welfare being conceived as a configuration of individual preferences and not as the power of the Prince. Both principles go without saying for most academic economists. It is worth recalling, however, that it has been a long-standing matter of controversy to decide whether a nation's power and opulence or a society's happiness was, or should be, the main object of political economy. The controversy between Thomas Mun and Dudley North, well-known by historians of economic thought, is a nice example of it. This debate is still on the agenda even if not explicitly. Let us briefly remind the reader of their relevant positions.

Thomas Mun (1664),[2] a partisan of the balance of commerce theory, maintained that an excess balance was the means to increase the wealth of a country (*England's Treasure by Foreign Trade* is the title of his most famous book). Consider a square matrix of payments where the hth row (column) shows the expenses (receipts) of a country h addresses to (coming from) other countries. Each country exhibits a positive balance if receipts (the sum of the column) exceed expenses (the sum of the rows) or negative otherwise. The algebraic sum of these balances is identically zero. According to the rules of the game of trade, a country with a positive balance gets richer comparatively to the others. If payment flows are made in gold or silver, enrichment takes the form of an increase in precious metals, very useful for financing diplomacy or wars. If payments use credit – money issued by monetization of capital – then enrichment takes the form of financial assets. In any case, these gains of trade are the way merchants and nations get richer. Thinking this way is far from stupid.

Sir Dudley North (1691), however, observed that an excess balance of trade means that the quantity of commodities (measured in money) flowing out of the country is greater than the one flowing into it. The consequence is clear: individuals living in a country have less quantity of commodities (measured in money) to consume. The country, *i.e.* its inhabitants are impoverished. Thinking this way makes sense too!

Who is right? Both of them! If wealth is conceived of as a relative advantage over other traders, Mun is right. If, on the contrary, wealth is the utility or happiness given by command over commodities, North is closer to the truth. The fact is that economic theoreticians have en masse decided to follow North rather than to develop Mun's argument. North and Mun may be taken as the emblems of the two major strands in economic analysis that Schumpeter (1954) proposes to distinguish in his *History of Economic Analysis*, respectively the *real analysis* or value theory and the *monetary analysis*.

> Real analysis proceeds from the principle that all the essential phenomena of economic life are capable of being described in terms of goods and services, of decisions about them, and of relations between them. (. . .) Monetary analysis introduces the element of money on the very ground floor of our analytical structure and abandons the idea that all essential features of economic life are represented by a barter-economy model.
>
> (*History of Economic Analysis*, pp. 277–278)

We will adopt Schumpeter's general view even if we will be more radical about the definition of monetary analysis: money will be considered not only as important but, in some sense, as the true substance of economic relations.

Schumpeter's observation has not received a sufficient attention by academic economists. They too easily agree about an *empirical* definition of the field of economics as *simultaneously* encompassing operations on commodities *and* monetary flows while they restrict that definition to commodities when they build their *theoretical* models. Whatever the school they claim to belong to, if they were asked about that schizophrenia, they would deny it. They would consider that economic theory does deal in fact with commodities *and* money. After reflection, some of them involved in monetary theory would accept that money is *in fact* excluded from modern value theory – the so-called integration of money into value theory is known as being a spiny task – but they would absolutely refuse to admit that a symmetric approach – excluding commodities and dealing with money flows only – would make sense. At most they would concede that during the pre-scientific era of economics, some authors, dubbed "mercantilists" by Adam Smith, have followed such a foolish track. Needless to say, such an orientation would be meaningless nowadays. Even theoreticians claiming to be true to Keynes and being critical of the mainstream for its neglect of money do not go as far as recommending an exclusion of commodities from the field of economics. They affirm that money is ever present together with commodities in economic life as in theory without providing any motivation for doing so without asking themselves about the legitimacy of such an accumulation of postulates. They assert that money is not neutral without establishing the conditions for neutrality. They seem not to be motivated by an inquiry into what makes their claims acceptable. Most of them are concerned more by empirical phenomenon than by giving strong logical foundations to their work

The present state of the art is a little bit paradoxical. While most of people, including academic economists, proceed as if commodities transactions *and* money flows are present in economic theory, a critical examination of most theoretical works convinces that such a co-existence is by no means effective and legitimate. As we shall see, (a) money finds no room in value theory, (b) it does not make sense to postulate a commodity space in addition to a payment system postulate. Most theoreticians are rarely so radical: value theoreticians try to find some room for money in their models while defenders of a monetary analysis exceptionally renounce to take for granted the existence of an *a priori* given commodity space. As a rule, the former are more rigorous than the latter. But this should not prevent us from taking seriously Schumpeter's proposition (more seriously than he did himself!) and from sharply distinguishing between different theories according to the predominance of one or the two postulates: commodity space or payment system (money).

It appears useful to cross that dichotomy with another distinction: do economic agents have the same status – it is the case in a pure exchange economy – or have they different conditions?

Doing so we get a grid based on these two criteria:

• The first one concerns the more or less hidden founding abstraction: a commodity space *or* a payment system.
• The second one concerns economic agents status; are entrepreneurs and wage-earners treated as homogeneous *or* heterogeneous.

Crossing these criteria gives four cases which correspond to some of our next chapters:

1 Commodity space and homogeneous condition (not to be confused with identity of endowments and preferences) for entrepreneurs and wage-earners: general competitive equilibrium theory illustrates the case. Integration of money into that value theory is examined in Chapters 1, 2 and 3 (Part I). We maintain that in spite of very sophisticated models built by very talented authors, money has not been satisfactorily integrated into value theory. General competitive equilibrium theory (and more generally

mainstream theory) remains still based on a commodity space postulate. It will be shown how the logical structure of that piece of real analysis is an obstacle to account for some fundamental features of a market economy.

2 Commodity space and heterogeneous condition between entrepreneurs and wage-earners: the typical example is Ricardian (and more generally English Classical economics) and Neoricardian theory (not studied in this book).

3 Payment system with homogeneous agents: pure market economy (Chapter 5). We show that a basic property of a market economy which is not accounted for in mainstream theory (a true decentralization of economic agents) receives the attention it deserves allowing us to deal with out-of-equilibrium positions. A specific dynamic approach is suggested in consequence. Commodities are not postulated but derived from the payment system postulate.

4 Payment system with heterogeneous condition between entrepreneurs and wage-earners: Keynes is the outstanding author here. We show that the heterogeneous condition follows from how economic agents stand vis-à-vis the payment system. This allows us to give precise foundations to Keynesian economics (Chapters 6 and 7). A comparison with what is going on in Keynesian economics at large (and especially SFC models) makes clear what a logically founded monetary analysis (without commodity space postulate!) may bring forth.

The subtitle of the present book – the case for a monetary analysis – gives a clear idea about our motivation. In order to give some substance to our motivation we are required:

- to prove that money integration into value theory has failed even if interesting propositions have been established thanks to the many efforts of general equilibrium theoreticians
- to build a logically coherent theory of both a market and a capitalist economy independently of any value theory (*i.e.* without postulating a commodity space).

In this book we try to partially contribute to that double task. Partially because, as Keynes justly reminds us, "the difficulty lies, not in the new ideas, but in escaping from the old ones, which ramify (. . .) into every corner of our minds" (*General Theory*, p. xxiii). The more or less implicit postulate of any value theory – an *a priori* given commodity space – appears to be so evident that it hardly needs any justification. It seems almost impossible and nonsensical to do without it. Neoricardians, although radically opposed to Neoclassical theory, share with it that postulate. Marx indulges himself in accepting it also. It is not easy to go counter a dominant way of thinking.

A further obstacle to overcome is the prevalence today in the academic world of the empirical studies over theory. As we shall see in due course, Keynesians of all sorts are more eager on showing that capitalist economies are not working satisfactorily than giving convincing reasons for the weakness of mainstream theory. More than often invoked by them, the lack of realism is an ambiguous critique since it takes for granted that reality is in some sense already known. If this were true why bother with theory? The affirmation of the predominance of demand over supply – a metaphor more than a clear-cut statement – may hardly be taken seriously either. Expressing that idea as an insufficient effective demand looks better but leads most often Keynesians to emphasize the occurrence in the "real world" of under-employment equilibria which is by no means a hard blow to mainstream when the cause is attributed to oligopolistic competition or other "realistic assumptions".

Whatever the difficulties to be overcome may be, we have to embark upon that double task assuming that most readers would agree that the two fundamental choices a theoretician has to decide for are (a) whether real *or* monetary analysis should be adopted, and (b) whether entrepreneurs and wage-earners should or should not be treated on the same footing.

The book is about theory, not about the history of economic thought. A detailed history relating how value theoreticians have solved the problems they have raised is far beyond the purpose of this book. Not only will the Ricardo-Sraffian tradition be ignored but many interesting debates in Neoclassical theory, or more generally academic theory, will also not be carefully studied. One of our aims is rather to understand the logical relations existing between the different issues about money characteristic of value theory (existence of a monetary equilibrium, money neutrality, the essence of money, etc.). An alternative way of expressing this objective is that we take a critical examination of the main propositions or statements that value theory has brought up so far.

Put in a nutshell, modern academic theory of money, which belongs to the real analysis, has gone as far as possible up to the point where it is no longer possible to go further without a radical change for an alternative view about economic theory, *i.e.* for a monetary analysis. This last approach has a long tradition and can be traced back to mercantilists and Steuart (1767). It leads to a very different view of what economics is about and of what its relations with other social disciplines could be. The case for a monetary analysis is due to a failure of the real one to take into account the fundamental properties of a decentralized economy. It is not easy to be aware of that failure since it comes as the paradoxical outcome of some great analytical advances in the field of general competitive equilibrium theory. Paradoxical because these great improvements towards rigour came jointly with the shrinkage of the field covered by analysis. A well-known example is the negative results of the global stability study that emerged in the 1970s which led to the abandoning of any research about the way a market economy could arrive at an equilibrium through a decentralized process of successive positions of disequilibrium. In the same manner, the great advances in academic money theory make easier to see its limits. An inadequacy of *fiat money* as the basic notion and an inappropriate view of the quantity of money as a parameter are two outstanding negative features calling for a change of approach.

The importance given in this book to a critique of the academic theory of money requires that the reader have some clear ideas of its basic reasoning and propositions. The first part of the book is devoted to that task. Technicalities will be reduced to what is strictly necessary for a good understanding of what modern academic theory says about money. What matters is less the details of the models, although they cannot be entirely neglected, than the concepts and the way basic questions are formulated. It is only at this level that an alternative theory makes sense and may be discussed. The alternative theory in question – *monetary analysis* – is by no means new. It belongs to the long tradition initiated by the so-called mercantilists and Steuart.

The other and more important aim of this book is to precisely defend and illustrate the monetary analysis. We do not attempt to give a detailed account of how many authors have progressively developed the monetary analysis. Some special steps will be mentioned in passing – John Law (1705) and Steuart (1767) being the most outstanding figures from the past and Wicksell (1935), Schumpeter (1970), Hawtrey (1919) and Keynes (1973) in more modern times. But, in any case, a reformulation of the monetary analysis is in order. It will be done more in accordance with modern standards, namely a quasi-axiomatic presentation allowing a clear discussion and a rational separation between what is due to philosophical convictions and prejudices (barely debatable) and what results from a logical and consistent reasoning (which is possible to seriously discuss).

Consequently, the book is in two parts and dedicated respectively to a critical examination of modern academic theory of money and to a presentation of an alternative theory based on the idea that money, market and capital are intertwined concepts.

At this point of the introduction an important remark must be made. Even if we think that a monetary analysis is more fruitful and more relevant than value theories, we do not maintain that the former brings better answers than the latter to the questions the existence of money commonly raises. As a matter of fact *value theories and monetary analysis do not address the same issues*. One contribution of this book, if any, is to make it clear that value theory and monetary analysis are not in competition about particular common monetary questions but on *a general attitude towards what economic theory is and what it is about*.

Value (or real) analysis to money has been adopted by the academic profession (or at least by those economists concerned with money theory). In that spirit, a good theory must first of all justify that money be introduced amongst commodities. This is done by proving the *existence of a general equilibrium with a positive price for money*. Then, it must be checked whether or not the introduction of money modifies the main properties of the economy (the so-called question of *money neutrality*). That money has a positive price at equilibrium is not enough; its presence in the economy has to be accounted for. This is achieved by comparing non-monetary equilibria with monetary ones. Money is said to be *essential* (in the sense of Wallace) if the latter is better than the former from a welfare point of view. In this case, it is possible to make precise what "frictions" money remedies and what makes it essential: absence of double coincidence of wants, lack of information about commodities' quality, impossibility of commitment, etc.

This methodology is a powerful and versatile one. Many important results are due to it. Its weakness lies in its unduly restricted field of validity. All the models alluded to above incorporate equilibrium conditions amongst their equations. Consequently, their solutions are necessarily equilibrium ones. *By construction, out-of-equilibrium situations are left unexplained and undescribed.* But there are no convincing reasons to exclude such situations from the study of decentralized economies. Quite the opposite! For more than two centuries, the problem of global stability of market economies has been the main concern of authors. From Cantillon to Marx, Classical economists have inquired into the gravitation of market prices around natural ones and into the general overproduction crisis. From Walras (1988) to Arrow and Hildenbrand, general competitive equilibrium theoreticians have tried to demonstrate the global stability of general equilibrium until Sonnenschein (1972), Mantel (1974) and Debreu (1974) definitively showed the impossibility of it. As a result, the longstanding issue at stake for all value theories – the property of self-regulation of market economies – has been left unexplored since the beginning of the seventies. What common wisdom considers a typical feature of our economies – the so-called market sanctions and adjustments – is out of reach for real analysis theoreticians!

Investigating the reasons for that unacceptable oversight leads one to realize that its origin lies mainly in the way money is conceived of. Money theory and market theory are so strongly inter-related that the former should be built in mind of the latter (Cartelier, 2007).

The second alternative, the monetary analysis, is scarcely adopted nowadays. For the economists following this track, market economies cannot be thought of without money. Consequently they take it for granted, without bothering with its (logical) origin and genesis. The existence of a general equilibrium with a positive money price is no longer a relevant issue, no more than neutrality. The differences between the general visions on which value and monetary analysis rely, respectively, are responsible for the diversity of the issues which are dealt with. Monetary analysis makes sense, by comparison with value theory, because it is not restricted to viewing economic relations as exchange ones. It encompasses *every type of social relations mediated through money*. A major issue is the issuance of a means of payment and how different people are situated from that point of view. Monetary relations are thought of as not reducible, neither for exchange nor for power. They are beyond exchange and predation. They must be studied for themselves.

Accordingly, what has to be discovered are the rules of the game played by humans when their relationships are mediated through money. Chess players are human beings. When they play chess they are more than pure human beings. They have also to comply with chess rules. Nothing of interest can be said about a game by an observer who does not know the rules of chess. But, while it is easy to learn *these* rules in a book, the rules of monetary mediation are written nowhere. The present book is a tentative effort to modestly remedy that absence. The main purpose of monetary analysis is to make them explicit. Discovering the dynamic properties of a monetary economy is part of that issue. Such a program belongs to an older tradition starting with the so-called mercantilists and encompassing some very different authors but who all share a common concern. It is the case for the writers listed above, John Law, James Steuart, (partially) Marx, Wicksell and the Swedish School, Hawtrey and Keynes.

Real and monetary analysis offer advantages and difficulties. Are there criteria for choosing between them?

A pure methodological argument should be avoided at this point. Some commentators argue that philosophical or methodological considerations are decisive. It is a commonplace to maintain that academic theoreticians adhere to methodological individualism which makes them start from supposed independent, egoistic and rational individuals groping into Nature without any *a priori* social bond. Not only commentators but theoreticians themselves share that view. However, a straight examination of how general competitive equilibrium theory *effectively* proceeds shows that such imputation is not valid. In fact, despite their methodological or philosophical convictions, theoreticians have to presuppose something common to all individuals before they could articulate any proposition about them. They have first to assume a commodity space (Debreu's Euclidian space R^l) which is common knowledge. Without that commodity space, it would be impossible to describe individuals as they are in that theory, *i.e.* as initial endowments (points of R^l) and preferences functions (defined on R^l) as well as production techniques.

The commodity space is the common language individuals use to communicate their demands and supplies to others. It is also the language theoreticians use to describe the economy and to demonstrate its properties. Being logically prior to the assumption of individual economic agents, the commodity space may be called an *institutional assumption*.

Two other institutional assumptions are necessary for general competitive equilibrium theory to be consistent: (a) for the study of equilibrium existence, an auctioneer (a non-individual entity having no endowment and no preferences) must propose parametric prices; (b) for the study of global stability, another auctioneer (or the same one!) must modify parametric prices according to an *a priori* given rule, improperly called the "law of supply and demand". That so-called "law" is nothing but an assumption and, as it has been shown, an (inefficient) algorithm for solving the system of excess-demand equations (Saari & Simon, 1978). These assumptions may be interpreted (as Walras did) as a *social mechanism* – competition – triggered by an institution.[3]

In brief, value theory, as represented by general competitive equilibrium, should not be condemned for its supposed methodological individualism or for inappropriate methodological considerations.

At this point, the reader may ask: what use is it to show that general equilibrium theoreticians comply with methodological principles very different to those usually imputed to them and that they adopt, even if not consciously, those of their opponents? The answer is straightforward: a critique based on the methodological argument above is a poor one. If this academic theory is to be criticized (and it certainly should be), it is not for the absence of institutional hypothesis but for the irrelevance of those which are effectively made. As a sign or consequence of that irrelevance, general equilibrium theory describes an economy very different to what is generally considered as a market economy. The question is not whether institutional hypothesis should or should not be made, but to determine the ones which will allow us to give an interesting and fruitful account of a decentralized economy.

Here, the question of money is crucial. Presupposing money as an institution – *i.e.* a given set of rules – instead of a commodity space (with or without fiat money) radically changes our perspective about economy. Money is an important mediation in the mutual relations that individuals entertain amongst themselves. Taking money as granted is not *adding* an institutional hypothesis to academic theory but *replacing* the commodity space postulate with a nominal unit of account postulate which will prove to be more relevant. It will lead us to make the mode of issuance and cancellation of the means of payment – the *minting process* – the central institution of market economies. Here too, this may interpreted as replacing an inefficient institutional hypothesis – the so-called "law of demand and supply" does not guaranty global stability of general competitive equilibrium – with a more relevant one.

In what follows, what will be at stake is an assessment of the relative fruitfulness and the relative limits of validity of the real and monetary analysis. Far from accumulating anathemas against one or the other, our purpose is to broaden the scope of discussions around money theory. If it seems rather clear that money theory relying on a real analysis has limited perspectives – which makes absolutely necessary the search for an alternative – it is also true that its available results deserve to be known and discussed, if only for generalizing and overtaking them.

Notes

1 It is my great pleasure to recognize that this book owes much to a collaboration over more than thirty years with Carlo Benetti (as the bibliography testifies). Moreover I am grateful for all his remarks and suggestions after a reading of a first version of this book. Perry Mehrling and Ghislain Deleplace have made many useful and important suggestions. I am also grateful to them and to three anonymous reviewers. The usual disclaimer applies.

2 Names followed by a date refer to the bibliography appended at the end of the book.

3 Institutions are understood as supra-individual entities by authors defending a holistic point of view. We abstain from that view in the present essay, less because we disagree but because such a view is by no means necessary to our argument. Institutions here will be any set of rules which has not to be micro-founded even if these rules concern only individual inter-relations.

Part I

Money in value theory

Value theories in general, and modern theories of value in particular, proceed from the conviction that money is an "artificial" wealth opposed to a "natural" one, as Nicolas Oresme (1990) once wrote. Commodities (Classics's use values or Debreu's commodity space R^l) are thought of as being *natural*; their presence in a social science does not need any justification. By contrast, money is a social device; it has to be defined; its existence and its use have to be explained. Thus, money is an optional (and special) commodity. Its existence alongside other commodities is a problem to be solved: its (positive) price and neutrality of its quantity (hopefully) have to be proved; the reason for its presence has to be explained and its essence (what money does) elucidated. Commodities and money are not on the same footing.

Relevant prices for evaluating wealth are not money prices but real (relative) prices. They are solutions of systems of equations in which money does not enter. Money – to assess whether it is or not an element of wealth is sometimes a bone of contention – enters value theory on a particular footing. It has to be a commodity – if not, nothing could be said on it – but not a usual one – if it were, money theory would not make any sense. Money in modern value theory is not an empirical object but a concept whose intelligibility is internal to a real analysis. Money does not exist here but as *fiat money*, the definition of which is linked to the use it is designed for.

The research program for the academic theory of money forms a diptych; one part is devoted to integration and neutrality of fiat money, the other to its functions and essence. The intricacies and complexities of the matter should not make us forget the logical nexus which gives sense to academic money theory.

Part I

Money in value theory

Chapter 1

A bird's-eye view

The following propositions form the background of modern academic value theory:

- Society should not be considered as an entity *per se*: society is a set of inter-individual relations based upon the voluntary exchange of commodities; money, if any, is one of these commodities; money has nothing to do with the State and should not be manipulated by any authority.
- Society should be considered from the point of view of its members only (their happiness or utility) and not from the point of view of the State (wealth and political strength).
- The myth of a social contract provides the philosophical basis for that view. Society proceeds from its members only: *society is the involuntary outcome of voluntary individual actions.*
- Value theories pretend to be scientific because they go beyond the monetary appearances of economic affairs and reveal their essence, *i.e.* the relative values are determined either through production relations (Ricardo-Sraffa) or through generalized exchange (Walras-Arrow-Debreu); relative values are expressed in a *numéraire* which can be any commodity (fiat money included but not exclusively).

The propositions above are not to be discussed as such. They have been listed here only to clarify the intellectual context which gives its meaning to mainstream monetary theory. We should take that context as granted and we do not need to discuss or criticize it now.

The most outstanding outcomes of value theory – determination of the rate of profit and prices of production for the Ricardo-Sraffa theory or existence of general competitive equilibrium prices and Pareto-optimality of these equilibria for the Walras-Arrow-Debreu theory – are demonstrated in a moneyless economy. Money appears in value theory as a second thought.

What economic theory tells us about economic relations (their essence or nature) is to be discovered less by examining the philosophical convictions of the theoreticians than by scrutinizing the assumptions necessary to the system of equations whose relative prices are the solution. In the general competitive equilibrium theory of value – the one mainly considered here – relative prices reflect relative scarcities, *i.e.* equilibrium rates of marginal substitution between commodities.

Economic theory deals with relative prices established for natural commodities. Can it apply to money prices, which amounts to determining a price for money? Clearly it should be. Money exists and it must find room in value theory. *Integration of money into value theory* is the most traditional issue in standard monetary theory. Basically, this means that the system of equations designed for commodities should be extended to fiat money in order to determine its price (in terms of a *numéraire*). The integration of money into value theory is considered to be achieved when fiat money is proved to have a positive price at equilibrium along with the other commodities in the general model.

Classical (Sraffian) and modern general competitive equilibrium systems of equations leave no room for fiat money. In order to deal with money, an equation at least should be added or appended to these original systems. Commodity equations reflect production (and production techniques) or consumption (and individual preferences and allocations). As it is not introduced from the start in these systems, money should be deprived from any use for production or for consumption. Consequently money has to be thought of as not entering production functions and utility functions (it is improperly said to have no intrinsic utility). Moreover, money, not being a natural commodity, cannot be privately produced.[1] Such a special commodity, not used for production and consumption and not privately produced, is called *fiat money. The fact that money appears as fiat money is neither a deliberate abstraction nor an induction from observed facts; it is the unavoidable consequence of the internal logic of value analysis, namely of the commodity space postulate.*

Thus, the only use fiat money may have is to circulate commodities. Circulation is the third of the traditional fields of economic theory, production and consumption being the other two. In spite of what has been often maintained, introducing a money equation into the system of production and consumption equations does not raise any difficulty *in principle*. Taking into account the circulation or transaction technique, in addition to production techniques and utility functions, makes it possible to add an $l + 1$th equation to the l commodity-equations to form a complete system of $l + 1$ equations (of which l are independent as a consequence of Walras's law) determining l relative prices, the price of money included. By contrast with that thesis, most commentators (and sometimes eminent authors) have maintained that money integration into value theory was an intrinsically difficult, even impossible, task. Hahn's celebrated paper of 1965 is an outstanding example of that position. We will show that it relies on a misunderstanding of the Walrasian tradition unduly restricted to the Arrow-Debreu model.

But determining a positive relative price for fiat money (*i.e.* integrating money into value theory) is not the end of the story. Since money is not generally considered as a necessary ingredient for value theory, it would be embarrassing if introducing money would change the emblematic propositions established for a moneyless economy. The founding act of value analysis – getting rid of money – has to be justified by demonstrating that integrating money into value theory does not alter its main propositions. Money should be *neutral* in that precise sense: different quantities of money should not have any influence on non-monetary variables. *Neutrality of money is a fundamental issue which is hardly separable from money integration into value theory.* Quantitative theory of money is providential in this perspective. Its main proposition is that the quantity of money variations leave unchanged the equilibrium relative prices; they proportionally affect money prices. However, neutrality, if it justifies *a posteriori* an *a priori* exclusion of money at the very starting point (the Occam's razor argument), may require unduly restrictive assumptions, as we shall see. Let us accept these restrictions for the moment.

Showing that fiat money has a positive price at equilibrium and that it is neutral is the joint product of the exercise called "integration of money into value theory". From Walras (1988) to Patinkin (1987) via Hayek (1967),[2] integration has been the central objective of monetary theory. This must be kept in mind in order to understand what money theory has been about during a long time and is still about nowadays. However, even if that objective were fulfilled – which is far from being the case – it would not be the last word. As fiat money is a social entity, it is not enough to prove the existence of a general equilibrium with a positive price for fiat money and to show that money is neutral. Theoreticians have also found it highly desirable to explain why or how fiat money could be an element of the entire commodity space. The solution is straightforward for some modern academic theoreticians: since money is introduced into value theory as a transaction technique, it has to be proved that money has been chosen against other available transaction techniques (typically barter). In the current modern terminology this is called "giving microeconomic foundations" to monetary theory.

Modern theoreticians affirm:

1   Money has a positive price at equilibrium because it is an equilibrium technique of transaction. If money allows for having better equilibrium allocations than other available techniques, money is said to be *essential* (in the sense of Wallace).
2   Essentiality of money is the cause of its adoption by the whole economy.

Even if the preceding proposition were acceptable – which is doubtful as we shall see – it would still remain much to do. We do not yet understand what money really does. We know only that it is the best technique of transaction from the point of view of welfare but we do not know its *essence*. The common saying in money theory runs: money is what money does. But precisely what does money really do?

Here again, the answer modern theoreticians propose is simple. They take Arrow-Debreu's model as a benchmark. In that model transactions are centralized; a clearing institution makes sure that individuals respect their budgetary constraints. Moreover, transactions are costless. By contrast with that benchmark, transactions do not go as smoothly in a market economy. Transactions take time, are costly and are not feasible sometimes. Let us call all these deviations "frictions". When individuals are specialized in production and consumption and when they bilaterally meet, a lack of double coincidence of wants may happen which prevents all desired transactions from taking place. This is also the case when private information on the quality of commodities makes exchange difficult. When these "frictions" are important enough, resorting to money provides a solution; a monetary equilibrium exists. One may say that money remedies market "frictions".

"Frictions" is the general heading under which money enters modern value theory. These "frictions" are not considered equally typical of a decentralized economy. Amongst them, the absence of a credible commitment to do something for somebody in the future is viewed as crucial for assessing the essence of money. In an economy without any double coincidence of wants where anonymity is the rule and where individuals make transactions one at a time, no credible commitment can prevent an autarky equilibrium. Kocherlakota notes that two alternative devices may help in overcoming that situation. The first one is a central control which would allow individuals to produce for would-be consumers without equivalent if they could check that these agents have done the same in the past (*gift-economy*). The other one is fiat money. A would-be consumer, by holding money, informs the would-be producer that he has already produced in exchange for money, which means that he has followed the rule. Kocherlakota concludes that money is memory. He should have written rather that *money is a decentralized control over individuals*.

Integration of money into value theory, neutrality, essentiality and essence of money are successive aspects of a unique research program commanded by the logic of a value analysis. It is important to understand all these links and to realize that the issues above are not necessarily the relevant ones to an alternative analysis. At the end of this brief overview on the modern analysis to money theory, it will be clear that, despite the cleverness and skill of many recent authors, the current state of thought in academic money theory is far from satisfactory. Fundamentally, money theory does not meet with what would be required by a rigorous study of a market economy.[3]

Let us briefly review, successively, the four issues above: integration, neutrality, functions and essence of money.

Notes

1 That property is to be interpreted with care. In Ricardo's theory of money, for instance, money has a standard which is produced along with other commodities (see Deleplace, 2017 for an original and convincing defence of Ricardo).

2 Note that Hayek (1967) is a rare marginalist economist considering neutrality as a norm for monetary policy and not as a property of money.

3 The critique of the standard theory of money proposed here has nothing to do with the usual ones. Aydinonat (2011) gives some good reasons for being sceptical about critiques such as (a) ignorance of institutions, (b) ignorance of pre-existing forms of money, (c) failure to take history into account, (d) not being aware that money is a social fact, etc. All these critics, although interesting in their own way, are naïve. They are off the mark since they do not address the core of academic theory.

Chapter 2

Integration of money into value theory and neutrality in a nutshell

The problem of integration

By contrast with many commentators who think that integration of money into value theory has failed, we will maintain that no basic obstacle prevents it from being realized. The delicate issue is not integration but neutrality.

A basic presentation

Value theory deals with three domains: production, consumption and circulation of wealth.

Classical tradition emphasizes production: the quantities of produced commodities being given and taken as physical units for each of them, a price determination may be summarized by Sraffa's (1960) well-known system:

$$(1 + r)Ap = p \qquad (2-1)$$

with r being the rate of profit, p the vector of prices and A a non-negative (irreducible) square matrix showing how commodities produce commodities (production technique). According to the Perron-Frobenius theorem, system (2–1) has a solution for the rate of profit: $r^* = \dfrac{1-\alpha}{\alpha}$ where α is the maximum eigenvalue of A and prices: p^* being the price vector defined up to a scalar (eigenvector of A associate to α). Let us take the total value $e'p^* = T$ evaluated in whatever *numéraire*; T is the value which has to be circulated amongst industries.

According to Neoclassical tradition, prices are determined by simultaneous equality between supply and demand on all markets. This condition is expressed by the well-known system of equations:

$$D(p) = S(p) \rightarrow Z(p^*) = 0 \qquad (2-2)$$

where $D(p)$ and $S(p)$ are respectively the aggregate demand and supply functions for commodities, $Z(p)$ being the market excess-demand vector function,

p^* the vector of equilibrium price defined up to a scalar factor and $q = q^*$ the quantity vector given by $D(p^*)$ or $S(p^*)$. Let us take $q^{*\prime}p^* = T$ as the *numéraire* and the value to be circulated.

In both cases, relative prices are p^* and value of circulation is T.

In spite of their differences in the treatment of production and consumption, the two value traditions above share the same view about circulation. Money is the name of this technique and to keep the story simple, this technique is roughly described by V the velocity of circulation of money.

It is of utmost importance to understand (and to keep it in mind) that systems (2–1) and (2–2) do not host any money. Integrating money into systems (2–1) and (2–2) would imply money being necessary for production or consumption, as any other commodity. If so, money would not be a special commodity and no specific theory for money would make sense. Consequently, money must be defined as a commodity without any intrinsic use – which means neither for production nor for consumption.[1] The only specific use of money – in the framework of value theory – is for circulation. But circulation does not enter systems (2–1) and (2–2) which appears now to be incomplete. Circulation, besides production and consumption, should enter the picture. Therefore, a further equation is needed.

The history of economic thought is full of affirmations about the lack of utility of money as opposed to that of ordinary commodities. From Hume[2] to Menger[3] quotations are abundant. They should not be literally interpreted as saying that money is useless but only that money is exclusively needed for circulation or transactions.

Integrating money into value theory consists then in adding to systems (2–1) or (2–2) an equation describing the circulation of commodities by means of money. A transaction technique completes the traditional primitives: initial endowments, production techniques and preferences. So, how to deal with money, once it is conceived of as a transaction technique? The simplest way to do so is to assume a given velocity of the circulation of money V interpreted as an institutional data. Considering money as a special commodity and applying to it the supply and demand apparatus is the usual strategy. Money supply is taken as a parameter (since money is not privately produced) while demand is for using money as the technique of circulation. In both traditions of value theory, the Exchange Equation is the same:

$$\frac{M}{P} = \frac{T}{V} \tag{2–3}$$

where M is the quantity of money expressed in monetary units (the \$ for instance), T the value of total transactions in a *numéraire* (corn for instance) and P the price of money, expressed also in corn.

Contrary to what most of theoreticians have maintained, there is no problem *in principle* for integrating money into value theory along this line *if a transaction technique is made explicit*. This is the case in Walras's *Éléments d'économie politique pure* where agents perfectly know the dates of payments to be realized during the "week". Once a transaction technique is considered as a primitive of economy *on the same footing as preferences and initial endowments*, it becomes quite obvious that money price should be determined by system (2–1)-(2–3) or system (2–2)-(2–3), under the usual mathematical assumptions (Perron-Frobenius theorem for Sraffian systems and fixed-point theorem for general competitive equilibrium theory).

But until recently, most theoreticians failed to explicitly recognize transaction techniques as a primitive. Therefore, they define money as a special commodity with "no intrinsic utility" forgetting that transactions should be detailed as an integral part of price theory. They seem unaware that "no intrinsic utility" means in fact that "money is only a transaction technique". Until the 1980s, the absence of the utility of money was widely taken at face value by academic theoreticians without any concern about transactions. Martin Hellwig (1993) lists five questions to be solved in order "to find appropriate conceptual foundations for monetary economics". The first questions reads: "Why does fiat money have a positive value in exchange against goods and services even though it is not intrinsically useful?" Hellwig calls it *Hahn's problem*. Analytically, the problem is whether an existence theorem may be established with a positive price at equilibrium for *fiat money*. It seems an impossible task, even if Walras had already done the job but theoreticians of money had failed to notice it! As we shall see, Frank Hahn's incorrect lecture of Walras is responsible for the misunderstanding which has disoriented academic monetary theory for more than twenty years.

A quick rationalization of the Walras-Patinkin approach to money

Walras and Walrasian tradition take for granted that transactions are carried out exclusively through money. Theoreticians of this tradition care for transactions but do not introduce in their models alternative techniques of transaction. Money is the only one. Consequently, the problem is not to reveal the conditions under which money is chosen – that problem will come later on – but whether money, the exclusive intermediary of exchange, has or not a positive price at equilibrium. Only when this has been proven does it make sense to ask whether quantity of money influences the real variables of the economy, *i.e.* the relative prices of commodities and the level of economic activity.

Walras carefully describes the way transactions are carried out. At the beginning of the market agents know perfectly the parametric prices and the dates at which commodities will be delivered and at which payments have to be made. When equilibrium prices are known, it is very easy for them to calculate the amount of money they need in order to meet their commitments to pay during the market period. There may even be a problem of adjustment, since a modification of the demand for money may have a feedback on the demand for commodities, Walras assumes that in the end the process will converge so that money prices will be perfectly determined at equilibrium.

Nothing would prevent us from thinking of money as IOUs issued by individuals by means of a bank, these IOUs being cancelled at the end of the market. But Walras did not follow that track. He chose instead to treat money as a circulating capital, another way to assume that money is a durable commodity whose services – *i.e.* making realization of transactions possible – are priced, the price of money being nothing but the capitalization of the value of these services. Treating money as a capital was by no means a logical necessity for Walras. But it was tempting to do so since money as a store of value seems to be a by-product of treating fiat money as a capital.

But this is not quite exact. There is an apparent paradox in the way Walras considers money. Walras's model should not be confused with Arrow-Debreu's one. The former is a temporary equilibrium model (in the sense of Hicks); Arrow-Debreu's model is an inter-temporal one. Capital pricing in Walras's relies on future prices expectations. For the sake of simplicity, Walras assumes that expected future prices of capital services (money included) are equal to present prices. That money has a positive price at equilibrium surely means that agents think it will have the same positive price in the next period. But that belief will make sense even *if money is not durable but simply renewed by the bank (in the case of IOUs)*. Moreover, it makes sense even if money will not *effectively* have a positive price next period. As Hicks reminds us, we should not confuse prices equilibrium at a given point of time (temporary equilibrium) and prices equilibrium over time (full equilibrium). Later on, Jean-Michel Grandmont will explore systematically that vast family of models (see below). The apparent paradox – in fact error – lies in the interpretation of the Walrasian theory of money as if it would hold in Arrow-Debreu's model.

Antoine Rebeyrol (1999) has convincingly shown that Walras's theory of money does not rely on the idea that money is a store of value. His theory is free from the difficulties met by later models of general competitive equilibrium in the 1970s and in the 1980s. Rebeyrol proposes a consistent model where money *services d'approvisionnement* only are responsible for the positive price of money at equilibrium (see Rebeyrol, pp. 239–246). These *services d'approvisionnement* are the exclusive consequence of money being the unique transaction technique of the economy. Jacques Drèze & Herakles Polemarchakis (2000) have tried to give a new life to that approach in recent times.

Acknowledging that Walras's money theory does not raise problems in principle does not mean that it is relevant. It may lack relevance, as Pascal Bridel (1997) reminds us. It is nevertheless necessary to underline that it is consistent, contrary to what has been maintained by many subsequent authors, like Frank Hahn. There is no contradiction between its assumptions and its main outcome (the positive price of money at equilibrium).

The inopportune proposition of Frank Hahn (1965)

The axiomatic presentation of the general competitive equilibrium theory of Arrow and Debreu makes it possible to debate with clarity; every notion is well-defined and the chain of reasoning can be checked. But Arrow-Debreu's model differs from Walras's model not only in its rigorous mathematics but also in two characteristics that are important for the question of the integration of money into value theory:

1 Arrow-Debreu's model does not deal with any decentralized technique of transaction; instead a centralized clearing is presupposed making sure that budgetary constraints are respected; as a consequence money has no room in this model: "No theory of money is offered here, and it is assumed that the economy works without the help of a good serving of a medium of exchange" (Debreu, 1959, p. 28); however, in Walras's model as noted above, money is presupposed as the exclusive transaction technique.
2 Arrow-Debreu's model is inter-temporal while Walras's is a temporary equilibrium, as it is well-known; budgetary constraints faced by individuals differ according to the model considered: one unique constraint in Arrow-Debreu's setting, one constraint by period of time in Walras's model.

It is the particularity of the Arrow-Debreu environment which makes Hahn's proposition apparently reasonable: even if a monetary equilibrium would exist – and in 1965 it was by no means certain – an equilibrium with a zero price for money would in any case also exist. An immediate corollary is that a future demonstration of existence of a monetary equilibrium would not be the end of the story since a selection between (at least) two equilibria would still to be solved.

In other words, *money theory, in the context of general equilibrium, cannot avoid addressing the choice between a monetary and a non-monetary equilibrium.* This decisive turning point occurred with the publication in 1965 of Hahn's article. *After 1965, instead of taking for granted that money is the transaction technique inherent to a market economy, theoreticians have to prove it and to explain why.* The quest for so-called micro-foundations of money theory takes its intellectual origin in Hahn's proposition.

This debate is totally foreign to a monetary analysis spirit as we will see in the second part of this book.

Hahn's argument

Hahn's argument is very simple. In a competitive l-commodity-economy, under the usual assumptions (continuity and homogeneity of excess-demand functions bounded from below and subject to Walras's law), an equilibrium exists with positive prices, if at a zero-price p_i excess-demand for commodity i is strictly positive for all i (Hahn calls that last property the scarcity assumption).

Let us introduce commodity $l + 1$, fiat money. There is now a problem since the scarcity assumption does not apply to money. If $p_{l+1} = 0$, the demand for money is nil since at a zero price money can be neither an intermediary of exchange nor a store value; it cannot even be used for expressing prices. Its quantity (supply) is positive; consequently, excess-demand (demand *minus* supply) for money is negative for all positive price vectors having the $(l + 1)^{th}$ component equal to zero. Zero is an equilibrium price for money. Hahn goes on applying its argument to Patinkin's model, which was the reference at the time.

Hahn's argument seems devastating. Money appears quasi-impossible to integrate into value theory. Its quantity is normally greater than demanded so that an equilibrium with a zero price for money cannot be dismissed and equilibria with a positive price for money difficult to imagine. In any case, the road toward the solution of what was considered THE PROBLEM of money theory appears to be very difficult to follow after Hahn's demonstration.

Discussion of Hahn's argument

Hahn's argument is not convincing at all. Drèze & Polemarchakis consider it as "an artificial conundrum". Hahn's central proposition does not make sense, as Carlo Benetti (1996) has ably shown. Its weakness lies in the confusion between an economy with a zero price for money but *without any other transaction technique*, on the one hand, and an economy without money, on the other. The second one does not need money, as Arrow-Debreu's model testifies: transactions are carried out by means of a central clearing. There is no monetary problem there. By contrast, an economy with a zero price for money exhibits a completely different situation. The impossibility of using money would impede any transaction from being realized. Excess-demands could not be satisfied and desired allocations would not be implemented. Does it make sense to call equilibrium such a situation? Obviously not! The only conceivable equilibrium in that economy would be autarky. Money would not even exist! Speaking of a zero price for money in that case is absurd.

While Debreu is consistent (but not relevant) when he replaces money by a central clearing allowing desired allocations to be realized, Hahn is not consistent (and not relevant either) when he assumes money without making explicit any transaction technique. If he had thought about it he would have been aware of the necessity to offer an alternative to money (decentralized barter for instance) in view of giving some sense to an economy with a zero price for money. Search theoreticians will follow that track twenty years later (see below).

Table 1.1 Different consequences of $p_m = 0$ according to the techniques of transactions which are considered

Walras	Arrow-Debreu	A-D for Hahn	Iwai (1988)	Kiyotaki & Wright (1993)
Money	Central clearing	Money No clearing	Many including fiat money	Barter money
$p_m = 0$	$p_m = 0$	$p_m = 0$	$p_m = 0$	$p_m = 0$
Not an equilibrium	Irrelevant: there is no money!	Not an equilibrium	Fiat money not chosen	Barter is chosen

The table above shows the different consequences of $p_m = 0$ according to the techniques of transactions which are considered (second row).

Hahn's critique of Patinkin addresses the wrong target. In the Walras–Patinkin model, a technique of transaction is assumed (even in a somewhat rough way). This technique absolutely requires a positive price for money. If money could not be used because of its zero price, no transactions would occur and the economy would not be in equilibrium. Saying that such an economy may have equilibrium with a zero price for money is self-contradictory. Why did Hahn not realize that? The fact that he never accepted the Walrasian mode of dealing with money may be an explanation. This clearly appears when Hahn presents Patinkin's arguments as well as those of Tobin or Baumol: "All assume that no transactions are possible without the intermediate use of money. It is, I think, evident that none of these rationalizations can be taken as an explanation of the positive exchange value of money since that is already assumed". In other words, he does not adhere to the idea that the purpose of money theory is to state that money has a positive price at equilibrium *as a consequence of being a transaction technique*, in the same manner that a pure means of production has a positive price at equilibrium as an effect of its use in production, or goods purely for consumption because it is an argument of an agent's preference. Choosing an Arrow-Debreu framework, Frank Hahn is led to depart from a Walrasian approach and to address a wrong point. In an economy without any specified transaction technique, there is no point to search for a positive price for money which has no reason to be there, exactly like a pure means of production would be useless in a world without production.

Hahn's proclaimed result is neither a positive nor a negative one. It is a nonsensical proposition. It has nevertheless been largely accepted because Arrow-Debreu's model has replaced Walras's one (probably the intricacies of the Patinkin controversy have paved the way for that substitution). Theoreticians were not aware that Arrow-Debreu's model was not well-suited to deal with the question they were raising. Arrow-Debreu's model may be used for money theory only if a transaction technique is explicitly added to it.[4] Frank Hahn abstained from doing it. Iwai did it successfully more than thirty years after.

Kiyotaki and Wright followed. In the meantime, a lot of energy and talent have been spent in vain.

Failing to focus on the right problem – does money as an intermediary of exchange have a positive price at equilibrium? – money theoreticians took a wrong track – does money as a store of value (*i.e.* as capital) have a positive price at equilibrium? The answer to that last question is trivial but it did mobilize a lot of clever writers in the 1970s and 1980s.

THE CONSEQUENCE OF THE LARGE ACCEPTANCE OF HAHN'S ARGUMENT: MONEY AS CAPITAL

Accepting Hahn's argument, some money theoreticians considered that Arrow-Debreu's framework should be put aside or transformed. By the same move they insisted less on the intermediary function of money than in its role as a store of value.[5] Fiat money was supposed to be durable, in addition to not being privately produced and useless for production and consumption. Fiat money was treated as a special asset, as a particular kind of capital. Whereas *confusion between money and capital* could be avoided in Walras's model (see Rebeyrol), it became from Hahn onward, the main weakness of academic money theory. Two types of models were successively in fashion. In the first type a temporary equilibrium method is adopted; in the second one, an infinite horizon assumption transforms Arrow–Debreu's model into an overlapping generation framework. Let us now see two simple versions of these models without too much detail and technicalities (basic equations of both types of models are given in appendices 1 and 2).

Money as capital: temporary equilibrium models

As noted above, in Arrow–Debreu's model, agents face one budgetary constraint only. Markets exist for each commodity at each period for all states of nature (complete markets hypothesis). There is no room for any inter-temporal allocation. Introducing incomplete markets creates a "friction". At each period only spot markets are open. Money is supposed to be the unique durable commodity (capital). Fiat money is transmitted from one period to another. Agents must take into account that fact and make explicit their expectations about money prices and about what will happen in the future periods. Their excess-demands will depend on these expectations so that equilibrium today is influenced by what agents expect for the future. Hicks named this method "temporary equilibrium".

In that context, it is quite possible to list the conditions under which money may have a positive price at equilibrium. It is the case if expectations about the future price of money do not tend towards zero (Grandmont, 1983). The intuition for that proposition is immediate: if money is a unique durable commodity, any individual may accept to hold it at the end of the present period only if he/she thinks that it will have a positive price next period. If it is the case, there will be a price of money at the present period at which that demand will be equal to the exogenous supply.

In this general framework, Grandmont shows that:

1   The real balance effect, advocated by Pigou and Patinkin, is generally not sufficient to ensure the existence of a monetary equilibrium; it must be completed by an inter-temporal substitution effect which depends on expectations.
2   Money has a positive price at equilibrium if money price expectations are bounded from above (the future price does not tend to infinity). Money has a positive price if individuals expect it will have a positive price in the future. In other words, the price of money is governed by a *bootstrap effect*. This means that money does not depend on the primitives of an economy (preferences, technique and initial endowments) but on beliefs. The model gives support to the old idea that money is conventional (due to a bootstrap effect).

That conclusion is welcomed by economists belonging to a real analysis – money, after all, is not part of the economy on the same footing as "natural" commodities; it is a kind of arbitrary addition – but also by many so-called heterodox economists who find here a formalized expression for the notion of *trust*, a possible foundation for money theory.

Temporary equilibrium models may be said to be in the Walrasian tradition since money neutrality is still the leading concern, as Grandmont's book made clear. However, these models are not true to Walras. In order to be in line with Walrasian tradition, money should function only as an intermediary of exchange. But, in the simple model above it is not the case. Money functions as capital, that is as a store of value. Money does not play any role for transactions. It is just a bridge between past and future, as Keynes (1973) put it in his *General Theory*. It is only as a store of value that money gets a positive price at equilibrium. In a sense, Grandmont (1983) proceeds to a misinterpretation of Walras. Intelligent as his book may be, it remains a misinterpretation. Patinkin's model should not have been referred to, since, for the author of *Money, Interest and Prices*, the positive price of money rests upon its role as an intermediary of exchange (as a consequence of a non-synchronization of payments).

Money as capital: the overlapping generation models

Temporary equilibrium models are not the only ones proposed as a solution to Hahn's problem. In the 1980s overlapping generation models were much in fashion not only in money theory but also in dynamics and macro-economy. Their interesting and somewhat surprising properties may explain their success. As far as money is concerned, a significant conclusion was that money's positive price at equilibrium was not due to a bootstrap effect, as was the case with a temporary equilibrium approach, but to the primitives of the economy.

Overlapping generation models exhibit rational expectations equilibria. The positive price of money depends on the real rate of return of money. It is no longer a psychological or conventional phenomenon which rules the roost: money is demanded as a consequence of the primitives and not for speculation or by virtue of trust.

The fact that equilibria are rational expectations means one is obliged to abandon Arrow-Debreu's framework where time horizon is finite. In a finite horizon economy, there cannot be a positive demand for money. The reason is simple. At the last period nobody has any interest to demand and hold money since it will be useless. Nobody would hold it at the end of the preceding period since it would be impossible to get rid of it at the last one. By backward induction, nobody would demand money at the first period.

We have thus to adopt an infinite horizon economy. The infinite horizon hypothesis is not properly a "friction", as it was with incomplete markets; but, in that case also, theoreticians leave Walrasian tradition without always being aware of the problems generated by this "farewell" to Walras. In order to get an infinite horizon, models deal with an infinite number of successive generations of people living in only two periods which overlap. In each period people co-exist, the young – having still one period to live – and the old, who die at the end of the period.

The story told by these models about money is rather simple and easy to understand. But the formal properties which are responsible for the outcomes are sometimes difficult to interpret and there is no general agreement amongst economic specialists. The most schematic story is as follows. At each period there co-exists a young person who receives an endowment of a unique non-durable commodity (ice cream) and an old person who receives nothing. The preferences of the young are such that he would like to consume less than his endowment right now and have more than his zero endowment when old. The problem is that ice cream melts and cannot be kept over time. The young cannot propose an inter-temporal exchange with the old since in the next period the old will not be alive to honour the contract. This unique equilibrium is an autarky one, which is clearly not Pareto-optimal.

Introducing a durable commodity, even without intrinsic utility, may remedy the sub-optimality of that economy. Let's endow the old with a given quantity of a durable commodity (typically fiat money). Now the old may propose to the young to buy the fraction of the ice cream endowment that he didn't consume. Why would the young accept the fiat money which is deprived of any intrinsic utility? Because at some cost he could proceed to the same operation when old (recall that a rational expectations equilibrium is searched for)!

In that economy, there are two possible equilibria: a sub-optimal autarky one, in which money does not exist or is not accepted in exchange (which amounts to the same thing), and an optimal monetary one, in which money is accepted and has a positive price (in terms of ice cream). In accordance with what Frank Hahn's proposition has stated, the monetary equilibrium does not come alone but with its companion, the barter or autarky one. This way of tackling money radically differs from Walrasian tradition. Money here is not a necessity. It could be absent not because it is forgotten in the model's hypotheses but because, being a possible option, it is not chosen by economic agents. The fact that money is chosen, *i.e.* has a positive price at equilibrium, depends on some features of the model or on some values of the parameters, all these circumstances being susceptible to being interpreted as many explanations for the existence or for the essence of money.

Interpreting these results is by no means simple.

Some commentators have been tempted to attribute the positive price of money to trust. The young would accept money from the old only because he would expect that the young of the next generation would have the same behaviour with the elderly next time. That interpretation is misleading. Trust does not enter at all in the story. The point is that amongst all parametric prices, which are taken as equilibrium prices by price-taker agents, only two correspond to rational expectations of equilibrium configurations of excess-demands. The existence of these two equilibria results simply from the mutual compatibility of decentralized decisions determined through a standard program of maximization. One of those prices is zero, the other is positive. Trust has nothing to do with that traditional method.

Moreover, the price of money is positive only if certain conditions on the primitives are satisfied. A quick examination of equations (see below Appendix 2) shows that the young must have more than half of the total endowment and choose to consume less than their endowment but more than half the total quantity available. The two prices are symmetrically treated. Trust is outside the model. Trust could be possibly invoked to solve the selection problem. But nothing is said on this point in the literature to my knowledge.[6]

Another interpretation is more interesting: in this model money would remedy the problem of the absence of the double coincidence of wants. Instead of a store of value function, money would act as an intermediary of exchange. Young and old are impeded to transact when they meet at period (*t*). Money would allow some mediation between them, avoiding the inconvenience of barter. The best authors have maintained that, in these models, money is an intermediary of exchange because it is also a store of value, endorsing a point made by Frank Hahn (1971) many years ago: "Money cannot act as a medium of exchange if it does not also act as a store of value". This assertion is however not convincing at all. In the model, money is, and is uniquely, a store of value. There is no intra-periodic transaction. Money could be replaced by a pension fund or by any other durable asset. What matters here is the rate of return of the durable commodity, *i.e.* the efficiency of the storage technique. Nobody can reasonably maintain that a storage technique is an intermediary of exchange.

The application of overlapping generation models to money theory has been criticized on this very point. The monetary equilibrium vanishes as soon as another store of value with a higher rate of return is introduced. Treasury bonds (risk-free assets bearing a positive rate of interest) would eliminate money were there not the famous legal restrictions evoked by Wallace.

A more profound interpretation, but also more difficult to understand, is suggested by John Geneakoplos (1987) who compares some properties of the overlapping generations models with those of Arrow-Debreu's model. What is responsible for most of the strange results of the former (the positive price of money included) is the infinite horizon due to the infinite number of genera-tions. "The explanation of the puzzles of OLG equilibria (. . .) is the lack of market clearing at infinity". "It can be shown that there is a 'finite-like' Arrow-Debreu economy whose 'classical equilibrium', those price sequences which need not clear the markets in the last period, are isomorphic to the OLG equi-libria. Lack of market clearing is also used to explain the sub-optimality and the positive valuation of money" (Geneakoplos, 1987, p. 207).

We are left with the idea that money as a store of value, but not as an intermediary of exchange, may have a positive price at equilibrium in mod-els where that function is taken into consideration. If we accept to reduce money to the function of value storage, even if we know that it is not specific to money, we could content ourselves with that conclusion. But this would amount to reducing money to capital and to showing that, when money is the only capital, money has a positive price at equilibrium; a poor result indeed!

Appendix I: A simple model of temporary equilibrium

A representative individual is supposed to live during two periods. We are inter-ested in the first period equilibrium only. The second period market for com-modity is not open but the individual forms expectations on the future price. Individual behaviour is given by a standard maximization of utility function which depends on the present $x(t)$ and the future consumption $x(t + 1)$ only.

$$Max \ \{alnx(t) + (1 - \alpha)lnx \ (t + 1)\}$$

under the following constraints

$$px(t) + m(t) \leq pe(t) + M$$
$$\varphi(p)x(t + 1) \leq m(t) + \varphi(p) \ (1 - e)$$

where M is the initial money endowment, e and $(1 - e)$ commodity allocation in first and second period respectively, m the desired money balances, p the money price of the commodity and $\varphi(p)$ the expectation function of the second period price of commodity. We assume $e > a$.

A standard calculation gives the excess-demand of commodity and, by virtue of Walras's law, that of money:

$$z = a(1-e)\frac{\varphi(p)}{p} + a\frac{M}{p} - e(1-a)$$
$$z_m = pe(1-\alpha) - \alpha\varphi(p)(1-e) - \alpha M$$

We are interested in the equilibrium of the first period only.

Patinkin's model is interpreted by Grandmont as a special case where $\varphi(p) = p$. In this case, money price of commodity is:

$$p = \frac{aM}{e(1-a) - a(1-e)}$$

Money price is positive if $e(1-\alpha) - \alpha(1-e) > 0$, *i.e.* if $e > a$, an assumption already made above.

The general case is less favourable. Everything depends on the properties of the function $\varphi(p)$.

We have drawn on the graph below Patinkin's case and an example of zero price (or infinite price of commodity).

The price of money $(1/p)$ is given by putting $z_m = 0$:

$$\frac{1}{p} = \frac{e(1-a)}{aM + a(1-e)\varphi(p)}$$

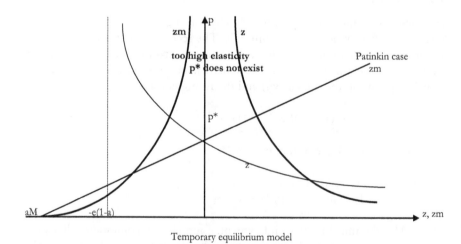

Temporary equilibrium model

Figure 2.1 Temporary equilibrium model

Appendix 2: A simple overlapping generations model

Representative individuals (young and old), living in two periods, have the same Cobb-Douglas utility function where α and $1 - \alpha$ are the coefficients corresponding to the ice cream consumed when young and when old respectively. Endowments of ice cream are denoted in the same way by e and $1 - e$. The autarky equilibrium implies that relative price where $\frac{p_{t+1}}{p_t} = q** = \frac{e(1-a)}{a(1-e)}$ is the price of ice cream consumed at t (when young) in terms of ice cream consumed at $t + 1$ (when old). If an inter-temporal allocation were possible (a durable ice cream), another equilibrium would be found.

For the young born at $t > 0$, excess-demands are determined by the standard program:

$$Max\{a lnx(t) + (1 - \alpha)lnx(t + 1)\}$$

under the constraints:

$$x(t) + \pi(t)m(t) \le e(t)$$
$$x(t + 1) \le \pi(t + 1)m(t) + (1 - e)$$

where π is the price of money in terms of ice cream.

A straightforward calculation gives the excess-demands of the young:

$$z^t(t) = \frac{a(1-e)}{\theta(t)} - e(1-a)$$

$$Z^t(t + 1) = \theta(t)(1 - \alpha)e - \alpha(1 - e)$$

with $\theta(t) = \frac{\pi(t+1)}{\pi(t)}$.

For the person born at $t = 0$, who gets money in addition to ice cream, excess-demand is simple: being the only one to live, he/she consumes all of his or her endowment and keeps the money M if it has a positive price or throws it away if it has a zero price. His or her excess-demand when old is simply:

$$Z^0(1) = \pi(1)M$$

Stationary equilibrium requires $\theta(t + 1) = \theta(t)$ for $t > 1$; this is true if:

$$(*) \qquad z^t + z^{t-1} = 0 \leftrightarrow \frac{a(1-e)}{\theta} - e(1-a) + \theta(1-a)e - a(1-e) = 0$$

While equilibrium at $t = 1$ requires:

$$z^0\left(1\right)+z^1\left(1\right)=0 \leftrightarrow \pi M +\frac{a\left(1-e\right)}{\theta}-e\left(1-a\right)=0$$

Condition (*) has two solutions $\theta* = 1$ and $\theta** = \dfrac{a\left(1-e\right)}{e\left(1-a\right)}$. It is easy to check that the first solution only gives a positive price for money:

$$\pi = \frac{e\left(1-a\right)-a\left(1-e\right)}{M}$$

The second one implies $\pi = 0$.

The graph below illustrates these results.

Autarky equilibrium is the only one when there is no durable commodity susceptible to be used as a store of value. The representative agent then has no choice: he or she must consume his or her initial endowment. He or she cannot modify it through exchange or through storage (the ice cream would melt).

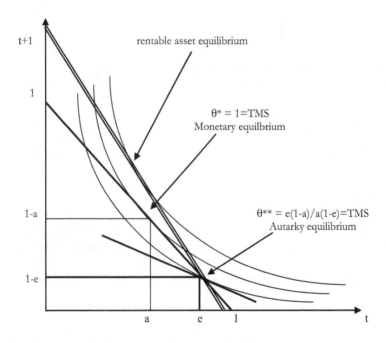

A simple overlapping generations model
Multiplicity of equilibria according to the durable asset

Figure 2.2 A simple overlapping generations model

A horizontal line starting from his or her initial endowment exhibits a gross rate of return equal to zero. When there exists a store of value with a unit rate of return (durable *fiat money*) – which may be read by the unit slope of the budgetary constraint – an equilibrium with inter-temporal allocation exists. It may be called monetary equilibrium to remind the reader that money is that store of value. But if another asset exists, with a rate of return greater than that of money, money disappears because the agents prefer that asset (this is shown on the graph by the slope greater than one).

In any case, two equilibria exist; one is autarky – Hahn's proposition – the other is monetary or else according to the rate of return of the store of value adopted.

A modern solution to the problem: the search-theoretic analysis

As we have seen above, neglecting transactions has been responsible for Hahn's inopportune result. Transaction realization had to be introduced into general equilibrium models but in a way different from Debreu. Central clearing does not suit a decentralized determination of market allocations. In a market economy transactions are performed by individuals themselves. However, a decentralized process is not easy to conceive and formalize. At the beginning of the 1970s Ostroy & Starr showed in a famous paper (1974) that such a decentralized process could generally work only under severe restrictive hypotheses. In fact, Ostroy & Starr's assertions were devastating.

What is at stake with the question of transactions?

Transactions are the link between market equilibrium prices, on the one hand, and individual market allocations on the other. Arrow-Debreu's existence theorem makes sure that individual desired allocations are mutually compatible at equilibrium prices. But once central clearing is no longer allowed, individuals have to effectively get their desired allocations by themselves, starting from their initial endowments. No money, no central clearing means they have to engage in a decentralized process of exchange.

Is it possible, in Arrow-Debreu's framework, to shape a decentralized process at the end of which individuals will generally get their desired market allocation? The answer is not a trivial one. The inconveniences of barter have been commonplace in economic theory since the middle of the 18th century and have often been invoked in the past as a justification for money. Veendorp (1970) had pointed to some problems of indirect barter four years before Ostroy & Starr's (1974) paper. What is at stake is no less than the validity and relevance of the two welfare theorems. *To know that desired equilibrium allocations are Pareto-optimal is useless if individuals are not able to get them through a decentralized process of transactions even at equilibrium prices.* The existence of desired equilibrium allocations is not enough. At equilibrium prices, we have to make sure that individuals are able to effectively obtain their desired allocations through a decentralized exchange process. If they do not, welfare theorems cease to be relevant and theorems of existence are incomplete.

Of the three pillars of general competitive equilibrium theory – existence, Pareto-optimality and global stability – only the first one (albeit incomplete!) would stand intact. At the beginning of the 1970s, the third one was destroyed by Debreu, Mantel and Sonnenschein's papers. What would happen if the second one was recognized to not be valid? To prove (under sensible assumptions) that a generally successful decentralized process of transactions could make all desired transactions realized was an absolute requisite for general competitive equilibrium theory. Curiously enough, few theoreticians have taken seriously that challenge. But two of them have performed so well that they have done the job and paved the way for a future analysis.

Ostroy & Starr's devastating assertions

Ostroy & Starr's propositions are mainly negative. Unless a centralized mechanism be in charge of permuting goods amongst individuals respecting the *quid pro quos*, individuals working by themselves would generally not succeed in getting their equilibrium allocations, even when prices are equilibrium ones.

Let us try to give an idea of a demonstration whose details are rather complex but whose inspiration is quite simple. Consider the matrix of excess-demands at equilibrium prices. The scalar product of each row (individuals) by the vector of prices is zero (individual budgetary constraints are respected), and the sum of each column (commodities) is also zero since it is the total excess demand for each commodity (general equilibrium).

Three notions need to be defined in order to understand the demonstration: a round, an exchange rule and what is, precisely, a decentralized process.

A *round* is a succession of bilateral meetings such that everybody has met everybody once (the meetings order matters but may be neglected here). A round is a good approximation for a market procedure. When two individuals meet (formally this amounts to comparing two rows of the matrix of excess-demands) they exchange according to a *rule*. The rule runs as follows for any commodity: (a) if excess-demands have the same sign no exchange takes place; (b) if excess demands have opposite signs positive exchange takes place, the quantity exchanged being the lower absolute amount; (c) once all these exchanges have been realized a balance will generally exist; an individual with the negative balance settles his or her balance by means of a basket of goods for which he/she has a negative excess-demand. No credit is allowed and goods are consumed only after the end of the market. The market closes when the round is complete.

If the matrix of excess-demands were a *chain* – a chain is a configuration of excess-demands such that the rule above allows a realization of transactions in a unique round – no problem would arise. An example of a chain is

$$\begin{pmatrix} 4 & -4 & 0 \\ 0 & 4 & -4 \\ -4 & 0 & 4 \end{pmatrix}$$ for prices (1 1 1). Successive bilateral meetings 1–2, 1–3

would do the job.

Decentralization and centralization are defined by the information individuals have about the economy. A process is fully *decentralized* if individuals only know the excess-demand vector of people they meet and *centralized* when they know the vectors of excess-demand of all other individuals.

The basic argument relies on an interesting property of the matrix of excess-demands. That matrix, which is not a chain in general, can always be written as a sum of submatrices each being a *chain*. In a centralized process everybody knows, whenever he/she meets somebody, the transactions he/she has to perform, since he/she knows the configuration of all the chains. When h meets k, both know their situations in chain 1, in chain 2 and so on. They are able to manage their transactions applying the rule to each chain. They make sure to complete all their desired transactions taking care of the different chains they belong to.

Hence the first Ostroy & Starr assertion: *there is a centralized trading procedure – the rule above – that achieves the equilibrium allocation.*

In a decentralized process when h meets k, both ignore the chains they belong to. "Without some central direction and notification there is no reason why a trader should have any idea about the chains to which he is assigned and who the other members are" (p. 158). Due to that lack of information they cannot respect the global scheme which would ensure that their desired transactions will be fully realized. The process may be blocked. Some mutually advantageous transactions will not take place because some inappropriate ones have occurred before.

Hence the second assertion: *there does not generally exist a decentralized procedure to achieve the equilibrium allocation.*

That negative result is disastrous. It means that economic agents may not succeed in getting their desired allocations in a decentralized economy. As a consequence, the welfare theorem is no longer valid when transactions are taken into account (as it should be!).

Is it possible to remedy that terrible drawback? Ostroy & Starr's answer is positive. But the cost is high as shown by the alternative assertions which mitigate the preceding result.

- If some agent h has initial endowments such that the quantity of each commodity is greater than the sum of all positive excess-demand of others, then all desired transactions will be realized in a round; agent h acts as an intermediary of exchange.
- If a commodity m is such that the value of endowment in this commodity for each agent is greater than the value of their positive excess-demands,

then the rule assumed above allows all desired transactions being achieved according to a decentralized process, commodity m acting as an intermediary of exchange.[7]

In both cases, Arrow-Debreu's model has to be modified in order to account for transactions, assuming that a central clearing is closer to Debreu's spirit – even if his central clearing is not part of his theory and is only a comment – than to Walras's one. Two examples of post-Walrasian authors may be mentioned here. The first is Clower's cash-in-advance constraint – the money value of total excess-demands of an individual must not be greater than the amount of his/her money holdings – which makes sure that Ostroy & Starr's last condition is fulfilled. The second one is Shapley & Shubik's (1977) seminal model of strategic market games where prices come from realized transactions and not from excess-demand cancellations. However, most of the academic theoreticians have not followed that track: either they have kept the dichotomy between price determination and transaction realization or they have denied the necessity of presupposing money.

A new direction

Fifteen years later, however, a new literature emerges. Some interesting authors (Jones, 1976, for instance) paved the way for a more sophisticated positive solution to the Ostroy & Starr problem: the Iwai and Kiyotaki &Wright models.

In order to get the demonstration of the existence of a monetary equilibrium with money used only as an intermediary of exchange, some "frictions" are introduced into the economy. "Frictions" are to be understood by reference to the Arrow-Debreu model in which there is no explicit process of transactions, as if transactions were carried out instantaneously and without any cost (by a central clearing). "Frictions" is a misleading term but we can interpret it as having some normal features of a decentralized market economy. Ostroy & Starr's (1974) article gives a precise idea of what kind of "frictions" they may be. Bilateral transactions instead of multilateral exchanges, specialization in production and/or in consumption with problems of double coincidence of wants and imperfect information on commodities' quality are some examples of "frictions". If these different problems are sufficiently important, and if there exists a special commodity called fiat money, then search models show that agents choose fiat money to carry out their transactions rather than any other transaction technique. At equilibrium, fiat money "without any intrinsic value" has a positive price nevertheless.

The basic idea of search models is that equilibrium conditions, which concern traditionally prices and allocations determination, should be extended in order to encompass the technique of transaction.[8] The economic calculation is not only about prices and quantities but also about the best strategy for the realization of transactions. Typically, an individual has to choose between barter and money, but this choice may be richer and encompass credit and competition between different means of payment.

In view of these objectives, search models are different from the traditional general competitive equilibrium. The non-individual (auctioneer) posting parametric prices in the Arrow-Debreu model is (in principle) no longer at work; there is generally no aggregation of individual functions, and alternative strategies for transactions realization are specified. To the usual primitives (initial endowments, preferences and production techniques) a description of the way individuals meet is added (bilateral stochastic meetings following a Poisson process, for instance). Individuals have to decide their participation to the market and the level of their activity taking into account all these elements.

Typically, these models generate "coordination failures", which means a multiplicity of equilibria ranked according to welfare. In the Kiyotaki-Wright model (1993), which may be considered as the canonical model of the first generation, existence of barter and monetary equilibrium is proved depending on the value of some parameter. The monetary equilibrium is proven to be better in terms of welfare than the barter one. Before presenting that model, it is worth expressing the general logic of the search analysis in the context of Arrow-Debreu's model completed by a description of transactions realization. This will make clear what the general idea exactly is.

The general idea (Iwai, 1988)

Let us assume a situation of general competitive equilibrium where prices are known and where individuals have just to decide how they will get their desired allocations at those prices. Transactions are decentralized as in Ostroy & Starr but money is not presupposed – which differs from Walras. People just have to decide the markets they need to visit in order to get their desired allocations.

In an l-commodity economy, there are $\dfrac{l(l-1)}{2}$ markets or trading posts. Several strategies are open to an individual who has apples and desire pears. The barter one is to visit the market for apples and pears hoping to meet somebody having pears and looking for apples (the double coincidence of wants). An indirect barter one is also possible: the first time to visit the market is for apples/cherries and the second time is for cherries/pears. Here, since prices are fixed, the time used to achieve desired transactions is the unique variable cost (due to time depreciation). Indirect barter takes more time but one also has to take into consideration the time necessary to find a coincidence of wants in a given market. That duration depends on the number of people choosing that market, which in turn depends on individual strategies. If a lot of people think that cherries will be chosen as an intermediary – that means that the $l-1$ markets in which cherries are exchanged are expected to be highly frequented – most people will choose a strategy of indirect barter using cherries as an intermediary of exchange. As a result, these strategies will be effectively advantageous and will be equilibrium ones (self-fulfilling prophecies).

The physical particularities of commodities matter less than expectations about frequentation of their markets. This may explain why for a commodity without intrinsic utility (typically *fiat money*), if expected for any reason to be chosen by people, everyone has an interest in choosing also that commodity as an intermediary of exchange. As a consequence, that commodity will have a positive price at equilibrium.

Giving a formalized expression for that simple and deep idea is not easy. Iwai derives from his complex model several interesting propositions:

1   There are a lot of equilibria. Amongst these equilibria the barter one is subject to very restrictive conditions which make it hardly likely (completely connected economies, *i.e.* with a general double coincidence of wants).
2   The commodity on which individuals coordinate is completely arbitrary since commodities' intrinsic properties do not matter much when compared to individuals' expectations; what Menger called *Absatzfähigkeit* (Menger, 1892) appears to be more a social characteristic than a natural one; the choice of an intermediary of exchange relies on a *bootstrap effect*, another name for a self-fulfilling prophecy.
3   Consequently, a commodity without intrinsic utility may be chosen at equilibrium as the general intermediary of exchange.

Iwai's model had the great interest of being built as a prolongation of that of Walras, where a multiplicity of transaction strategies replaces the *services d'approvisionnement* (some kind of a cash-in-advance constraint). That feature allows one to understand exactly what is at stake. But, at the same time, Iwai's model is not very tractable. It could not provide a convenient basis for developing a search-theoretic program. More tractable models were required. Nobuhiro Kiyotaki & Randall Wright (1993) offered to economists a first generation of search models.

Kiyotaki & Wright model (1993)

This model is simple but needs some interpretative remarks in order that its link with Iwai's general idea be understood. It is presented with some of its technicalities (which may be omitted by non-economist readers) because they matter to the model's interpretation.

Consider an economy populated of a continuum $[0,1]$ of individuals living forever. The individuals are specialized. Each can produce only a fraction $0 \leq x \leq 1$ of the continuum of non-storable commodities $[0,1]$ at a zero cost;[9] each can consume only that fraction x with a positive utility u but cannot consume its own production. Individuals have the same rate r of depreciation of future. Preferences, production techniques and endowment are described in a very simple and special way. It is thus possible to build a tractable model. In the same spirit assume that a fraction M of individuals hold one unit of indivisible money and that storage capacity is limited to one unit. Individuals holding money cannot produce.

A given individual either holds a unit of money or is a potential producer. What determines the level of activity and the choice of a transaction technique (money or barter) is the mutual compatibility of individual actions which in turn depend on a maximization of the present value of the future utility flows. The hypotheses on the way individuals meet (bilateral and stochastic) and transact (exogenous prices or bargaining) make models differ according to authors and dates. They do not significantly alter the main results. In Kiyotaki & Wright's (1993) model, prices are given exogenously and individuals meet by pairs according to a stochastic Poisson process of parameter β.

The value of an individual's position is equal to the present value of the expected flow of utility attached to the position. Using discrete dynamic programming (Bellman equations), one period is enough to calculate that value. When a money holder meets a potential producer (with a probability $1 - M$), the producer effectively produces for the money holder if (a) producer and money holder specialization are mutually compatible (simple coincidence occurs with a probability x) and (b) if money is accepted by the producer (with a parametric probability $\bar{\pi}$). In this case, the money holder consumes (gets utility u) and becomes a producer. In all other cases, the money holder keeps his or her position. His or her value at t, $V_m(t)$, is then:

$$V_m(t) = \frac{1}{1+r\Delta}\left[\begin{array}{l} \beta\Delta(1-M)\bar{\pi}x\big(u+V_s(t+\Delta t)\big) \\ +\big(1-\beta\Delta(1-M)\bar{\pi}x\big)V_m(t+\Delta t)+o(\Delta) \end{array} \right] \qquad (2\text{--}4)$$

where $\beta\Delta(1-M)\bar{\pi}x$ is the probability of transacting during interval Δ and $u + V_s(t+\Delta t)$ the value obtained during $t+\Delta t$ thanks to that transaction, while $\big(1-\beta\Delta(1-M)\bar{\pi}x\big)$ is the probability to keep a money holding position, which has a value $V_m(t+\Delta t)$ and $o(\Delta)$ being the approximation term.

Developing that expression and simplifying by Δ and making Δ tend toward zero leads to the following differential equation:

$$rV_m(t) = \beta(1-M)\bar{\pi}x(u+V_s-V_m)(t)+V_m'(t) \quad \text{with } V'(t) = \frac{dV}{dt} \qquad (2\text{--}5)$$

By the same procedure we get the value of a potential producer, $V_s(t)$:

$$rV_s(t) = \beta(1-M)x^2(u(t)) + \beta Mx\pi max_\pi(V_m - V_s) + V_s'(t) \qquad (2\text{--}6)$$

The interpretation of this last expression is straightforward. The instantaneous expected utility flow is equal to the sum of two products: on the one hand, the product of the probability to meet another producer with a double coincidence of wants $\beta(1 - M)x^2$, by the gain of the transaction, u and, on the other hand, the product of the probability to meet a money holder with a simple coincidence of wants $\beta M x \pi$, by the gain which results, which depends on the producer decision to accept money. Money acceptation probability π, depends on V_m which depends in turn on $\bar{\pi}$, parametric probability of accepting money (see below).

The two value expressions above form a non-linear system of differential equations. It is almost impossible to get general propositions from such systems. It is why Kiyotaki & Wright limit themselves to a study of stationary solutions. Stationary solutions are given by the following Bellman equations (putting $V'_m(t) = V'_s(t) = 0$):

$$rV_m = \beta(1 - M)\bar{\pi}x(u + V_s - V_m) \tag{2-7}$$

$$rV_s = \beta(1 - M)x^2(u) + \beta M x \pi max_\pi(V_m - V_s)$$

The properties of equilibria crucially depend on the producers' acceptation of money when they meet money holders with a simple coincidence of wants. Accepting money generates a utility flow $V_m - V_s$. If this flow is positive, the best decision is $\pi = 1$. If it is negative, the best decision is $\pi = 0$. If $V_m - V_s = 0$, the producer may choose whatever value $0 \leq \pi \leq 1$. A key element of the decision is the parametric probability of money acceptation $\bar{\pi}$.

Individuals take $\bar{\pi}$ as an equilibrium value (otherwise they would not accept to take it as a data for utility maximization). They are wrong to do that. Obviously, the only equilibrium values are those which generate individual decisions which confirm them. If for $\bar{\pi} = 0$ individuals do not accept money ($\pi = 0$) – a very plausible decision since if you think that nobody will accept money you have no reason to accept it – it is clear that $\bar{\pi} = 0$ is an equilibrium value. In the same manner that in a Walrasian model, prices posted by the auctioneer are equilibrium prices when they cancel market excess-demands, $\bar{\pi}$ is an equilibrium degree of money acceptation if everyone validates it, *i.e.* whenever $\pi(\bar{\pi}) = \bar{\pi}$. We must precisely look for the exact form of correspondence $\pi(\bar{\pi})$ whose fix-points will determine equilibria.

Condition $V_m - V_s = 0$ will give us the critical value $\bar{\pi}°$, of $\bar{\pi}$; producers will accept money if $\bar{\pi} > \bar{\pi}°$. From the expressions above, it is easy to derive that value. $V_m - V_s \geq 0$ if $\beta(1 - M)x(u)(\bar{\pi} - x) \geq 0$. Producers will accept money if the following condition is met:

$$\pi = 1 \qquad \text{iff } \bar{\pi} > \bar{\pi}° = x \tag{2-8}$$

The best response correspondence and its fix-points are shown on the graph below:

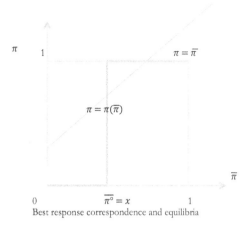

Figure 2.3 **Best response correspondence and equilibria**

Kiyotaki & Wright's model exhibits three equilibria:

- A barter equilibrium at which money is not accepted ($\bar{\pi}^\circ = 0$) and not used.
- A mix equilibrium at which money is accepted with probability $\bar{\pi}^\circ$.
- A monetary equilibrium at which money is always accepted ($\bar{\pi}^\circ = 1$); not only are double coincidence of wants transactions realized but also purchases and sales take place (commodity against money).

In brief, money is accepted if parametric acceptation is high enough in regard of preferences and production specialization, even higher if impatience is great (high r). Our special case $c = 0$ is interesting since it makes the basic point absolutely transparent. Variable x measures the difficulty of meeting somebody else with a double coincidence of wants. Hence, x measures the probability to get a consumable commodity when being a producer (x^2); x may be said to measure the degree of *liquidity* in a barter economy. The probability to get a consumable commodity for a money holder is $\bar{\pi}x$. The choice for an individual boils down to accepting money *if money is more liquid than commodities* ($\bar{\pi} \geq x$), which may seem trivial once the mathematical apparatus of Bellman equations of the original model are put aside.[10] Menger adopted that view a century ago with his concept of *Absatzfähigkeit*.

Kiyotaki & Wright's model exhibits not only a multiplicity but also a ranking of equilibria. The monetary equilibrium is the best one according to the sum of individual values. The reason for that is clear: at that equilibrium transactions against money are added to barter ones which still take place whenever possible. Calculation confirms that intuition. This model is characterized, as noted above, by a situation of *coordination failures*. In these types of models, equilibrium selection, a very delicate problem indeed, is crucial.

A more elaborated version of this model relaxes the fixed price hypothesis and replaces it by a bilateral bargaining (Trejos & Wright, 1995). Despite that improvement, the model does not bring new results and will not be presented here.

The search-theoretic approach to money may be credited for having demonstrated the existence of a monetary equilibrium with money serving exclusively as an intermediary of exchange. In a sense, money theory was replaced on the right track, the one initiated by Walras. These authors may rightly claim that they have found an elegant solution to an old problem. Money is now integrated into value theory in a more elegant and rigorous model than those of Walras and Patinkin. But search-theoreticians claim far more than providing a solution to an old problem. They think they have given *micro-foundations to monetary theory*. In more precise terms, they claim to have raised and solved a question unduly neglected by Walrasian tradition: how is it that money is adopted for transaction when other possibilities exist (barter, for instance). Presupposing money as the exclusive transaction technique, as Walras and Patinkin did, is no longer acceptable. Elucidating the mechanism by which money is selected as the best technique of transaction amongst all others is what monetary theory should be about. Search models do that job, and they kill two birds with one stone since they exhibit not only a monetary equilibrium but also a non-monetary equilibrium which is inferior in terms of welfare.

Is the Kiyotaki & Wright model really more micro-founded than the Walras one?

Micro-foundation is claimed by Shi (2006) to be an achievement owed to search models. Shi sees in micro-foundation the signs that money theory has filled the gap between price and money theory. Presupposing money, according to Shi, exposes any theory to the Lucas critique about monetary policy. We should be able to verify that an inflationary policy does not contradict money acceptation and does not incite people to switch to another technique of transaction. Besides, following the Walras-Patinkin approach amounts to considering real balances as an argument of utility functions, which is not compatible with the idea of *fiat money*, the central concept of money theory. It goes without saying that a cash-in-advance constraint is also rejected by Shi in the name of micro-foundation. However, despite Shi's assertions, it is far from being clear whether or not search models give the alleged micro-foundations to money theory.

A problematic micro-foundation

What search-theoretic authors mean by micro-foundation is that the trans-action technique (barter, *fiat money*, credit, etc.) should not be presupposed, but be the outcome of the model. They wish or they claim that transaction technique should be determined by equilibrium conditions as are other eco-nomic variables. Even if we can agree with the desire to make endogenous the greatest number possible of variables, it is by no means sure that it is legitimate to go any further along in this than Walras and neo-Walrasians have done.

WHAT KIND OF MICRO-FOUNDATION?

A misunderstanding should be avoided: micro-foundation of money is not a magic trick. Money is not to be invented starting from scratch. In search models the quantity of *fiat money* is given and the question is whether money is or is not chosen at equilibrium as the transaction technique. In other terms, we face here *a problem of choice of techniques for the whole of economy* and we do not try to make the reader think that money will emerge from this nothing-ness (he/she would legitimately be worried if the purpose was to accomplish such a miracle!).

At this point, an important remark is in order: choosing a transaction technique is different whether the choice is between barter and money, or between two different monies. In the latter case, we can compare two mon-etary economies whose logic is more or less the same. One may expect that what matters is a simple comparison between transaction costs (the dollar and peso, for instance, in the study of dollarization). But, in the former case, one may suspect that a monetary and a barter economy work according to different logics. The question is now: to what extent is it acceptable to con-sider that barter and money may be alternative transaction techniques of the *same economy*?

It is legitimate to examine that point since, *from the very point of view of search models, barter and money economies are different economies*. In the moneyless econ-omy, individuals do not need more information than the commodity space (continuum $[0,1]$), the degree of specialization (x) and the matching technique (Poisson process with parameter β). In an economy with money, there must be an *additional information*, the average attitude toward money (parametric degree of money acceptance $\bar{\pi}$). An additional institution is thus required, making sense of $\bar{\pi}$. Does an auctioneer gather and deliver information by asking people if they intend to accept money? If it is not the case, how do people know what others intend to do? Variable $\bar{\pi}$ has to be explained. To my knowledge, search authors have not yet given much of an explanation. Therefore, a barter econ-omy ($M = 0$) should not be considered as equivalent to an economy in which individuals have chosen barter instead of money ($M > 0, \pi = \bar{\pi} = 0$).

AN ILLUSORY MICRO-FOUNDATION

Parameter $\bar{\pi}$ plays a crucial role since its value is decisive for the choice between the two available strategies (to accept money, to refuse money). How may we interpret that parameter?

Two interpretations of $\bar{\pi}$ seem possible. The first one is that $\bar{\pi}$ is synthetic information about other people's behaviour freely available to everybody. When taking the decision of accepting ($\pi = 1$) or not accepting ($\pi = 0$) money, each individual takes into account what other people do ($\bar{\pi}$).[11] In other terms, according to that first interpretation, when two people meet they know what other people do (complete information). Such a situation is not compatible with the fact that a market economy is a decentralized one. In a decentralized economy it is admitted that any pair of would-be partners only know their own history and their disposition to exchange. A second interpretation is to consider $\bar{\pi}$ exactly as Walrasians consider the auctioneer's parametric prices. The centralized character of the economy would be incarnated, if one may say so, in an institution.

In both cases, equilibrium requires that individual decisions be compatible with the information which has prompted them. This occurs in pure strategy equilibria, either when all individuals decide to accept or to not accept money. How may individuals know which equilibrium is implemented?

According to the first interpretation, global economy is transparent for each individual (complete information). Everyone is able to check if his or her own decision is in accordance with those of others. But nobody has the possibility to decide which of the two pure strategy equilibria will be implemented. The choice between barter and monetary equilibria requires unanimity. Everyone knows the consequence of his or her choice since they know what others are doing, thanks to $\bar{\pi}$. If this is true, how could anybody choose a strategy other than $\pi = 0$, $\pi = \pi°$ or $\pi = 1$? Any other strategy would be absurd since it could not bring about any equilibrium position. In other words, everyone is reduced to acquiesce to what other people have decided. As a consequence nobody can select equilibrium. Indeterminacy of which equilibrium will be selected ensues.

According to our second interpretation, $\bar{\pi}$ is fixed by the auctioneer. If the auctioneer "prefers" the monetary equilibrium, it just has to post $\bar{\pi}$ above its critical threshold $\pi°$. The selection of money as the equilibrium transaction entirely depends on the auctioneer. In that case, far from micro-founding money theory, search models would just give a sophisticated version of Knapp's theory – money as a creation of the State or of the law – which is definitely not what they are intended for!

Is it for that reason that the first interpretation is the most common? Yet, even so, money micro-foundation is an illusion.

CHOICE AT EQUILIBRIUM VERSUS CHOICE OF AN EQUILIBRIUM

Micro-foundation is illusory in search models because individual choice between diverse transaction techniques (money and barter) is fundamentally different from individual choice between diverse consumption baskets or between diverse production techniques:

1   When a consumer chooses his or her optimal consumption basket as the solution of their utility maximization program he or she have not to take into account what other people do; by contrast, when he/she chooses a transaction technique he or she must take into consideration what other people do.
2   In the first case, if that choice is not compatible with other people's choices, the auctioneer applies the "law of supply and demand" and triggers a dynamic process of adjustment; in the second case no adjustment process is available; the auctioneer has simply to decide whether money ($\bar{\pi} = 1$) or barter ($\bar{\pi} = 0$) will prevail.

In search models exhibiting coordination failures as in Kiyotaki & Wright (1993) the monetary equilibrium is no more micro-founded than the barter one, if micro-foundation is understood as it is in traditional economic theory. The story told by Kiyotaki & Wright's model about money does not differ in essence from that told by Knapp or other institutionalists: in both cases money is accepted by virtue of an exogenous variable. Search models do not perform better, from that point of view, than a standard general equilibrium model to which a Clower constraint (*horresco referens!*) would have been added, leaving open the question of the commodity adopted as a means of payment. In such an economy, as nobody would know in advance which commodity will be selected, they would have to calculate their excess-demands for each parametric prices vector and for each commodity selected as a means of payment (which intervenes in the Clower constraint). As no reason exists that the same commodity would maximize utility in any case and for all individuals, no decentralized procedure may be implemented for solving the problem. The auctioneer has to arbitrarily choose the intermediary of exchange. Holding that commodity would be nothing but a cash-in-advance constraint.

We should not confuse individual choices at equilibrium (individuals take parametric prices as equilibrium ones) and individual choices between equilibria. Micro-foundations are relevant only for the former, not for the latter. Either the auctioneer decides which equilibrium will be selected by individuals by fixing $\bar{\pi}$ at an appropriate level or the type of equilibrium (money or barter) is undetermined.

To remedy that indeterminacy, one may resort to "focal points", "correlated equilibria", etc., all additional procedures revealing that a simple coordination of maximizing individuals cannot account for the existence and use of money as a transaction technique. In any case, one must add *some institutional variable*. Here too an institutional assumption is required. Why not recognize that search models fail to micro-found money? Because, some authors think, the essentiality of money – which holds in the Kiyotaki-Wright model – guarantees that monetary equilibrium will ultimately be selected.

Shi, for instance, maintains that "*a monetary equilibrium that is inferior to a non-monetary equilibrium could not have survived the test of time*" (Shi, 2006, p. 644) (my italics). It is Shi's argument which cannot survive a test of logical consistency. In order to justify a trend toward the better equilibrium, we would need a global stability analysis. It is precisely what is lacking (and not only in search models). This absence cannot be evoked specifically against search models since it is general. But it makes Shi's proposition totally arbitrary. The dynamics of the basic search model are very complex and its dynamic properties are out of reach. We must content ourselves with stationary solutions only. In that poor state, insistence on essentiality as a justification for the choice of money is hardly acceptable. It tends to accredit that Dr Pangloss's motto – *tout est pour le mieux dans le meilleur des mondes possibles* – is a scientific one. From the logic of the model itself, there is no reason for the economy to select monetary equilibrium instead of the barter one, except if one thinks that the auctioneer is a benevolent one. A strange idea for a micro-foundation oriented theory!

AN ARBITRARY MICRO-FOUNDATION

In the Kiyotaki & Wright model, primitives of the economy are the same when money is and is not accepted. As we have seen, only $\bar{\pi}$ makes a difference. That point raises problems. Either money is just an option which may be added to a barter economy – this is exactly what monetary equilibrium is – and money essentiality is trivial (since it allows additional transactions) or money is an alternative to barter. But to compare money and barter assuming the specialization is constant is completely arbitrary. Assuming specialization to be independent of the technique of transaction is difficult to stomach. How can we imagine that rational individuals will specialize without considering the transaction technique? In the absence of money, it is not very rational, to say the least, to specialize up to a point where there is no longer any double coincidence of wants. Ironically, it is that starting point which should be micro-founded instead of money!

If specialization and money acceptation are two related variables, does it make sense to compare a monetary and a barter economy? The answer is: yes, if they have the same primitives. But, at this point, it is the notion of primitives which comes under discussion. Whatever their position may be, primitives are data that economic theory refuses to explain or, in other terms, refuses to micro-found. As already noted, all value theories rely on the same postulate: a commodity space is common knowledge to individuals who are defined in relation with it. To my knowledge, no value theoretician has proposed to micro-found the commodity space. Even Marx, who sometimes affirms that use values reflect social relationships, adopts that postulate at the beginning of *Capital*.[12] A commodity space postulate is probably the bottom line for value theoreticians, in the same manner as a nominal unit of account is for monetary analysis partisans (see Part Two).

Reasoning along a value-theoretical analysis makes money theory problematic. On the one hand, value analysis allows for raising the question of acceptance of an *a priori* given money, which amounts to preaching for a micro-foundation of money theory. But, on the other hand, this makes that micro-foundation arbitrary. Search models assume at the same time that specialization is such that no double coincidence of wants exists and that money is not the current transaction technique. These two assumptions are difficult to reconcile. In that approach, money appears at the final act for a happy ending: if money should exist, everything would go smoothly; money is so desirable in that context that discovering that an additional commodity without any intrinsic utility, called money, may overcome "frictions" comes as no surprise. Search theoreticians discover the rabbit they have put into the hat beforehand.

If that reasoning is widely accepted by academic economists and if money micro-foundation seems an acceptable objective, it is probably because money and transaction techniques occupy a very special place in value theories. As already mentioned, money has to be considered as a social device whereas ordinary commodities are natural ones. Consequently, money prices are not on the same theoretical level as relative prices, rates of interest and market allocations. Money is an option. Money acceptance proceeds from a bootstrap effect (a social convention). Money arbitrariness is a fundamental feature of value theories.

A non-orthodox variant of money micro-foundation: the logical genesis of money

Orthodox economists are not the only one who chase after a micro-foundation of money. Under the heading "the origin of money" many authors have tried to give an account for the presence of money in our societies.

It is quite natural that historians may be interested in "the origin of money". They try to explain how coinage of precious metals or how paper money have appeared in the past. Their conclusions or hypothetical explanations are backed by testimonies, contemporary material, etc. When economists embark upon "the origin of money", what they are looking for is a *logical genesis* of it, which in most cases is another term for micro-foundation.

Marx, for instance, announces in *Capital* that he is about to provide "what bourgeois economics has never attempted at doing, that is a genesis of money form". What is behind that ambitious program is to make explicit how phenomenal forms of social life are linked into a complex nexus with the market division of labour and its obliged complement, the exchange of commodities. Marx aims at giving a critique of political economy and at showing the transient historical character of our institutions and of our social relationships. A careful examination of Marx's forms of value theory, *from an internal critique point of view*, shows that it is a failure (Cartelier, 1991). Later, Carl Menger (1892) again tackled the problem of "the origin of money" and he delivered a logical genesis for money which paved the way for all the search models.

Recently there has been a tentative step in the same direction by Michel Aglietta and André Orléan (1982, 2002), two leading "heterodox" authors in France. They present their theory as anthropologically founded and as a charge against academic theory. By contrast with Marx and Menger who tried to derive money from commodity exchange, they place themselves at a logically prior stage. They share with Benetti & Cartelier (1980) the idea that any market economy is a monetary one but they reject the latter authors' view because it presupposes money. Aglietta & Orléan would like to explain "institutionalisa- tion and collapse of monies"[13] as starting from competition between monies.

Their main idea is the mimetic hypothesis borrowed from René Girard. They already explored this track in a preceding book (Aglietta & Orléan, 1982) but they intend in their more recent work to give that idea its maximal extension. They transpose Girard's critique of the "romantic lie" into a critique of *homo oeconomicus*. Instead of the face-to-face subject/object, they adopt the triangular subject/model/object. Imitation expresses the incompleteness of those who do not master their desires. "The essence of wealth is intersubjective" is the mes- sage conveyed by imitation. They describe a three-stage sequence more or less parallel to that of Marx's value forms theory.

The uncertainty two individuals are subject to when they ask themselves about their desire for wealth and its content (dubbed Stage F1 with reference to Marx's theory of value forms) turns into *essential violence* (F2) as a generalization. Such a scenario is thought to be the earliest kind because it informs the funda- mental point about market society: "the unanimous desire for wealth under its more immediate form before its transfiguration through money". According to the authors, this point comes as an opposition to orthodox theory where individual preferences are well-defined on the commodity space and are such that equilibrium generally exists. Against that determination, the authors wish to demonstrate the consequences of wealth indeterminacy.

These first stages generate by themselves a dynamics which leads towards a third stage (F3). It is then possible to show that "in a group where everyone is linked to everyone else (. . .) stochastic dynamics of imitation necessarily con- verges toward unanimity". The commodity toward convergence takes place; it is arbitrary. That unanimity is interpreted by Girard as the expression of a *social violence*. According to the authors, the point of Girardian thought is to understand that between order and extreme violence the difference is minimal. It is very easy to pass from one to the other. This is the fundamental idea, and that intrinsic instability explains why and how monetary crises occur and why money is precarious.

This logical genesis of money bears a problematic relation to economic theory. Despite being apparently extraneous to economics, Aglietta & Orlé- an's thesis is not free from the critiques addressed to money micro-foundation above. Both approaches are in fact more or less parallel. Aglietta & Orléan's propositions are very close to those of the mainstream. This is true, for instance, for the arbitrariness of the selected commodity, a result demonstrated by Iwai (1988). In 1892, Carl Menger described an evolutionary process led by a successful elite and imitated by the masses which brought about money. Moreover, Menger is aware of the circularity or of the conventional character of his *Absatzfähigkeit*: the saleability of a commodity is more affected by expectations than by a commodity's intrinsic properties. In the terms of search models, equilibrium multiplicity and selection are arbitrary. They cannot be deduced from the primitives of the economy. Aglietta & Orléan do not add much to the academic theory they are minded to criticize. They propose an anthropological interpretation and another way of reading it. However sympathetic we may be with their view about money, we cannot help thinking that their opposition to orthodoxy is more philosophical than analytical. Bootstrap effects are well-known by academic theoreticians – who have formalized them for a long time and call them sunspot equilibria. They do not mention social violence – which may be regrettable – but they are aware of the conventional character of equilibrium selection.

Another difficulty with Aglietta & Orléan's presentation is a certain lack of precision about their main notions. For instance, the agents who intervene at stage F1 are not defined. What is an economic agent when money is about to be selected? What are the commodities or wealth components amongst which the competition is supposed to select money? The alleged incompleteness of individuals should not preclude from defining them precisely. Marx is clear about it when he talks about the independence of people having an obliged expression in the mutual dependence of things. Benetti & Cartelier (1980) use the concept of *separation* to indicate that economic subjects are such only once the market is over. The market ensures the transition between would-be economic subjects and effective ones.

To conclude, Aglietta & Orléan succeed no better than any other academic theory and for the same reasons despite proclaimed differences in providing a logical genesis of money. The reader also faces an additional difficulty. While academic theory's failure is clearly seen in the equilibrium selection problem (and also in the inadequacy of the concept of *fiat money*), the origin of Aglietta & Orléan's failure is in the indeterminacy of their initial hypotheses. Initial assumptions show what the theoreticians choose not to explain. It is very difficult to make explicit what Aglietta & Orléan accept to not account for. Discussing the results of a theory when its postulates are not clear is almost impossible.

How is it that authors so philosophically opposed may share a common thought of a logical genesis of money? The answer is not obvious. We could conjecture however that they all adhere to the idea that it is possible for a social science to tell us the truth about society. That conviction originates in a common belief that our societies proceed only from ourselves. Even if Marx was not explicitly fond of the myth of social contract, he was certainly confident in the possibility to scientifically study societies. Social scientists influenced by Marx may join those following a "social contract" line of reasoning (academic economists) on this particular attitude. It is not the proper place to develop this point. We would suggest nevertheless that our critique and our reluctance to embark upon a quest for a logical genesis – which is justified rationally by their failures – is the expression of a diffidence about the founding myth of our societies, namely the conviction that we do not need any myths but only science and especially the social sciences. Against that view, it should be recalled that thinking of ourselves as overhanging above our social reality and observing it as external to us is presumptuous and politically not innocuous.

A debatable orientation

Maintaining that money theory should be micro-founded means that Walrasian-Patinkin models were not! This is clearly false: the price of money is determined in those models – once correctly interpreted – in the same way as the prices of other commodities. Here it appears how inopportune Hahn's proposition has been and how it has contributed to give a very special orientation to money theory. The misinterpretation of Walras's model and its replacement by the Arrow-Debreu one have led the best theoreticians to conceive micro-foundation in a way not conforming to tradition. For them, micro-foundation does not mean only that prices and market allocations are determined by a condition of mutual compatibility between decentralized individual actions – which is the traditional meaning – but also that the "institutional framework" which gives sense to individual behaviour must also be determined in the same way. Mechanism design is now fashionable. Theoreticians try to extend the property of optimality from prices and allocations to the mechanisms and procedures which are implemented. Money – both a commodity and an institution? – is a privileged field for applying the new view of micro-foundation.

The orientation of money theory toward micro-foundation is certainly interesting but illusory.[14] It raises a very general problem, far beyond money: *how to account for the existence of institutions or of institutional rules in a theory where only individual behaviour is considered?* In other words, the academic *motto* – we should give micro-foundations to everything – is far from being clear and well-founded.

Micro-founding money, the State, transaction organization, etc., implies that a model of a minimal economy without institutions is conceivable and could be used as a benchmark.

Let's consider Arrow-Debreu's model, for instance. The economy described by this model is logically possible – a general equilibrium exists – and desirable – this equilibrium is Pareto-optimal. To introduce the State in the model, it is necessary to add an assumption, the existence of collective goods which cannot optimally be allocated through a market-like procedure. The State will be present as a remedy to a market failure. Similarly, the introduction of some "frictions" (bilateral transactions between specialized agents) may generate another type of market failure: money will be accounted for since it will remedy those types of "frictions".

Such a method raises two types of interrogations:

- What are the minimal institutional hypotheses compatible with the existence and optimality of equilibrium? Is it possible to think of a zero-institution economic model which could be used as a benchmark to appreciate the extent of micro-foundation of any added institution?
- Does it make sense to adopt the normative point of view according to which the best equilibrium in terms of welfare will always be implemented? More decisively: why would our societies adopt the diverse particular settings which generate optimal outcomes (mechanism design)? Why should economists adopt a Dr Pangloss vision of society? Are there analytical arguments in favour of such a social philosophy?

We have noted above that the *a priori* less institutional model (Arrow-Debreu) relies at least on three institutional hypotheses. Is it possible to eliminate one of those hypotheses and to make endogenous the commodity space, the posting of prices and the "law" of supply and demand? Some efforts have been made in the past. One already mentioned has been the elimination of the "law" of supply and demand consequently to its inefficiency. As a result, the whole domain of the global stability of a general equilibrium, considered as crucial for a long time, has fallen into oblivion. By the same token, the field of economic theory shrinks to equilibrium existence and optimality, which is a pity in regards to the whole of economic tradition. Another possibility is to suppress parametric prices and replace them with a strategic foundation of perfect competition. It is probably too early to assess the success of such recent efforts.

A completely different strategy would be to give a foundation outside economics for some institutional hypotheses. Let us quote Wallace on the commodity space and preferences postulates: "*Tastes and technologies are given building blocks of economic models mainly because the assumed description can, in principle, be provided by other disciplines. Agronomists describe the various ways to grow wheat, chemists describe how molecules are constructed, and so on. But no other disciplines will tell economists how real cash balances contribute to utility or reduce time spent shopping or what constitutes those real balances*" (Wallace, 2001, p. 849) (my italics).

Wallace's argument is not receivable. The way economic theory treats commodities or goods (Euclidian space in Arrow-Debreu's models, continuum in search models) owes nothing to other disciplines, except for mathematics. Postulating a Euclidian commodity space has nothing to do with agronomy, physics or chemistry. It is an abstraction of its own which can be justified (or not) only by theoretical economic considerations.

We can go even further in questioning the *motto* of micro-foundations of institutions. It is well-known and even proclaimed that economic theory is about private ownership economies. Should we chase after the micro-foundations of all the institutions making private property possible and viable? Should we explain why economic agents are supposed not to rob, not to cheat, not to murder?

Piccione & Rubinstein (2007) have shown that two economies populated by individuals having the same commodity space and the same preferences, but differing by the mode of allocation of commodities (respectively exchange and predation) share the same basic properties: the general equilibrium exists and is unique; moreover it is also Pareto-optimal! Should we elaborate a meta-model allowing people to choose (endogenously) between exchange (or market) and predation (or jungle)? To my knowledge, nobody has maintained that such a task is possible and even desirable.

We have to endure that economic theory does not explain everything and that economic theoreticians (and other social scientists too) have to make explicit what their postulates are; this is tantamount to listing the institutions they accept to renounce to micro-found (without being ashamed to do so). Academic theoreticians insist on the necessity to micro-found money. Do they succeed in making money emerge from a spontaneous coordination of individualistic agents? As we have seen, they do not. This could be a sufficient reason to embark on exploring an alternative route, the monetary analysis. But there is still some work to be done before.

Neutrality of money: the grail of money theory?

The quest for the conditions of money neutrality is inherent in value theory. Money is not considered there as a primitive. Fundamental theorems are demonstrated for a moneyless economy. The Walras-Patinkin tradition explicitly introduces money as the exclusive transaction technique. Later theoreticians aimed at justifying the presence of money. In both cases, the only question which matters is whether money circulation affects real variables or not. As we shall see, Walras's answer is "no" but he is uncomfortable when he has to justify it. Since money is a component of wealth (money has a positive price at equilibrium), a variation of the quantity of money may affect the whole economy. We have to make precise the conditions under which it does not. Patinkin has done part of the job but modern trends in monetary theory have raised new challenges.

The way of looking at money neutrality has changed with the development of search models. At first sight, essentiality, which makes sense only when nonmonetary or monetary equilibrium exist depending on the values of some parameters, is difficult to reconcile with neutrality; if money is essential, how can it be neutral? However, one exercise is to compare two identical economies with different quantities of money – a neutrality problem – another is to compare two identical economies with barter and money as respective transaction techniques – an essentiality problem. *Essentiality and neutrality are analytically distinct questions.* The fact is, as we shall see, that models adapted for dealing with essentiality – search models – are not well-suited for discussing neutrality (the quest for the optimal quantity of money in search models is a symptom of this difficulty). The price paid for money essentiality seems to be a farewell to money neutrality.

Money neutrality: an elementary solution

Let us come back to Exchange Equation (2–3) in the basic model above. If the following additional assumptions are made: (a) V and T are independent from M, (b) M is an independent variable determined from outside systems (2–1) or (2–2), we get the Quantity Theory of Money (QTM).

The interesting property of QTM, in that simple and crude formalization, is money neutrality. What does it mean? Analytically, it means that multiplying M by a factor γ does not change equilibrium value of p and multiplies P by a factor γ (homogeneity of degree 0 of p and of degree 1 of P); it means also that the preliminary rejection of money – which founds value approaches – is a good research strategy since money does not affect the basic propositions of value theory, all of which only concern real variables.

But the debates about neutrality show that the story is not that simple. Two important considerations – dynamics and distributional effects – make neutrality a too expansive property in terms of restrictive assumptions.

Neutrality, comparative statics and dynamics

Neutrality proposition results from a comparison between two equilibria, where money quantity is respectively M and γM. Neutrality is a matter of comparative statics. But comparative statics does not make sense unless some transient trajectories are stable.

A strong belief was common to economists during the interwar period and immediately after WWII: money is not neutral in the short-term (transient adjustment) but is neutral in the long-term (comparative statics). Patinkin's strong attack in the 1950s and 1960s against the current state of art of monetary theory (say systems (2–2) and (2–3)) was precisely motivated by its inability to deal with neutrality. There is an incompatibility, maintained Patinkin, between two sacred cows of general equilibrium theory: the homogeneity of zero degree of excess-demand functions and Walras's Law. Whereas QTM entails that a change of money quantity triggers disequilibrium on the market for money, homogeneity precludes any change in excess-demand equations of system (2–2). Walras's Law makes impossible such a situation (equilibrium in all markets but one). Patinkin suggested to remedy that contradiction by breaking with the homogeneity of excess-demand functions and introducing a real balance effect into them. The story then becomes the following: if money quantity is doubled excess-demand functions of system (2–2) change as well as equation (2–3). If general equilibrium is unique, the only possible equilibrium after a doubling of M is one with p unchanged and P doubled. If we assume global stability, the transient disequilibrium trajectory will tend toward that equilibrium when time tends to infinity. Patinkin (1987) had given some firm foundations to the belief in long-term neutrality of money compatible with a non-neutrality in the short-term.

The controversy triggered by Patinkin gave birth to a huge amount of literature and to a great expense of ingenuity, mathematics and subtle economic reasoning. For us today, it has only a historical interest since a seismic event in general theory put an end to the controversy: Debreu (1974), Mantel (1974) and Sonnenschein (1972) informed the profession that the global stability of a general competitive equilibrium is out of reach with the existing hypotheses (those which are sufficient to demonstrate equilibrium existence). Global stability was no longer a current topic in academic literature and these transient trajectories cease to haunt most theoreticians.

Neutrality and distributional effects

Independently of that earthquake, some authors had realized that the crude expression above for QTM was not entirely convincing. Walras was aware that any variation of the quantity of money generates distribution effects. Rigorously, these effects are not compatible with neutrality since they will affect excess-demand functions of system (2–2) (unless some very restrictive assumptions are made as Patinkin will remark later). Walras, however, assumes without any verification that these effects compensate. It is not without some trouble that he concludes his studies by this astonishing assertion: money neutrality is a statement "*à très peu près rigoureusement exact*". Of course, such a proposition cannot be accepted by modern standards. Later, an interesting debate placed Patinkin in opposition to Gurley & Shaw (1960). A clarification of the conditions under which money neutrality was valid ensued. Basically, the absence of any distribution effects following a variation of the quantity of money depends on the structure of the totality of assets.

When Patinkin's controversy – *i.e.* a lot of books and articles published by eminent theoreticians – came to an end, two points characterized the agenda of monetary theory:

1   The choice between alternative transaction techniques is not yet a fundamental issue, even if the myth of barter is used as cheap talk to justify that omission.
2   What dominates the so-called "integration of money into value theory" is not the positive price of money but the conditions of its neutrality.

As we know, modern developments have brought into the foreground the choice between alternative transaction techniques as the main problem to be solved. But the assumptions under which search models are built make it more difficult (and even not appropriate) to deal with neutrality.

Neutrality and modern theory of money

In the modern theory, the quest for neutrality has not disappeared. No wonder: it is a necessary component of value theory. Even if non-neutrality may justify and guide monetary policy, it would be embarrassing for those theoreticians who think money is optional to renounce money neutrality. In any case, neutrality conditions must be carefully established in order to understand the conditions which make a monetary policy possible and efficient. But, at the same time, if these conditions appear too restrictive to be respected, the very foundations of money value theory are put into danger.

Although transaction techniques are amongst the primitives of an economy, it is clear for most authors that money is not on the same level as the others. The mere idea that a positive price for money at equilibrium is due to a bootstrap effect shows that money is not treated on the same footing as production and consumption. *Money neutrality is the norm in value theory as the obliged consequence of money being "artificial".*

At the first stage of search-theoretic models, neutrality was not really addressed. Diverse assumptions, or possibly the general structure of these models, made it irrelevant to inquire into neutrality. Consider for instance the Kiyotaki & Wright model of 1993 (see above). Money holders are assumed to not be capable of producing commodities. Moreover, money is assumed to be not divisible and money holdings are limited to unity. In that environment, increasing the amount of money clearly means diminishing the number of potential producers. By construction of the model, money cannot be neutral. When money holders are permitted to produce (Siandra models), money quantity affects the meeting probabilities and hence the final allocations. Models which allow for the proving of the existence of monetary equilibrium appear to be those which prevent the establishing of money neutrality. Models of second and third generations address that general question but they rely on such epic assumptions that we may have to doubt their relevance.

Neil Wallace (2001) opposes two sorts of models. In the first one, money is essential, which means: "trading intrinsically useless objects is necessary for the achievement of at least some allocations, and in particular, good allocations" (Wallace, 2001, p. 847). In the second one, the advantage of money over the other transaction techniques is presupposed but not proved (cash-in-advance models, typically). On that basis, these models deal with monetary policy. They are well-adapted for the study of money neutrality. Alas, declares Wallace, models of that second type are not compatible with models of the first one. In any case, the use of money to carry out transactions at equilibrium has to be justified. Explaining the choice of money amongst other transaction techniques should be a prerequisite for dealing with the more traditional problems of money influence on real variables.

Thus, the orientation prescribed by Wallace is to modify models of the first type, where the essentiality of money is proved, to make them suitable for the study of neutrality and, by the same topic, useful for monetary policy. An example of this new path is the search models of Lagos–Wright, which give conditions for essentiality and neutrality to be compatible (Lagos & Wright, 2005). The cost paid for that, in terms of additional assumptions, seems, however, too high.

Let's see briefly the origin of this drawback and how the Lagos–Wright type of models try to remedy it.

There is nothing new concerning the obstacle to be overcome: the distribution effect of money is the villain as it was in the case of Walras and Patinkin. What is specific with these search models, however, is that these effects exist even without any change in the total quantity of money! This is the case with the search models of the third generation in which money indivisibility and limited storage assumptions are relaxed. In that general environment, transactions stochastically modify the distribution of money amongst individuals. It is no longer possible to track the distribution of wealth amongst individuals. "One of the main problems with the model is the endogenous distribution of money holdings across agents, F(m), is non-degenerate, and hence the model has a built-in heterogeneity that is hard to handle analytically" (Lagos & Wright).

To overcome that heterogeneity, "tricks" (Lagos & Wright's own term) have to be imagined. The one adopted by Lagos & Wright is to assume two types of markets: one works along the search analysis, the other is centralized in a Debreu-like manner. The strategic point is an individual's behaviour about money holdings when they leave search markets and enter a centralized one. They have to decide the best amount of money to hold at equilibrium. At this point, Lagos & Wright introduce their special assumption of linearity either of the utility function or of the cost of production of the general good. Thanks to that "trick", it can be shown that individuals will choose the same quantity of money so that distribution of money holdings over individuals is known.

Models of the Lagos & Wright type are tractable (even if they are complex) and allow the discussing of monetary policy questions. They link search-theoretic approach to the usual macroeconomic concerns. In that sense they accomplish part of the program sketched by Wallace. Classical neutrality holds in the Lagos & Wright model and welfare comparisons are possible between economies characterized by different parameters (time depreciation, bargaining power and so on). But it seems not possible to relax the opportunistic linearity assumption of cost or utility function, which is, however, a very arbitrary one. It is not yet clear which path will allow academic theoreticians to get out of the woods.

* * *

The creativeness of the authors of the third generation of search models obviously deserves admiration. Old and new discussions about neutrality meet the same fate, however. The cost paid for proving money neutrality is so high that we cannot help thinking that we are in a dead end. The dilemma is the following:

- Either money is conceived of as a special commodity (fiat money); then it is a component of wealth (it has a positive price at equilibrium); money neutrality holds only under very special assumptions having nothing to do with the specific function of an intermediary of exchange (absence of any distributional effects); this means that money neutrality is not an acceptable statement; money is not neutral, and except for very special cases, it should be present at the very starting point of value theory since a later introduction changes the deal (a contradiction of value theory?)
- or money should not be conceived of as a commodity but as an institutional hypothesis, *i.e.* as a mechanism of coordination specific to market economies; in this view money exists and its neutrality does not make any sense; money should be presupposed from the start (as in a monetary analysis).

Does inquiring into the second part of the diptych of the academic theory of money help to get us out of that dilemma? The next chapter addresses that point.

Notes

1 Here again, Ricardo is an exception as Deleplace makes it clear in his book (Deleplace, 2017).
2 "Money is not properly speaking, one of the subjects of commerce; but the instrument which men have agreed upon to facilitate the exchange of one commodity for another" (Hume, 1970, p. 33).
3 "Why it is that the economic man is ready to accept a certain kind of commodity, even if he does not need it, or his need of it is already supplied, in exchange for all the goods he has brought to market, while it is none the less what he needs that he consults in the first instance, with respect to the goods he intends to acquire in the course of his transactions" (Menger, 1892, p. 68).
4 Or, as R. Starr (2011) assumes, if a compulsory money payment is imposed to economic agents at the end of the last period (tax payment).
5 An example is D. Gale's (1982) position: "In general equilibrium theory money has one function. It is a store of value. There is no useful distinction to be made between its role as an asset and its role as a 'medium of exchange'" (p. 231).
6 Things will be different with search models (Araujo & Guimaraes, 2014).
7 This condition means that the cash-in-advance constraint is not binding.
8 Two surveys deserve to be read since their authors have contributed much themselves to the development of that approach (Rupert et al., 2000; Shi, 2006).
9 In the original model a positive cost c was assumed with $u > c$. Assuming a zero cost simplifies the presentation without loss for what we are concerned with.
10 If not very familiar with academic literature, the reader may think that it is not very useful to mobilize all that mathematical apparatus for such a common sense conclusion. That reader will be both right and wrong. Wrong because we never know how long

a seemingly trivial proposition will hold when subjected to a strict examination of its validity and consistency (see below what happens when the quantity of money is endogenous). Any statement consistency has to be carefully checked. Being strict on this point sometimes allows you to get counterintuitive and interesting results. The reader will be a little bit right, however, because part of the mathematical refinements is often a requirement to be published in high-ranked academic reviews.

11 It makes sense to sum up other people's behaviour by $\bar{\pi}$ because the model is symmetric. A more general presentation is possible but would not add anything to our discussion. In Iwai's model, for instance, the available information is the expected vector of markets frequentation.

12 "(Use values) constitute the material content of wealth, whatever its social form may be" (Marx, p. 126).

13 "l'institutionnalisation des monnaies comme leur dépérissement" (Aglietta & Orléan, p. 37).

14 Patinkin (1965) shows a great lucidity when he notes that a conversion of a barter economy to a money economy was a "difficult, if not impossible" task "because the system of excess-demand equations of the two economies differ so fundamentally" (p. 75).

Money

Fiat money or social device for coordination?

The dilemma just mentioned haunts this chapter. Striving for the essence of money, theoreticians come to a point where it is no longer possible to deal with money as if it were a commodity. Sticking nevertheless to that position, academic economists reach a limit and are caught in a dead end. The situation calls for another analysis giving a chance to the idea of money as a device for coordination.

The essence of money

Fiat money, as an intermediary of exchange, has a positive price at equilibrium but is generally *not neutral*. Fiat money is *not useful* for production or consumption. It is *not privately produced*. That is all we have learnt about fiat money so far. But what is *positively* fiat money? Suggesting that "money is what money does" does not answer the question since that is precisely what theoreticians try to find out. The traditional functions of money do not teach us much about it either. Being a possible expression of relative values is not specific to fiat money (any commodity with a positive price at equilibrium is eligible for that) any more than to be a store of value (any durable commodity shares that property). Being an intermediary of exchange helps a little bit more, but other transaction techniques may also do the job. What defines fiat money beyond its negative characteristics (not privately produced, not useful)? What is its essence?

In the good old days of value theory, the "myth of barter" – which, properly speaking, was not a part of value theory – explained why money was present in our economies. Nowadays, to elucidate the essence of money, theoreticians make great efforts in integrating the "myth of barter" into value theory. This myth is re-written following a new syntax and new rules – mathematical models – which makes it the intellectual basis of money theory. Two types of exercises are possible and are currently made.

The first one consists in comparing the different equilibria of an economy (typically barter and monetary ones) and in selecting the one which ranks first in terms of welfare. If monetary equilibrium ranks first, money is said to be *essential; "Otherwise, why bother with money?"* asks Wallace (Wallace, 2001, p. 849) (my italics). If essentiality could hardly justify a collective choice in favour of money over barter, it could give some hints at what makes money a better intermediary of exchange; what money effectively does may reveal what is the essence of fiat money.

The second one consists in comparing two economies having the same primitives but endowed with different institutional devices, money being one of them. Even if it is not mentioned by authors, Ostroy & Starr's (1974) paper gives sense to that exercise. What makes that exercise different from the former is that it concerns economies *which are not market economies*. If identical allocations may be implemented in both economies, money will be said to be equivalent to the alternative institutional device. Some authors pretend to deduce the essence of money from that observation. This is the case with Kocherlakota (1998) who affirms that *money is memory*.

Money a remedy for "frictions"

Money essentiality is a property common to many search-theoretic models. The modern quest for essentiality may be viewed as providing an analytical foundation to the old myth of barter. Obviously, if monetary equilibrium is better than barter it is because money remedies the inconveniencies of it. Thanks to rigorous modelling it should be possible to make precise what money does that barter cannot do. But this implies a break in some ways with Arrow–Debreu's model where no decentralized transaction technique is to be found. "*For at least 2000 years, it has been asserted that monetary exchange is helpful in overcoming difficulties of exchange, difficulties which fall under the heading of absence-of-double-coincidence difficulties. Because the general-equilibrium part of the classical model has complete competitive markets,*[1] *and, therefore, does not depict any such difficulties, it cannot display any sense in which monetary exchange is helpful*" (Wallace, 2001, p. 848) (my italics).

The question which allows that break is: *what "friction" does money remedy?* The term "friction" is written between quotes to indicate that its meaning has to be made precise. "Frictions" are to be understood by reference to Arrow-Debreu's model viewed as a frictionless model. This may be very surprising since the Arrow-Debreu model is unanimously considered as a bad representation of a market economy (but a good one of a private economy).

Transactions there are centralized, multilateral and costless. Introducing "frictions" amounts to amending what is an irrelevant representation of the market and to sketching a more adequate view. This is a very interesting approach in that it reveals the view about market theoreticians have in the back of their minds.

To begin with, multilateral transactions are judged inopportune. They are replaced by an alternative assumption of bilateral meetings (either stochastic or endogenous) which are thought to give a best representation of how markets work. Bilateral meetings are at the very first steps of value theory with Turgot and Smith. They are still present in some modern general competitive equilibrium models. In a sense, bilateral meetings are archetypal. Paradoxically enough, such a representation excludes any form of market organization. The only one dealt with boils down to bilateral bargaining. One can hardly speak of markets for commodities, contrary to strategic market games. Equilibrium prices are bargaining solutions *à la* Rubinstein under assumptions making them also Nash solutions. This is the case in the Trejos & Wright (1995) model for instance.

In a centralized market, what matters is the *value* of initial endowments and not their *physical composition* (as the Walras equivalent distribution theorem reminds us). Assuming bilateral meetings dramatically changes that characteristic. Now, the physical composition of initial endowments matters. It is therefore possible to deal with a fundamental characteristic of a market economy (forgotten in Arrow-Debreu's model): individuals freely choose their specialization or, at least, they are supposed to be already specialized, so that exchange is a necessity (in search models individuals cannot consume their own production). Emphasis is nowadays put again on that feature of a market economy considered long ago as a typical one (from Steuart (1767) to Marx (1976), passing by Smith (1996) and Ricardo). The double coincidence of wants is thus a problem money theory has to deal with.

Bilateral transactions and specialization are sufficient "frictions" for determining conditions under which a monetary equilibrium exists. What money does in that case is easy to understand. Money remedies the absence of the double coincidence of wants, a very old idea but recast in modern terms. Barter makes the time before consumption shorter since it dispenses with the detour through money,[2] but the greater the specialization, the more severe is the lack of double coincidence of wants and the more probable is monetary equilibrium.

In Arrow-Debreu's model, a commodity's quality is common knowledge. Introducing specialization makes plausible some private information on commodities. If the knowledge about commodities depends on specialization, we could admit that individuals may have difficulties in assessing the quality of commodities they do not produce. Imperfect knowledge about a commodity's quality suggests another "friction". Williamson & Wright have discussed that point with the help of a model where people could imperfectly recognize a commodity's quality. Without going into too much detail about that complicated model, it is worth reminding the reader that money is the unique commodity which is perfectly recognized by all. Two qualities are possible for other commodities: a bad one (utility and cost are equal to zero) and a good one (utility and cost are positive, the former being greater than the latter). One interesting conclusion of the model (with no problem of the lack of double coincidence of wants) is that a monetary equilibrium is more probable when the private information problem is important. In this model, money remedies imperfect information about a commodity's quality. Money is, in that case, the best common language; a not uninteresting conclusion in view of what will be developed in the second part of this book!

Money conceived along that line is not the same as the one which remedies a lack of double coincidence of wants. Their properties are different. Kiyotaki &

Wright's model deals with money as an intermediary of exchange by virtue of a bootstrap effect. Williamson & Wright's model emphasizes the problem of information imperfection: money is that commodity which is unanimously recognized. Information problems (managing metallic currencies, counterfeiting, etc.) greatly differ from specialization ones. If money is the unique commodity which is perfectly known in a private economy, it follows that money is in fact the unique non-private commodity. Not being used in consumption and in production, on one hand, and being a non-privately produced commodity, on the other, are two characteristics of *fiat money* in academic theory. Being the only one to be common knowledge – a strong qualification for the commodity space postulate – money becomes the language unanimously adopted by individuals. We are not very far from the monetary postulate, a characteristic of the monetary analysis, as will be clear below.

Other "frictions" may be worth considering. A farewell to centralization has important consequences. In Debreu's central clearing economy, budgetary constraints are observed and individual accounts are monitored. In fact, a kind of auctioneer makes sure that nobody violates his or her budgetary constraints. The control over individuals disappears with the euthanasia of the auctioneer. Moreover, the fact that individuals transact only one at a time would require that commitments to complete transactions at another time be possible. Obviously, in an economy with a continuum of individuals and anonymity there is no credible commitment to doing something at a later period. The necessity to remedy the lack of commitment induces Kocherlakota to enunciate (and to prove with the help of a very impressive model) a now widely approved proposition: *money is memory*. The next section is devoted to a critical examination of Kocherlakota's view about the essence of money.

Money is memory

Kocherlakota proclaims a fundamental proposition which holds valid in most of the models currently used in academic circles: "*any allocation that is achievable by money alone could be achieved instead by allowing agents costless access to a historical record of past actions that I term memory; I conclude that the role of money is to serve as a (typically imperfect) form of memory*" (Kocherlakota, 1998, p. 233) (my italics). What Kocherlakota interprets as memory is more precisely a free access to the past history of transactions for the two individuals who meet. In that case each agent may know thanks to a central accounting system what his would-be partner has done in the past as it may be the case with the blockchain technique used in bitcoin.

The question Kocherlakota answers with his proposition is no longer: *for what "friction" is money a remedy?*" but, when money is used in a given economy, "*what does it do which could equivalently be done by another device?*" Answering that interrogation is not proving that money is essential – this is supposed already to be done since the economy is a monetary one – but revealing what money really does, its very essence. Now here comes the second type of exercise we mentioned above.

Equivalence between the two competing devices – money and free access to past accounts – is considered as effective when market allocations are identical.[3] Kocherlakota not only considers that the sentence *money is memory* displays the essence of money but also that it justifies its existence: "I believe that this paper represents an advance over the usual justifications for the existence of money" (Kocherlakota, 1998, p. 250).

Kocherlakota's demonstration is beautiful and impressive. It seems very general since it holds for a large variety of models (turnpike, search, etc.). In the following lines, we will allude only to search models in order to keep the story simple.

The alternative mechanisms

The economy is described in a very general and abstract way. We will consider only a very simple case. In our economy there exist K types of individuals $(i, i + 1)$ *modulo K* producing only commodity i and consuming only commodity $i + 1$. They bilaterally meet according to a stochastic process. Barter is impossible since there is no double coincidence of wants. If no other institution is assumed, only autarky equilibrium exists with zero utility for all individuals.

Introducing money would allow a monetary equilibrium to exist for any positive value of the parametric money acceptation (think of parameter $\bar{\pi}$ of the Kiyotaki & Wright model). But this exercise does not interest Kocherlakota since it is not a new one. What he is looking for is another mechanism which would give the same allocations as monetary equilibrium. He will call that mechanism memory (improperly as we shall see).

The crucial point for Kocherlakota is that the economies he has considered so far "do not have any technology of enforcement" (Kocherlakota, 1998, p. 239). When a bilateral simple coincidence of wants meeting occurs (the only possible ones in his model), the would-be consumer cannot persuade the would-be producer to effectively produce for him or her by promising to do the same for him or her in the future. Such an engagement is not credible when there is no monitoring and no punishment for defecting. Due to this "no commitment problem", the best strategy is always autarky, *i.e.* do not produce when there is no credible counterpart.

No commitment seems typical of any individualist society where people care only about themselves and never about society as a whole. Promises of future actions have a negative net utility (to produce is costly and there is no reward); consequently they are not credible and are not believed; thus they are not even formulated. We shall see below that this is not so crystal-clear. In any case, the equilibrium is that of autarky.

The story changes when either money or memory is introduced. Kocherlakota's money is *fiat money*. Initial endowments in money are given at the beginning and evolve according to realized transactions. Kocherlakota's memory is the possibility for individuals to have free access to the past transactions of the would-be consumer he meets.

How does that memory make it possible for the economy to get the same equilibrium allocations as *fiat money*? The answer is simple indeed (even if the demonstration is much more complex). Memory allows the would-be producer to check what the would-be consumer has done in the past whenever he/she was a would-be producer. If he/she had effectively produced without counterpart, the strategy is: to do the same, *i.e. to produce without counterpart also*. If he/she had not, the strategy is: do not produce. In that symmetric economy, everyone follows the same strategy. Therefore, thanks to that possible control and punishment, equilibrium with positive activity exists (if I do not produce for free, nobody will produce for me without counterpart in the future). Without such a mechanism, autarky is the unique outcome. Kocherlakota calls that type of society *gift economy* in which social control makes people avoid autarky and starvation.

Money and memory are equivalent

Kocherlakota demonstrates that the set of equilibrium allocations permitted by money is a subset of the set of equilibrium allocations permitted by memory. In short, *money is no better than memory*. Taking into consideration the incentives associated to the two alternative mechanisms, Kocherlakota may assert: "any incentive feasible allocation in an environment with money is an incentive feasible allocation (of the K perishable goods) in the same environment with memory".

We will limit ourselves to giving the intuition for that proposition, the demonstration being highly technical. The purpose is not to show that money is better than memory but only that it can be equivalent to it. The exercise is different from a comparison between money and barter. Money and memory are directly comparable since counterparts are obtained in the same future, *i.e.* with the same time depreciation. When money and barter are compared, time is important. In the present exercise *what matters is not time but information*. In an economy with memory, the would-be producer is informed by the past history of the would-be consumer transactions. In a money economy, holding money for a would-be consumer gives equivalent information to the would-be producer. Either this would-be consumer has not yet met anybody (money is his/her initial endowment) or he/she has met somebody in the past. The mere fact he/she holds money shows that he/she already produces against money (an intrinsic useless commodity). In both cases, the best strategy for the would-be producer is to effectively produce, exactly as if he/she had checked that the would-be consumer had had a good behaviour in the past. *Money holdings give the same information as consulting a history of past transactions.*

Critique of Kocherlakota's thesis

The proposition "money is no better than memory" is rigorously demonstrated but its validity and meaning are not those Kocherlakota thinks he has established. As already alluded above, it concerns more information than the durability of money. Moreover, the necessary assumptions are barely acceptable in the logic of money theory. At best, Kocherlakota's proposition holds valid only when money is the only existing capital and when transactions are only bilateral and do not take place in organized markets.

Capital rather than money is memory (a trivial proposition)

In Kocherlakota's model, money holdings at t may be interpreted as a summary of all transactions individuals have realized since date $t = 0$. Consider, for simplicity, Kiyotaki & Wright's model of 1993 in which an individual cannot hold but one unit of money. There is no ambiguity: observing the money holdings of an individual gives identical information as a reading of his past accounts. This is so not because of the simplicity of the model but because (a) money is assumed to be *durable* and (b) its *total quantity is fixed* forever; its distribution amongst individuals changes only as a strict consequence of transactions.

Durability is an absolutely necessary characteristic that money should have in order to be said to be memory. But if money is specifically defined as an intermediary of exchange (or as a transaction technique) durability is no longer a necessary property. IOUs paid back at the closure of transactions are not durable but are a possible transaction technique. In the application of Occam's principle (assumptions parsimony) one should not assume that money is durable when it is considered as an intermediary of exchange, as is the case in Kocherlakota's model.

Let's assume that money is no longer durable in that model. At each opening of the market, individuals should receive one unit of money or nothing. In order to keep valid Kocherlakota's reasoning, the rule of allocation of money units by the Bank should be the following: give a unit of money only to individuals who had produced for other people during the preceding market (or who hold money at the end of the preceding market, which is equivalent). Any other rule would invalidate Kocherlakota's proposition because *it would break the link between money holding at t and transactions realized between $t = 0$ and $t > 0$.*

Does it make sense to stick to that rule? Certainly not! In any monetary system, metallic systems included, the quantity of money is determined by a confrontation between demands from individuals and decisions of a monetary authority. At any time, the money holdings of any individual express some compromise between the individual needs for a means of payment and the sovereign actions of the monetary authority. In a pure metallic system, if the Mint's rules do not change and if the total quantity of coins is fixed, then Kocherlakota's intuition is valid. In any other system, the evolution of money holdings is not exclusively determined by the story of past transactions. *Money holdings and their evolution, on one hand, and access to the story of past transactions, on the other, do not provide equivalent information.*

That observation does not deprive Kocherlakota's proposition "money is no better than memory" from its validity but invalidates his *motto "money is memory"*. What does it mean for a would-be producer to observe that the would-be consumer holds money? Basically that the would-be consumer has a right to buy commodities. How has he/she got that right? If it is exclusively as a consequence of his/her past transactions we get the special case studied by Kocherlakota; money is memory in that case. If it is, on the contrary, because he/she has borrowed it from the bank in order to finance a future rentable activity, we get the special case emphasized by Schumpeter. In that case, there is no relation whatsoever between money holdings and past transactions. All the intermediary cases between Kocherlakota and Schumpeter are possible.

Assuming that money is durable is tantamount to saying that money is capital. When all other commodities are assumed to be perishable, as Kocherlakota assumes it, money is the unique capital. "Capital" and "money" are then two different names for the same thing in Kocherlakota's model. Asserting that money or capital is memory in that context is trivial and does not bring about any sensible information about the essence of money.

Despite its apparent generality, Kocherlakota's model deals with a very special case in which money is reduced to a homogeneous and indestructible capital; money cannot be distinguished from an exogenous capital. Against that confusion between money and capital, which is also a confusion between an intermediary of exchange and a store of value, a more rigorous approach to money should be elaborated. We will sketch it out in the second part of this book.

Money is not a remedy for no commitment

A no-commitment assumption is the clue to understand what money does in Kocherlakota's model: what matters is information more than memory. A would-be partner is unknown because of anonymity. Their past actions are private information. In a decentralized economy there is no social control. The fact that a would-be partner holds money is by itself information. It proves that he/she will behave honestly: their commitment is credible. But that nice scenario makes sense only because markets are not organized; individuals can transact only once during a given time.

In a more general context, Kocherlakota's idea is irrelevant. Think of the economic environment adopted in strategic market games (see Shapley & Shubik, 1977) where a market is open for each commodity. A "no-commitment assumption" does not convey the same consequences. At each *t* everyone simultaneously determines their desired sales and purchases and informs the different markets (sales orders backed by quantities, purchases orders backed by money or any other accepted means of payment). Checking in each market that the physical constraints are respected is sufficient. There are no parametric prices and, consequently, no verifiable *ex ante* budgetary constraints. Centralization within each market – compatible with decentralization between markets – makes sure that *ex post* budgetary constraints will be respected as a consequence of a market mechanism (Cantillon or Shapley-Shubik rule, see below).

Kocherlakota's view about money is a deep and clever one. Rather than memory, *money is a decentralized control on individual behaviour*. But, this view holds only in a very special environment, when meetings are bilateral and when markets are not organized, which is the view Kocherlakota shares with search-theoretic authors. It does not seem to be a good research strategy to restrict the validity of money theory to a special environment, even if we understand that Kocherlakota and others strive to make the least institutional assumptions as they can. Money is too serious a problem to only be correctly solved in a special case where money is (the unique) capital and individuals can transact only once at a time.

Beyond Kocherlakota's model, the critical observations above concern the view academic money theoreticians have about a market economy. That view is often made implicit and can be decoded only through many "technical" assumptions. The growing complexity of these models should not make us forget what is essential: money theories have their field of validity determined by the basic features attributed to market economies. Put in these terms, a consensus certainly exists about the necessity to keep a correspondence between what we think money does, on the one hand, and what we think the fundamental characteristics of a market economy are, on the other. This link may be found within academic theory, as we shall see. If that theory has to be rejected it is not for not having complied with that principle but for having an inappropriate view about the market. The case for an alternative theory of money is also the case for an alternative theory of decentralized economies.

But, before embarking upon the task of precisely defining the specifications of a market economy, it is worth explaining why going beyond academic theory is necessary and why developing an alternative theory is highly desirable.

The incentives for going beyond academic theory

Fiat money is the fundamental concept of the academic theory of money, as Shi makes it clear: "Despite this reality [some examples in history], I would argue that monetary theory should not be built upon the intrinsic value of money or government intervention. Any such theory would fail to account for the additional value that money has in the market over and beyond its intrinsic value and government intervention, and hence the theory would fail to uncover the critical differences between money and other assets. (. . .) Thus, fiat money should be the primary object to be studied in monetary economics" (Shi, 2006, p. 644).[4]

But this concept, although inevitable in a value approach to money, is inappropriate for the study of a market economy in general and for understanding our present economies. Even if academic theory may be credited for interesting propositions, fiat money appears to be a very special case. Not only is it not to be found in history but, more decisively from a theoretical point of view, it does not allow for grasping some basic issues such as the issuance of money or out-of-equilibrium positions. The main concepts and results of money academic theory should be either re-interpreted and generalized or rejected. In any case they appeal for new developments.

Money, decentralization and equilibrium

Money and decentralization go along together according to academic theory. For instance, the "frictions" of the Kiyotaki-Wright model introduce some decentralization in the Arrow-Debreu framework: (a) meetings between agents are effective and bilateral instead of being virtual and multilateral; the consequence is limited information about what is going on in the economy, and (b) agents are specialized in production and consumption; this is a possible rationalization of private information invoked in Williamson & Wright (1994). These features are responsible for the existence of a monetary equilibrium. Kocherlakota and Araujo & Camargo's (2015) articles add a new element: anonymity, which is the source of the no-commitment problem, typical of a total decentralization.

But *this general trend toward more concern about decentralization seems to contradict the exclusive attention given to equilibrium positions.* In equilibrium, each agent adopts the best action, actions of others being given. That point makes sense only if these actions are known. But a situation where the actions of everybody are known by everybody is characteristic of an extremely centralized society. Equilibrium is then another word for a totalitarian society where no individual action is possible unless it is unanimously accepted.

As a result, the idea that money is a decentralized control of transactions – a very meaningful proposition indeed – loses most of its relevance. It remains true that an agent observing that a would-be partner holds money gets decisive information since it triggers a transaction which would not have been taking place in the absence of money. But that information is not sufficient since that agent must know that everyone else behaves in the same way. He will sell his commodity to the money-holder only if this sale is compatible with the actions of *all* other agents.

Moreover, according to the logic of the so-called "micro-foundation" of money, the fact that money is used in the economy is an equilibrium property. There is no sense in inquiring into what would be the effective behaviour of an agent in an out-of-monetary equilibrium. In the framework of academic theory the idea that money is a general means of co-ordination, and possibly a device that makes convergence toward equilibrium easier, has no room. In mainstream models, money is an outcome of the theory (money has to be essential) and not an institution of a decentralized market economy.

We have thus to reconcile decentralization and money. Part of this task will be done in the second part of this book by linking the issuance of a means of payment and individual decisions about payments. Instead of being the mechanical consequence of past transactions with a constant total amount of money, an available quantity of the means of payment to each individual will depend on a minting process in which individuals and institutions participate according to specified rules.

The exclusivity of equilibrium positions or, equivalently, the incapacity to deal with out-of-equilibrium positions is a key problem. That bad state of affairs is not the result of a deliberate intellectual choice. It is rather the consequence of a great failure acknowledged in the 1970s in the study of global stability of general competitive equilibrium. *Tâtonnement* and *non-tâtonnement* models were rejected for different reasons. Concerning the latter – the only ones in which transactions were considered – the failure was less clear than for the former. Global stability has been proved under a very special assumption (no simultaneous rationing on the two sides of the market) which makes sense only if some general means of payment is presupposed. Mainstream theoreticians' willingness to micro-found money (and more generally institutions) has prevented researchers from exploring that track. Prejudices in social philosophy have surely played a negative role here (see Cartelier, 2007). Nowadays, academic theoreticians no longer have a concern in out-of-equilibrium positions and global stability. Self-regulation of a market economy (the traditional and most fundamental question of political economy for centuries) has disappeared from the agenda. Even the recent global financial crisis, although present in innumerable public debates, has not changed anything in the methods of academic theory.

The way economic theory deals with money plays an important role in that situation. It is a strong motivation for an alternative theory. The triptych *money-decentralization-equilibrium*, typical of academic theory, is not consistent and has to be deeply transformed. While a certain degree of decentralization is taken for granted – a minimum requirement for a market economy theory – out-of-equilibrium positions are the rule and must be dealt with. Money, as a decentralized control of transactions, can no longer be considered as an optional technique besides barter. Money has to be present at the very starting point along with the other primitives of the economy (preferences, techniques, in the case of academic theory, accounts and money transfers in a monetary analysis, as we shall see). The triptych toward which we must tend is a *money-decentralization-out-of-equilibrium* position. A first step in this direction is to adopt a *market mechanism* more general than equilibrium. Shapley-Shubik's rule can do the job here, and it comes from a long tradition (Cantillon, Smith, Keynes and strategic market games). That rule presupposes the existence of money. A second step is to inquire into the mere notion of money and into the different ways money fulfils the role of a decentralized control.

On the neglected problems in academic theory: issuance of money and nominal unit

Let us come back to money as a decentralized control. In Kocherlakota's demonstration, the fact that money quantity is constant is decisive. Total quantity of money does not vary over time. Initial endowments in money are given and transactions redistribute that money amongst individuals. At any time, individual money balances sum up the story of the transactions they have carried out. In this sense Kocherlakota is right when he interprets money as a memory.

But the case he considers is very special, as we have seen above. In any monetary system historically observed in developed market economies, individuals may get money not only by selling commodities but also through the issuance of money. The example of a strict gold standard makes that story clear. Agents holding gold have the choice to sell it or to bring it to the Mint in order to get legal coins. It is also true in modern systems where banks monetize capital (see Part Two). Banks are private but they have to take into account the legal constraints and the actions of the monetary authority. In any case, the *issuance of money qualitatively differs from a purchase or from a sale*. It changes the total quantity of money, and there is some idea of sovereignty in it. It implies a relation between any individual and the whole of society incarnated in the Mint or in a central bank. Introducing the issuance of money into the model radically changes some of the conclusions. It is no longer possible to strictly relate money balances and the story of past transactions. What has happened between the Mint or the central bank and the individuals may be essential. In most search models money quantity is treated as a parameter. It is, however, possible to introduce an endogenous issuance of money (see Cartelier, 2014a). Let's briefly see the consequence.

Money is generally issued against some commodity (gold) or some assets (IOUs). Consider Kiyotaki & Wright's (1993) model and, instead of taking the quantity of money as given, let any producer have the following choice: either to enter the market with the hope of meeting someone and to exchange or to ask the monetary authority to transform, without delay, his goods into a homogeneous means of exchange at an additional cost. There is now a trade-off: either immediately get some money at a given cost and wait until next market for somebody producing the desired good (simple coincidence) and accepting money or try to meet someone who will immediately exchange (double coincidence).

Two main results follow from that "minor" modification of the Kiyotaki & Wright model:

1   There exist three barter equilibria in which a zero quantity of money is associated with three different degrees of money acceptance. The first is trivial: nobody resorts to the Mint when money is never accepted. But this may also be true when a positive fraction of agents accept money (second

equilibrium) and it may even be still true when everybody is ready to sell their goods for money (third equilibrium)! In other words, a unanimous acceptance of money is not a sufficient condition for the existence of a monetary equilibrium, contrary to what most search models with an exogenous quantity of money seem to suggest; *an additional condition is that people have an interest in triggering the money issuance process.*

2 The existence of a monetary equilibrium depends, for a given cost of money issuance, on the absolute level of specialization and not only on a comparison between that level and the degree of money acceptation in the economy. Confidence in money, *i.e.* a positive degree of money acceptance, is a necessary condition for a monetary equilibrium but not a sufficient one. An additional condition must be satisfied which depends on the intrinsic properties of the economy, namely tastes and technology. *Money is no longer a pure bootstrap effect.*

Neutrality of money ceases to be a relevant question as soon as money quantity ceases to be exogenously fixed. Kocherlakota's theorem no longer holds. Allowing money to be issued according to a procedure involving both economic agents and monetary authority dramatically changes the basic conclusions of the theory. Issuance of money is clearly the Achilles' heel of academic theory of money and, by the same topic, a strategic question to deal with for any alternative theory.

Taking into account the way money is issued allows the explicit introduction of economic sovereignty into economic theory. Academic theoreticians are reluctant to do so. Their position is certainly philosophically respectable but leaves aside many fundamental problems of money.

In all modern monetary systems, a means of payment, *i.e.* "monetary things", are associated in virtue of monetary sovereignty with a certain quantity of nominal units of account.[5] Individuals may accept or refuse to endorse the decisions of this authority yet the fact that they exist should be taken into account in the models. But, in most academic models, the nominal unit of account is nothing but a *numéraire* amongst many others. Nothing would justify that such *numéraire* be exclusive or privileged. Prices may be expressed in any simple or composite commodity. There is a strong relation between the refusal to leave room for sovereignty and the absence of a special role for the nominal unit of account.

The issuance of money and a nominal unit of account are two decisive ingredients the absence of which prevents the academic theory of money from being relevant for the study of market economies.

Money: from fiat money to institution

Money in academic theory means fiat money, *i.e.* a commodity. Standard supply-and-demand apparatus is thus eligible, and value theory is extended from commodities to fiat money. But it is not certain that fiat money is effectively a commodity even from the point of view of academic theory itself. It looks rather like *an institution disguised as commodity*.

Is money really a commodity in academic theory?

In the academic theory of money, as in value theory in general, money is conceived of as a special commodity. The neglect of both sovereignty and a nominal unit of account are the consequences of that orientation. As a special commodity money is called *fiat money*.

According to academic theory three basic features make fiat money a special commodity: (a) it does not enter utility and production functions (in usual but misleading terms, *fiat money* has no intrinsic utility); (b) its unique use is to be an intermediary of exchange, negotiated against a commodity (sale) in order to be exchanged after for another commodity (purchase); (c) it is not privately produced (its quantity is exogenously given).[6] From (a) and (b) proceeds the basic problem of the academic theory of money: how may a commodity deprived from any intrinsic utility have a positive price at equilibrium?

Most academic theoreticians accept without discussion those properties of *fiat money*. It is, however, not superfluous to ask ourselves if it is really reasonable to accept that view. The specific features just mentioned are so special that one can suspect that they create in fact a non-commodity. A commodity having such features would have also the peculiarity of not being a commodity at all; a blunt knife without a handle can hardly be called a knife.

That *fiat money* cannot be used for consumption and production makes it a ghost commodity not to be seen in the traditional fields of economic theory. That *fiat money* may be used only as an intermediary of exchange does not say anything about its concrete aspects (for instance, is it a central clearing for a commodity?). Finally, that *fiat money* be not privately produced prevents one from applying to it the usual tools relevant for the analysis of private decisions. The identification of money to a commodity, even special, is therefore paradoxical since it is defined negatively by reference to ordinary commodities. Academic theory does not have the monopoly on that position. Keynes in Chapter 17 of *General Theory* indulges himself in the same exercise with the same paradoxical result. The special features he selects are (a) a zero elasticity of production (non-private production?), (b) a zero elasticity of substitution (money as the exclusive intermediary of exchange?), (c) "the characteristics of money which satisfy liquidity preference", basically "the low (or negligible) carrying-costs of money" (largely due to the fact that prices and contracts are expressed in money?). All the above features are not typical features of commodities. It remains to be understand why, despite these counterfactual properties, economists are so prompt to treat money as a commodity.

It is not very difficult indeed to answer that question. Value theory has its origin in a political philosophy that considers individuals rather than the Prince, the felicity of people rather than in the power of nations and views society as the result of a set of free individual decisions rather than the effect of an institutional entity (God, tradition, etc.). That philosophical position came along with a suspicion about nominal quantities related to the Prince.[7] "Monetary manipulations", and more generally State regulations, were an opportunity for economists and other social philosophers to rationalize their position against the Prince's pretentions. Value theory at large is the "scientific" expression and counterpart of that new philosophy that appeared in the 17th and 18th centuries. Commodities and not money are considered as the substance of wealth. Value has nothing to do with the Prince. It is entirely determined by "natural factors": difficulty of production for the English Classical School, marginal utility and market equilibrium for others. In both cases, the assumption of a given commodity space is the starting point. It supplies all the powerful tools of analysis used nowadays. Therefore it could seem a good strategy to extend these tools to money and to conceive money as a special commodity.

Money as non-commodity

However, that strategy is not as good as one may hope. Properties attributed to *fiat money* do not describe anything but rather suggest a set of rules or an institution:

1   *Fiat money* not being privately produced, money must be introduced into the economy by the means of an *ad hoc* procedure different to a sale or a purchase. When a monetary analysis will be presented in the next part of this book, this *ad hoc* procedure will be dubbed *minting process*. Specific to money, it will allow us to distinguish between, say, gold, which is a commodity, and legal coins, which are not a commodity. Legal coins, not gold, are an intermediary of exchange. Coinage and melting are the two operations through which money respectively enters and leaves the market, whereas gold, as a durable commodity, remains there as every other durable commodity. Coinage and coin melting are subject to non-market regulations. In a credit money system, we may distinguish between inside money, privately issued by commercial banks, and outside money, issued by a monetary authority according to non-market criteria. Outside money issuance is, amongst others, a mode of validation of inside money issued by the banks (the convertibility of bank money into proper money). Here also, sovereignty pervades the entire minting process.

2   The quantity of the non-commodity called money is not expressed in physical units as are commodities but in a specific unit, the nominal unit of account. The name of money (euro, dollar, etc.) is a prerogative of the State or of the Sovereign at large (think of the euro). Here again it would not make sense to deny the role of an institutional authority. The editing (and re-editing) of the "dictionary", Keynes reminds us, is a right of the sovereign.[8]

The attempt at a generalizing academic theory leads us to reject the image of money viewed as a special commodity. Far from being a commodity, *money is an institution*, that is, a set of rules not reducible to a private agreement between individuals (equilibrium) as the so-called "micro-foundation of money" tends to make us believe. But, with a presupposed set of rules, it is no longer possible to take for granted the usual definition of economic agents. Individuals cannot be described uniquely as points (endowments) or functions (preferences) defined in the commodity space. They are also defined as agents subject to some rules and mediations, money being the most typical. Economic agents in a market economy are not "natural human beings" but individuals defined by a structure of interdependence, by money relations.

Money versus value

An alternative to that approach – developed in the second part of this book – is to put money and the nominal unit of account in the centre of the picture right from the beginning and to consider money relations amongst individuals, *i.e.* payments, as the first object to elucidate. No commodity space is presupposed. If a notion of price and of commodity is needed, it has to be derived taking payments as a starting point. Value of money does not make sense here. Prices are objectively observable only through the quantities of units of account transferred from one agent to another when a (socially defined) commodity is sold. No need of value, as the money payments provide the relevant information.

Is there not some kind of money illusion in this view? No, there is no room for money illusion. Money illusion implies a comparison between two different evaluations (real and nominal). Since prices are determined by payments there are only money prices. In the same way as accounting does not measure something which would exist independently from the accounts, money evaluation does not measure something that would exist independently of that measure. Transfers of units of account measure, or more exactly, *are* economic relations. The system making these transfers possible – money as a set of rules – jointly with the currently accepted accounting conventions are the only means to socially measure wealth in a market economy. Individuals may have their private view about their own situation but their wealth is socially recognized only in terms of units of account written in a balance-sheet.

As a consequence, the relevant question about transactions is no longer whether they are realized by barter or by money or whether a given element of the commodity space is an accepted intermediary of exchange. *The decisive question is rather to make explicit how transactions take place, how units of account are transferred and how all that process is managed and controlled.*

In that context, two opposing solutions may be considered. The first one is a *direct* social control: a central clearing *à la* Debreu is in charge of the accounts, anonymity is broken and individuals are strictly subject to the equivalence principle. In that logic the central clearing will not accept transactions out of equilibrium.[9] The second solution is an *indirect* social control: a payment system permits individuals to get a means of payment, *i.e. a way for transferring units of accounts from one account to another in such a way that equivalence is imposed only a posteriori* (balanced accounts at the end of the market). Co-ordination amongst individuals does not require a full equilibrium but only that monetary constraints are respected. Transactions here are decentralized: contrary to a central clearing *à la* Debreu, a bilateral payment does not require unanimous approval.

To sum up, money is the "Great Accountant". *Money is not a thing or a commodity but the set of rules permitting the writing of units into the accounts and transferring them from one account to another in an economy subject to market rules (decentralization, equivalence, etc.).* Developing that view is the subject of the second part of this book.

Notes

1 Wallace should have been more precise: not only does a complete competitive markets assumption prevent "frictions" to show off in general equilibrium theory; the assumption of a central clearing matters too.

2 That last observation holds because transactions are bilateral which implies that individuals can make only one transaction at a time. It would not be the case if markets were organized and it were possible to order, simultaneously, purchases and sales.

3 Here, these two devices are substitutes. In another paper, Kocherlakota & Wallace (1998) have shown that they could be complementary when memory is imperfect.

4 The reader may be tempted to put Shi's statement in contrast with Keynes's in his *Treatise on Money*: "Money of account, namely that in which debts and prices and general purchasing power are expressed, is the primary concept of a theory of money" (Keynes, 1930, p. 3). As we shall see in the second part, starting from a monetary postulate leads to an alternative theory.

5 A unit of account is nominal even when defined by a legal weight of gold. The legal definition introduces a wedge between the commodity – gold as a metal – and the means of payment – the legal coin. That gap makes possible what is often called "monetary manipulations", a derogatory denomination coined by economists denying the legitimacy of any sovereign intervention in the field of money. In modern academic models money is reduced to being a special commodity, called fiat money, and the unit of account is nothing but the "physical" unit of that commodity. The question of sovereignty is swept under the carpet.

6 A characteristic often mentioned, durability, is not specific to fiat money. Although it allows economists to affirm that money is also a store of value, fiat money could be non-durable and simultaneously an intermediary of exchange. In order to transfer wealth over time we need only to buy capital today and sell it tomorrow. To be durable is a common property of all the elements of capital. The confusion between money and capital is the direct consequence of treating money as a commodity instead of a set of institutional rules.

7 Smith has invented a school called "mercantilism" in order to fight more easily against the chryso-hedonistic illusion.

8 Even ultra-liberals, advocating a cashless payment system breaking the relation between means of payment and unit of account, admit the legitimacy of the State to declare the unit of account.

9 Debreu is not explicit on that point. Note that the part of *Theory of Value* (Chapter 2) alluded to in the text is printed in roman, meaning that it is not part of theory *stricto sensu*.

Part II

The case for a monetary analysis

In spite of its important and interesting results – and of its prevalence in the academic profession – value analysis does not give an adequate account of market economies since, as we shall see, some essential aspects inherent in decentralized economies are not considered and cannot be. Not independent of that inadequacy, the role money plays in decentralized economies is not fully recognized either. The first part of this book has explained the reasons for its global failure. In the second part, an alternative, called monetary analysis, is proposed and defended.

Does a monetary analysis solve all of the problems left pending by value theories? Even if it is partially the case, a comparison between the two rival approaches should insist not only on that aspect but also on the differences in spirit and in scope. It is true, to limit ourselves to three major points, that Keynes's conjecture – the existence of general competitive equilibria with involuntary unemployment with flexible prices and wage – and Harrod's razor-edge dynamics are more congenial to a monetary than to a real analysis (see below) and that out-of-equilibrium situations – which are the rule in decentralized economies – may be dealt with in the former and not in the latter. But what is the heart of the matter is beyond these important but particular points: how are economic relations defined and conceived of? What is specific to economic relations and makes them differ from all other social relations? The answer to that question commands the way economics should be designed. A monetary analysis is to be preferred not only because it allows for "solving better the same problems than a value analysis" but also because it raises different questions with different purposes. A monetary analysis is open to a great variety of economic relations (not only exchange). Moreover, it allows for thinking anew about the links (or the absence of) between different social disciplines.

Part II

The case for a monetary analysis

Chapter 4

Primitives of a monetary analysis

What makes economic relations specific in comparison with social relations in general is that they are *quantitative*. In order to account for that specificity, value theoreticians discard the "appearances" – monetary magnitudes – for the "essence" – relative values as solutions of a system of equations. Here we choose to account for the quantitative character of economic relations by resorting to the type of mediation which makes them possible: *money*. "Appearance" and "essence" do not make sense here. Only the type of mediation matters.

As Simmel (1990) reminds us:

> Just as my thoughts must take the form of a universally understood language so that I can attain my practical ends in this roundabout way, so must my activities and possessions take the form of money value in order to serve my more remote purposes.
>
> (Simmel, p. 210)

In this perspective money cannot be viewed as a commodity or as a good. Mediations are not physical objects; they are not for sale; they are *a set of rules* which make sales or communication possible. They are institutions like the law, State, etc. We have to think of money as an institutional device allowing inter-individual relations to take place.

Rejecting any given *a priori* commodity space and adopting money as the expression for economic magnitudes leads to a defining of economic relations as monetary ones. In order to understand how they take place and how they may be interpreted it is absolutely necessary to free oneself from two related prejudices:

- An empirical one which reduces money to the thing used as a means of payment, most often to a special commodity (cowries, pieces of leather, stones, gold, banknotes, electronic bits, etc.).
- A theoretical one which interprets payments as exchanges between two equal values, one attributed to the commodity, the other to the means of payment; money has no value; money is one piece of what Simmel calls a *sequence of purposes*, which has nothing to do with equivalence and value.

Getting rid of those misleading views is difficult since they are largely inspired by academic economics which provides the basis for most current representations of social life.

The very basis of money mediation is the nominal monetary unit, conceptually distinct from commodities even if it may be related in some cases to precious metals. The nominal unit of account, in this case the dollar ($), is the *universally understood language* alluded to by Simmel. Economic magnitudes are expressed in that quantitative language. Transfers of monetary units from one account to another are carried out through a means of payment. A hierarchy may exist amongst the various means of payment and precise rules govern their issuance. We shall call the process of issuance of the means of payment, the *minting process*. A more precise description is given in the next chapters.

Let's content ourselves with a general definition:

Definition 1

The minting process is the procedure by which dollars are written down in individual accounts by an institution[1] (the Mint) issuing a means of payment.

In decentralized economies the monetary unit is the normal way by which individuals express their commitments. The buyer promises to transfer to the seller a determined amount of dollars at a certain date and place.

The constraint under which payments are promised comes from the rules which organize the issuance of the means of payment and their uses. Sovereignty pervades all systems of payment. Purchases/sales are not a mere bilateral relation; they imply a third element which makes that relation possible. Here *the third element is the minting process* which governs the issuance of the means of payment and determines individual capacities to intervene in the market.

In what follows, monetary magnitudes are recognized, no more no less, for what they are: quantities of units of accounts. Their name changes according to time and place (the pound, dollar, euro, etc.). But what matters is that the pound, dollar and euro are the language people speak when quantitative obligations are the subject. *Debts expressed in nominal units of account and their settlements define the proper field of economics.* Consequently, there is no need to postulate about a commodity space which would be common knowledge. It seems more accurate to start from the idea of money conceived of as a more or less complex set of rules, *i.e.* an institution.

While postulating a commodity space gives no indication about the way a society is organized – the more so if it is interpreted as Natural – starting with money is not socially neutral. Even if money at large may be compatible with many forms of society, which makes illusory the quest for a general theory of money (Cartelier, 2007a), in our societies *money means decentralization*. Decentralization of decisions is the general presupposition common to real and monetary analysis. But, as we shall see, only a monetary analysis takes it seriously. Simmel rightly emphasizes monetary interdependence as being the most accurate expression of individual freedom, a major moral value in our societies.

In order to keep things simple, the presupposition of money is done step by step: three successive postulates will set the environment of the economy: the unit of account, individuals and payments. These postulates taken together imply the working of a minting process. Specification of the minting process will depend on the nature of the economic relations considered. But, at this general level of abstraction it is necessary, however, to show how decentralization is implemented by the monetary organization of economic relations. It will be easier later to present different versions of decentralized economies, namely a *market economy* (to be compared to the general exchange economy of academic theory) and a capitalist economy where market relations are embedded in a general wage relationship.

The fundamental postulates

The first and fundamental postulate is:

There is a nominal unit of account and it is common knowledge, says the dollar

The nominal unit of account has no necessary relations with any goods or commodity. Some monetary systems display such relations (the Gold Standard for example), others do not. But, in any case, the nominal unit of account does not imply *per se* the existence of a commodity space.

This fundamental postulate has a long history. It is not the proper place to go into detail here but it is worth reminding the reader of some of its important successive steps.

Steuart (1767) is probably the first author to clearly and consciously enunciate this postulate:

> Money, which I call of account, is no more *than an arbitrary scale of equal parts invented for measuring the respective value of things vendible.*
>
> Money of account, therefore, is quite a different thing from money coin, which is price, and might exist, although there was no such thing in the world as any substance which could become an adequate and proportional equivalent, for every commodity,
>
> (Steuart, p. 526)

From that quotation we may infer that:

1   the nominal unit of account is, borrowing Keynes's formula, "the primary concept of the theory of money"

2   it has no relation with the physical world of commodities
3   it is an artificial (or social) entity not to be found in "Nature"
4   it is the measure of values or prices.

Schumpeter rehabilitates Steuart's idea but on a slightly different basis.

> [T]here is a scientific interest in demonstrating the complete logical auton-
> omy of the unit of account vis-a-vis the idea of something "having value".
> This demonstration likewise leads us to both the essence and the peculiarity
> of the institution of money.
>
> (Schumpeter, [1970] 2014, p. 223)

For the author of *Das Wesen des Geldes* social accounting is the suitable framework for developing money theory. Partially inspired by Solvay (see Lakomski,
2002)), Schumpeter links money to accounts, as we will do in a systematic way
below.

By contrast with value theories, goods or commodities are not given *a priori*
and are not the cornerstone of economics. Consequently, their presence in economic theory has to be socially motivated (see below). In a monetary analysis,
commodities are defined in a framework shaped by money; they are no longer
considered as representative of "Nature" upon which "Society" would be built.

Commodity space is often (but wrongly) interpreted as Natural. By contrast,
could we not maintain that a nominal unit of account is given by the State?
Keynes strongly suggests that type of interpretation in his *Treatise on Money*
when he attributes to the State the ability to edit and re-edit the "dictionary".
There is abundant empirical evidence that seems to support that view. But
one should refrain from succumbing to that temptation. Steuart (1767) rightly
speaks of an invention but does not mention the inventor. Simmel is even more
affirmative. There is no point in attributing the invention of money, language,
mores, law, religion, etc. to anybody:

> In fact, it is certain that, from the outset, they evolved as inter-individual
> structures, in the interaction between the individual and the multitude, so
> that their origin cannot be attributed to any single individual.
>
> (Simmel, p. 99)

He could have added "or to the State either".

From the fact that nominal units of account are not to be found in Nature,
one can deduce only that they are an invention of Society but not necessarily
of the State. The example of the *bitcoin* urges us to be prudent and to content
ourselves with the presupposition of a *common economic language* without specu-
lating on its precise origin.

Two further postulates and a condition are associated with the nominal unit
of account.

In the same manner as individuals are defined in value approaches as a consequence of the first postulate (R^l), individuals in a monetary analysis are the supports of the quantities of the nominal units of account.

Individuals are accounts where quantities of nominal units of account are written down

While individuals in academic approaches are conceived of as initial endowments (points of R^l) and preferences (functions defined on R^l), individuals in a monetary analysis are described as quantities of units of accounts, say quantities of dollars ($) written into the accounts.

Economists used to explain individual behaviour by way of diverse hypotheses: rationality, limited rationality, etc. In a monetary analysis no subjective considerations are in order, not for the sake of realism but because they are out of place. When expectations are considered, they have no explanatory virtue. What matters here is not welfare but the *rules of the game*. The questions needing answers are not whether the social situation, which results from individual actions, is or is not optimal but rather: (a) how quantities of dollars are written down in the accounts, (b) how dollars may be transferred from one account to another and (c) what are the rules to which accounts are submitted?, etc.

Retaining only objective and observable social facts makes it clear what monetary analysis is about. Its purpose is to give intelligibility to what may be observed rather than to establish a norm (Pareto-optimality) or pretend to explain stylized facts or predict future evolutions of the society. The illusion of economists to be social physicists, associated with real analysis and value theories, should be dissipated and criticized. Part of the critique may take the form of a theory parallel to value analysis – it's what Keynes did in *General Theory* against the "citadel" – but, on a more fundamental level, monetary analysis is conceptually independent from value theory. The way individuals are conceived of in these two respective approaches is a symptom of it.

A third postulate completes the first two:

Economic relations are transfers of dollars from one account to another; they settle mature debts

In the same way that permutation of commodities amongst individuals implies the postulate of a commodity space, transfers of dollars from one account to another requires the postulate of the dollar as a unit of account. A condition for economic relations taking place is a prior inscription of dollars into individual accounts. There cannot be any transfer of dollars amongst individuals if some quantities of dollars are not written down *beforehand* into the individual accounts. We have mentioned above the minting process (definition 1) which enables money to be the Great Accountant or the scribe of the economy.

Economic relations are dollar transfers amongst individuals; minting relations are dollar inscriptions into individual accounts by the Mint. At this stage it is worth distinguishing two kinds of individuals: (a) those who get dollars from the Mint at the beginning of the period are called *active individuals* and (b) those who do not get any dollars from the Mint are called *non-active individuals*. The former have the capacity to spend, *i.e.* to transfer dollars to other people from their own initiative, but the latter cannot spend unless they have received dollars from the former.

It may be useful to sum up the general framework in which real and monetary approaches respectively are enunciated:

Table 4.1 Real and monetary approaches

	General equilibrium theory	Monetary analysis
Basic postulate	Commodity space R^l	Nominal unit of account ($)
Active individuals	Preferences defined on R^l	Accounts where quantities of $ are written down
Relations	Generalized exchange: permutation of commodities	Dollars transfer from one account to another for settlements of debts
Conditions of relations	Positive initial endowments ($\in R^l$)	Eligibility for the minting process

The postulates are opposed, term to term, exhibiting the radical opposition between the two approaches. Such opposition will not prevent us, however, from establishing a comparison in order to justify a fundamental proposition about money (see below).

Even at this preliminary stage of presentation, it may be useful to announce and sum up some important effects of that difference between the two sets of postulates. They are as follows:

1   Different kinds of economic relations may be studied in a monetary analysis: exchange, domestic and wage relationships, etc.; the variety of economic relations is made manifest by means of specific forms of means of payment circulation; by contrast, a real analysis is limited to production (Ricardian or Sraffian value theory) or exchange (mainstream theory).

2   Monetary analysis is not normative; it does not require that individuals' preferences be made explicit; mainstream theory is necessarily normative as shown by the assumption about maximizing agents.

3   Real analysis relies on a central notion: *equilibrium*; this is related to the emphasis put on individual behaviour; monetary analysis is focused on the squaring of accounts as a condition for the observation of economic relations; *equilibrium* in the former case, *viability* in the other.

As a consequence, these opposed paradigms do not deliver the same propositions and do not deal with the same issues.

Concerning the first point:

1   Mainstream economic theory fails to account for the most fundamental characteristics commonly attributed to market economies, mainly the procedures of coordination *a posteriori* of individual effective decentralized actions; the so-called "market sanctions" – inherent in decentralized coordination – do not show off in the former while they are at the core of the latter

2   Monetary analysis proves the existence of involuntary unemployment equilibria (or steady-states in a dynamic context) in competitive economies with flexible prices and wages while mainstream theory is limited to the special case of zero involuntary unemployment; the origin of this outstanding difference is the ability of a monetary analysis to deal with the wage relationship as a *sui generis* relation different from exchange. Paradoxically enough, modern Post-Keynesians – as they claim themselves to be – forget about that fundamental result.

Concerning the second point:

1   The relevant domain of a monetary analysis is precisely defined: the payments; mainstream (real) analysis is considered as relevant for the study of any behaviour as soon as it is considered as rational, *i.e.* maximizing a function objective; it comes as no surprise that the relations between economics and other "social sciences" be conceived very differently according to the two approaches; we will draw some consequences of that in the conclusion of this essay

2   Amongst the philosophical foundations of the real analysis, the myth of the "social contract" is prevalent; the alleged spontaneous tendency for market economies to be driven by anonymous forces toward an equilibrium (the best one according to individualist criteria) was a major issue on the agenda of mainstream economists until the 1970s when it became clear that such a proposition could not be proven with the assumptions necessary for the existence of a general competitive equilibrium; nothing comparable may be found in the writings of authors belonging to a monetary analysis tradition; they were rather chasing for the conditions of viability of an economy; this implies basically that an authority being part of the economy raises and solves that question ("invisible hand" *versus* Steuart's statesman)

Money and accounts: a close connexion

The postulates above display a strict relationship between the unit of account, means of payment and accounting. Many examples of that connexion are well documented in the history of economic thought. From the "mercantilist" theory of the balance of commerce to Schumpeter's (1970) *Wesen des Geldes*, passing by Steuart's influence of flows-of-funds on the balance of wealth, there is a remarkable continuity. Money and accounting are the main components of economic reality for individuals who are immersed in it and observe it.

What are the conditions which make an economy objectively observable? It's a question scarcely raised, as if the answer were obvious. We have suggested above that the empirical reference for all value theoreticians (Ricardian, Marxian and academic ones) – a given commodity space – should not be interpreted as physically objective but rather as a language which implies a social objectivity and not a natural one.

When social objectivity is the issue, and more precisely quantitative social objectivity, money and accounting are better candidates than any arbitrary commodity space. The three postulates above are chosen with that view. All individuals in our society have an account attached to them. Banks, the State or other institutions manage these accounts and register all the economic operations they perform. The set of all these accounts, with their inter-connexions, is the "economic reality" we are continuously shaping and which we are interested in.[2]

But we cannot content ourselves with this basic assertion. Our economy is decentralized. It is conceived of as the involuntary outcome of voluntary individual actions. Decentralization does not imply a complete independence of individuals. As noted above, individuals are not defined but in a presupposed framework (R^l or \$). Rather than independence we should speak of *separation* (see Benetti & Cartelier, 1980). Individuals are autonomous but their autonomy makes sense only because they belong to a specified entity or institution (commodity space or monetary network). The question is now: *how can we observe the effects of individual actions, having admitted that these actions take place in a specified environment and that they are not spontaneously mutually compatible due to decentralization?* Mainstream economists do not meet that problem since they deal only with equilibrium situations (they turn a blind eye to the general situation of a decentralized society, disequilibrium and imbalances). The counterpart of that doubtful advantage is that mainstream economics has nothing to tell or to observe about the way equilibrium (and thus observability) comes about.

Primarily, the problem is the following: an individual, *i.e.* an account, is observable if it satisfies the rules of accounting. An account/individual does not exist unless squared, *i.e.* socially recognized. Formally, for a given period, if m_{hk} is the total payments[3] of h to k, the account of individual h makes sense only if:

$$\sum_k m_{hk} \equiv \sum_k m_{kh} \tag{4–1}$$

As a result, individual h is observable only if:

$$\sum_k m_{hk} = \sum_k m_{kh} \tag{4–2}$$

Identity (4–1) is relative to the instrument of observation – an account has to be closed – while condition (4–2) is an economic rule – an individual has to be solvent. From (4–1) and (4–2) it results that only solvent individuals are observable.

In a decentralized economy the evaluation an individual makes of him/herself (through his/her payments) has to be the same as that made by others (by their payments to him/her). But, at the same time, decentralization makes highly doubtful that such equality spontaneously happens. Accounts must be settled by means of *constrained operations* which are implicitly included in condition (4–2) as a complement to *voluntary payments*. Marx has stressed that double evaluation as the most fundamental characteristic of the market division of labour under the expression of the "dual character of the labour embodied in commodities".

Let's explicitly introduce these constrained payments into (4–2):

$$\sum_k (m_{hk} + \tilde{m}_{hk}) = \sum_k (m_{kh} + \tilde{m}_{kh}) \tag{4–3}$$

If condition (4–3) is not met, no account can be made up except by an *ad hoc* procedure (bankruptcy procedure).

Condition (4–3) is different to what equilibrium is in mainstream economics. What we observe in our economies is a mix of voluntary and constrained payments. It is only in the very special case when constrained payments are equal to zero that condition (4–3) is equivalent to equilibrium. Moreover, if constrained payments are not sufficient to ensure condition (4–3), bankruptcy occurs and accounts are no longer observable. But economic theory, whether "real" or "monetary", is at a loss for dealing with such situations.

In order to avoid the intricacies of bankruptcy (which do not belong to economic theory proper), we assume hereafter that no bankruptcy occurs, which means that the economy is *viable* (more on the notion of viability in Chapters 5, 6 and 7). Viability ensures that accounts are squared; they are thus effective and observable.

Hypothesis 1

Only viable economies are considered

The difficulty to empirically distinguish between voluntary and constrained payments must not prevent us from emphasizing the theoretical importance of that distinction. It is the price paid for making compatible the decentralization and observability of a market economy. By contrast, mainstream economists (if they are consistent, as is Robert Lucas) must maintain that crisis and disequilibria never occur; only equilibrium (and optimal) responses to external shocks are to be observed.

Here we touch upon a very deep question most often swept under the carpet. All theoreticians would agree that a decentralized economy differs from a centrally planned one by the fact that individuals do not know *a priori* if their plans (supplies and demands, for instance) will be agreed to by others. They would also accept that an individual effectively exists when they are socially recognized, which means that he/she is solvent at equilibrium. Consequently they imagine that some adjustment takes place in the market until equilibrium is eventually attained. The point is precisely that such adjustment is not conceivable in academic theory. In order to justify that only equilibrium situations are observed, academic theoreticians have to assume that adjustment to equilibrium is instantaneous and without cost as if a superior genius was at work. It is the price paid by academic theoreticians to justify their models. This price is far too high since doing so amounts to asserting that a decentralized economy is observable because it is a centralized-like economy, an illogical position indeed.[4]

To put it in a nutshell, we may say that an *economy becomes effective by observing itself by means of accounting.* Constrained payments square the accounts and allow individuals to be socially recognized. If constrained payments are not necessary (the special case of equilibrium), individuals are recognized at the very level that they have evaluated themselves. If constrained payments are necessary (the general case) individuals are recognized for a level different to what they have expected. In plain terms, these observable facts are called "market sanctions".

Constrained payments make accounts effective and observable. Such payments may be said to be "constrained" in several senses. First of all, they are such because the means of payment are used only to settle debts; they don't have to be durable; by virtue of Occam's razor they are supposed to be destroyed at the closure of accounts. Secondly, deficit individuals must square their accounts; they have to obtain directly or indirectly the required amount of dollars by giving up some counterpart to excess individuals; constrained payments lead to a reconfiguration of wealth amongst individuals. Thirdly, Hypothesis 1 about viability requires that imbalances settlement effectively takes place.

The minting process, a crucial element of a monetary economy

The minting process has been defined above in relation to accounting (definition 1). In spite of the flavour of a metal currency, the term *minting process* denotes the diverse modes of issuance of a means of payment in decentralized economies. As we will see in later chapters, the diversity of the means of payment in decentralized economies – legal coins, inconvertible banknotes, credit, etc. – does not prevent one from proposing a general and unitary theory valid for these various concrete historical systems. Paying attention to the minting process – trying to integrate it into economic theory – characterizes those authors reluctant or opposed to quantitative theory of money. Endogenous *versus* exogenous money is the modern version of this old opposition. Making the minting process the core of economic relations reminds us that money issuance is too important to be left outside economic theory and quantity of money is too essential to be treated as a parameter. It is the most obvious consequence of non-neutral money.

Cantillon (1755), writing about the effect of an increase in money quantity, notes its different effects according to the diverse ways additional money enters the economy. John Law (1705), followed later by Steuart (1767), strives for implementing a monetary system in which quantity of money follows the needs of the economy. Wicksell (1935), even if paying lip service to a quantity theory of money, destroys its basis by noting that banks, contrary to other agents, are not submitted to any capital constraint, which makes quantity of money endogenous.[5] Even if Keynes is not clear on this point, some Post-Keynesians have taken the endogeneity of money seriously. Making explicit the issuance of a means of payment, i.e. *making money issuance endogenous, is characteristic of monetary analysis by contrast with value theories in which the quantity of money is parametric.*

The history of market economies shows that many types of monetary organization are possible. Economic theoreticians have often considered that such diversity makes necessary a parallel diversity of money theories. Metallic money differs from fiat money, quantity theory not being valid for the former but only for the latter (Niehans, 1978), bank or credit money complies with other rules than fiat money, and so on. By contrast, we maintain that *money theory should be unique and sufficiently general to be relevant for all historically observed money systems in decentralized economies.*

From our three postulates and from Hypothesis 1 it results that active individuals initiate transfers of dollars to other individuals (active or not active) – which implies that means of payment have been issued – and that accounts are observed – which implies in turn that accounts have been squared by constrained payments. This is summed up in

Proposition 1

Issuance of means of payment (minting) and opening of accounts are one and the same thing; they are associated with forward-looking balance-sheets. Cancellation (melting) of means of payment and closure of accounts are one and the same thing; they generate backward-looking balance-sheets. Issuance transforms wealth (defined as a *minting basis*) into a means of payment; cancellation is the inverse transformation.

The minting process is presented here in abstract terms. Different versions of it, depending on the type of economic relations it shapes, will be detailed in due time.

Individual decentralized actions are *payments*, not receipts. Individuals decide only how much to spend, not how much they will receive from other people. *Primacy of expenses is inherent in a decentralized monetary economy.* All individuals decide how much to spend conditional to the required means of payment obtained from the Mint.[6] The quantity of the means of payment made available depends on what individuals demand, on what monetary authority decides and on the framework in which these actions take place. At the present level of abstraction it would be useless to say more. What is important is to emphasize that decentralization implies that agents could spend independently of what other people do. In other words, the means of payment which are spent are not those received from other people.[7] *The minting process is a generic term to denote the various ways through which people get money independently of their receipts.*

Minting is a transformation of wealth into a means of payment through an institutional procedure; *melting* – the symmetric of minting – is a transformation of a means of payment into wealth by another one. Minting issues, and melting cancels, the means of payment. Far from being a circular reasoning, this double bind between wealth and means of payment allows us to understand what decentralized activities are about. They are *a continuous transformation of wealth over time into money and of money into wealth.*

It is of the utmost importance to stress that minting and melting are specific operations. They are totally different from purchases and sales, for instance. Let's consider the archetypal system – the Gold Standard, well-suited for our terminology. Bringing gold to the Mint and having it as legal coins of the same weight (no cost, no seigniorage, to keep the story uncomplicated) cannot be interpreted as a purchase or a sale. It is not a gift either. Neither is it a piece of magic that makes a means of payment emerge from nothing and from nowhere (the famous *ex nihilo* creation of money currently met in textbooks!). Melting is not a private operation either. We just have to accept that being required to pay with legal coins and not with gold does not result from a purely private process. Besides individual behaviour (note that we speak about decentralized economies) we have to take into account an institutional entity, the Mint, and all its rules, even in the gold metallic system. Sovereignty, in all systems, is an inescapable element of minting and melting, which prevents us from dealing with money issuance and cancellation as we would with other economic operations.

In order to bring some intelligibility into that complex process, it may help to conceive it as a cycle which begins by transforming at a point of time part or total wealth into a means of payment (minting), goes on by voluntary flows of payment transferring units from an account to another and ends at another point of time by constrained payments transforming means of payment into wealth (melting). In the meantime, the structure and composition of the wealth of individuals will have changed.

In accounting terms, individual balance-sheets at τ show individual wealth and available means of payment, accrual accounts for period (t) of duration ε show the flows of payment in and out and balance-sheets at $\tau + \varepsilon$ show how these flows of payment have changed individual wealth and individual capacities to intervene in the market opening at date $\tau + \varepsilon$.

Note that, at a given date τ, two balance-sheets may be considered. One shows the consequences of what has happened during period ($t - 1$) to individual amounts of wealth (it is a backward-looking balance-sheet); the other shows what individuals have decided under the minting constraints for period (*t*), namely the amount of means of payment they intend to spend during the period (it is a forward-looking balance-sheet).

This way of looking at circulation and its relations to balance-sheets may be traced back to Steuart and Keynes. In his *Inquiry*, Steuart has extensively explored the effects of circulation on the "balance of wealth" (Chapter XXVI of Book II, "Of the Vibration of the Balance of Wealth"). He insists on the durability of purchased commodities and their ability to be a basis for minting. The impact of flows upon stocks analyzed by Steuart refers to backward-looking balance-sheets. By contrast, Keynes is concerned by forward-looking balance-sheets when he discusses the arbitrage between consols and liquidity. This point has often been misinterpreted. Some reputable commentators (Patinkin, for example) have criticized Keynes for taking into consideration two elements and having not considered all the markets simultaneously, as if Keynes's explanation was about a general theory of portfolio allocation. Things become clear when one realizes that Keynes was dealing with a forward-looking calculation: how much of the means of payment does an individual need for the opening period in order to be able to spend (transaction and finance motives) and to be covered against anything happening in the future (precaution and speculation)? Wealth does not change, at that point in time, before any expenditure has taken place; only its composition is affected: what part of wealth has to be turned into the means of payment. In a sense, when Keynes deals with the preference for liquidity, he is dealing with a minting procedure. He is perfectly right in considering only that part of wealth which is susceptible to be minted – the consols in *General Theory* – and not other items. Tsiang (1966) and Kohn have emphasized that aspect of Keynesian theory (see also Cartelier (2004)). After this short detour of antecedents, let us come back to our general schema.

The flow of payments forms the very structure of economic relations. That structure is well represented by a *matrix of voluntary payments* observed during a given period, where m_{hk} is the voluntary transfer of dollars from *h* to *k*:

$$M = \begin{pmatrix} 0 & m_{12} & \cdots & m_{1H} \\ m_{21} & 0 & \cdots & m_{2H} \\ \cdots & \cdots & \cdots & \cdots \\ m_{H1} & m_{H2} & \cdots & 0 \end{pmatrix} \tag{4-4}$$

Although aggregate decentralized payments are identical to aggregate receipts, there is no reason for such an equality to spontaneously hold for each individual. In general, individuals experience non-zero balances, either monetary deficits or surpluses. Some *procedure for the settlement of balances* must be built in as part of the money institution. Balance settlements make effective the *monetary constraint.* There is no *a priori* reason for allowing an individual to spend more than he/she receives. A balance settlement is the means of filling this gap. The individual in deficit is constrained to turn part of his or her wealth into the means of payment in order to respect the monetary constraint. This constraint works according to the rules of the particular payment system considered. The settlement of balances makes the monetary constraint effective and determines individual wealth at the end of the period (which generally differs from wealth at the beginning of the period). Accounts are squared and economic relations are observed and observable. This is the most obvious justification for the notion of a backward-looking balance-sheet alluded to above.

Minting and spending open the accounts for the period during which economic relations are observed, melting and settling balances close and square the accounts.

While *voluntary payments* result from individual decisions taken under the constraint of the minting process (availability of the means of payment), *constrained payments* ($\tilde{m}_{hk}$) result from forced transformation of wealth into the means of payment. *Co-existence of voluntary and constrained individual operations is a general characteristic of decentralized monetary economies.* In common terms, out-of-equilibrium situations are the general case. Monetary analysis enables us to deal with them; value theories do not leave any room for them, equilibrium conditions being a fundamental part of their models ($\tilde{m}_{hk} = 0 \ \forall h, k$).

Taking into account the co-existence of voluntary and constrained payments, the matrix of payments should be rewritten to make them both appear (respectively m_{hk} and $\tilde{m}_{hk}$):

$$M = \begin{pmatrix} 0 & m_{12} + \tilde{m}_{12} & \cdots & m_{1H} + \tilde{m}_{1H} \\ m_{21} + \tilde{m}_{21} & 0 & \cdots & m_{2H} + \tilde{m}_{2H} \\ \cdots & \cdots & \cdots & \cdots \\ m_{H1} + \tilde{m}_{H1} & m_{H2} + \tilde{m}_{H2} & \cdots & 0 \end{pmatrix} \quad (4\text{--}5)$$

with $\sum_k m_{hk} + \sum_k \tilde{m}_{hk} \equiv \sum_k m_{kh} + \sum_k \tilde{m}_{kh}$.

Individual actions appear as interdependent according to a matrix of payment. Money is the name of that specific interdependence associated with decentralization. *The matrix of payment is the quantitative and synthetic expression of what is individual freedom in a decentralized economy.* Money is the (economic) name of that structure. Simmel had expressed the same idea in philosophical terms (see Simmel, 1990, Chapter 4).

Theoretical developments are so far too abstract to be easily grasped. They need to be incarnated into more specific economies. Monetary analysis is open to a great variety of economic relations, while academic value theory is limited to voluntary exchange. Beginning with market relations may make a comparison between both approaches easier in this particular case. It will allow us to make more precise the different notions evoked so far.

Economists working along a real analysis tradition are convinced they are social scientists in the same level as physicists or biologists are natural scientists. The philosophical foundation provided by the myth of the social contract is more responsible for that than the use of mathematics and quantitative methods. The pretension to science pervades value economic theories since their emergence in the eighteenth century. Far from that illusion, economists belonging to the monetary analysis tradition are aware of the fact that economic theory is nearer to reasonably controlled knowledge than to science (an art according to Steuart, closer to dentistry than to physics for Keynes).

The following chapters are intended to illustrate what precedes. Chapter 5 is devoted to exchange relations in a market economy. Some fundamental notions as that of *legal money* (*i.e.* radically different from credit), the *double determination of social wealth* (thought of as a reformulation of Marx's incorrect but illuminating idea about the double character of labour in a commodity society) and an application of *viability theory* to the dynamics of a pure market economy. Chapters 6 and 7 deal with the wage relationship. It will be shown how and why a wage relationship is not an exchange. It is a *sui generis* relation conceived of as a *monetary subordination*, a notion foreign to and unthinkable in a real analysis, be it in a Ricardian or in a mainstream version. Some interesting consequence will be drawn of that specificity. An entrepreneur economy exhibits special properties not to be found in a pure market economy. Amongst these, the existence of equilibrium (or steady-states) with *involuntary unemployment* and Kalecki's principle are especially remarkable. Keynes, Kalecki and Harrod have more than paved the way for those conclusions but their path-breaking propositions and conjectures, misunderstood as relying on very restrictive assumptions (frictions and rigidities), will become demonstrated statements of a well-founded monetary analysis. The introduction of real and financial assets – on the basis of our postulates – will allow us to generalize Kalecki's principle to sketching a simple model of capitalism with an application of viability theory.

Notes

1 The logical necessity of an institution, claimed here, is not yet proved. One could object that a system of individual IOUs may be viable without any overhanging entity. It is why the minting process is introduced here as a definition and not as a proved proposition. The proof of the logical necessity of the minting process is postponed to the next chapter devoted to market relations since it concerns both approaches, real and monetary.

2 This point is emphasized by authors working along Stock-Flow consistent models (SFC). A special development will be devoted to these models.

3 Payments and expenditures are not equivalent notions: when h buys something from k, h may either pay for their expenditure or recognize a debt which will be paid later. More generally revenues and receipts have to be distinguished. However, when no confusion is possible we will use the two words indifferently.

4 Moreover, the global stability of general competitive equilibrium cannot be proved and, consequently, is no longer on the agenda. Interestingly, the same is true for Marx with his "*salto mortale*" of commodities. Marx's theory of the double character of the labour contained in commodities was designed to account for that adjustment. But that theory fails due to the absence of commensurability between concrete and abstract labour. Reasoning along a monetary approach changes the deal (see Benetti & Cartelier, 1999).

5 Wicksell's ambiguity explains why his works are invoked by authors so different as Hayek and Swedish School economists.

6 Another condition is the acceptation by the payee. But the payee has no initiative (except his/her own payments he/she has to recover in the market). We will assume for the sake of simplicity hereafter that payees always accept the means of payment the payers propose.

7 Clower's cash-in-advance constraint is the way academic economists express that idea without mentioning how means of payment are issued (Clower (1984).

Chapter 5

A pure market economy
Exchange relations

A combination of three principles may account for the diversity of human societies:

1   The feeling of belonging to human society; this feeling is logically prior to hierarchy and to social divisions; when it is not to be found, *i.e.* when a fraction of the people do not recognize the others as human beings, society runs into danger and the social bind can disappear (and typically lead to genocide).
2   Fairness or reciprocity which is the moral basis of exchange or market relations (Binmore (2005) and Seabright (2006)
3   Hierarchy; some people accept or recognize that they have a certain rank; reciprocity does not hold between them; asymmetric reciprocal obligations are the rule.

Academic theoreticians identify the market with the sole principle of reciprocity, forgetting what makes reciprocity possible. To be fair to some of them, we could add that common humanity may be expressed by the commodity space postulate (R^l) but correctly interpreted as a common language and not as Nature. Individuals would recognize themselves as interlocutors, as members of a same community. In monetary analysis, the common language is the unit of account (dollar) and individuals are linked by debts not necessarily due to reciprocity relations. As we shall see later, a monetary analysis is not restricted to exchange but provides hierarchy and reciprocity as well.

   In this chapter, however, only fair and reciprocal relations will be considered, recalling that it is a special case for a monetary analysis, whereas for academic theory it is the only one possible. Let us call these relations *market relations* and let's remind the reader that when contrasted with primitive communities, centrally planned economies, patriarchal economies, etc., the market ceases to appear as a natural entity, as academic economics tends to make us believe, but as a particular social construction. Consequently, it is worth making explicit what its basic characteristics are, keeping in mind that a pure market economy is less of a historically observed society than an intellectual representation useful to inquire into our decentralized modern societies.

A market economy: main characteristics

Three specifications for a market economy

Even if economic theory may not succeed in giving a complete view of the market, economists, however, can hardly disagree with the three following features each market theory (real or monetary) has to take into account.

1   A characteristic is fundamental and beyond contest: each individual is free to decide about his/her actions in the market. The most obvious requirement for any market theory is to allow for *decentralization*. Decentralization contrasts market economies with centrally planned ones or with economies ruled by custom or tradition. Individuals freely determine what, how, why and how much they produce or consume subject to technical and budgetary constraints. Those actions are not mere intentions, they are *effective*. As no one can read minds, individuals have to make their actions known to other people. Since no central authority knows an individual's intentions, individuals have no other means than to act effectively in some way: posting a price (for a seller), sending a purchase order backed by the means of payment (for a buyer), being present and exposing commodities in a trading post, etc. As freedom of thought significantly exists only if associated with freedom of expression, freedom of choice in the market implies some means of expressing it. Individuals carry out their decisions without being obliged to ask for the approbation of other people; let's call this feature *decentralization of individual actions*.

2   The outcomes of the combination of these decentralized actions are not known beforehand. Consequently, market coordination is only *ex post*. This is a consequence of individual freedom and of *general interdependence*. A consequence of decentralization is that agents take their decisions without knowing for sure what others are doing at the same time. Of course, every agent tries to guess what other agents are doing but decentralization is not compatible with a perfect knowledge of the actions of others. More precisely, *there is no general bargaining taking place prior to individual payment decisions*. If bringing to the market a given quantity of a commodity may be the result of a very sophisticated calculation taking into account past history and expectations, it cannot be determined by a direct observation of others' simultaneous actions. When he/she posts a price, for instance, a seller does not know the prices other sellers have posted (nor the purchase orders others have addressed to them). In other words, coordination *ex post* is compatible with a great diversity of meetings between agents (bargaining, markets, etc.) provided that no particular agent or no institution is able to master the entire process of coordination. If it were the case we would not be able to distinguish between a market economy and a centrally planned one. Coordination in the market takes the form of *ex post* confrontation

between *ex ante* mutually non-compatible individual actions. *Market* is the general name for the process through which agents adapt their own actions to that of others. The very idea of individual freedom makes sense only at the cost of a lack of transparency of society to its members. Complete transparency is not compatible with decentralization. The latter implies that *coordination between agents takes place once all agents have taken their decisions*. A spontaneous mutual compatibility of actions decided independently by a huge number of individuals is very improbable.

Hypothesis 1 (about viability) and constrained payments provide the conceptual contents of that coordination *ex post* whose equilibrium is a very special case.

3   Individuals are free and autonomous. The consequence is that their mutual relations are ruled by *equivalence*. No individual can oblige another individual to do something; each of them is only subject to the mutual compatibility of the actions of everybody else. *Equivalence in exchange is a straight consequence of assuming free individuals having the same rights and the same condition*. No agent can impose a transaction on another. Equivalence does not preclude gains in exchange. All agents may be better off after the market from the point of view of their personal utility. Some of them may be worse off as well, depending on the rules of the market. Equivalence does not concern utility but prices or exchange values. Prices are objective be they expressed as ratios between quantities of exchanged commodities (in value theories) or as quantities of a monetary unit.

Equivalence means that all agents accept *ex ante* that the exchange value of what they buy should not exceed the value of what they sell (including inter-temporal transactions). It means that actions in the market (sale or purchase orders, posting prices, etc.) are subject to a budgetary constraint. An *active* individual chooses *ex ante* to fix his/her payments to the level of the receipts they expect to get from the activity corresponding to that level of payments.[1] Although all agents *ex ante* respect their budgetary constraint, differences between sales and purchases may arise for some individuals (at least for two of them) due to decentralization of actions. Coordination *ex post* is relative to individual deficits or surplus. These deviations from equivalence can be corrected only *ex post*. Once deficits are settled and excess means of payments are melted, an agent's wealth (calculated at market prices) is known. Some people gain, some people lose. This is not an exception to equivalence but the very *consequence of equivalence combined with decentralization*. The market determines the individual's wealth and their variations through those constrained operations. The settlement of imbalances leaves individuals free from any mature debts.

The three features above – decentralization, *ex post* coordination and equivalence – may be largely accepted as being three basic characteristics of a market economy by contrast to other forms of social organization (traditional, feudal, centrally planned economy, etc.). These specifications should be met in any economic theory claiming to give an account of the workings of a market economy. *Any economic theory should exhibit these three properties in order to be agreed upon as a market theory.*

As simple as this criterion might be, it excludes most academic models from the list of acceptable ones. The crucial point is that conditions of equilibrium are amongst the equations of almost all current general models, making them unable to represent out-of-equilibrium solutions. By construction, only situations of equilibrium resulting from *a priori* mutually compatible actions are to be found. Monetary analysis is not submitted to that limitation. Equilibrium is just a special case. Differences between receipts and voluntary payments are the rule. As alluded to in the preceding chapter, disequilibria *ex post* are resolved through constrained operations which impose a squaring of accounts for all active individuals. They are typical of any market economy. The fact that they do not show up in current academic theory is an obvious sign of its irrelevance.[2]

The three features above are implicit in Marx's definition of market as a particular social division of labour where the useful forms of labour "are carried on independently and privately by individual producers". He draws its consequences in a felicitous sentence which may help to understand how and why real analysis may miss the point of inter-individual relations because they are hidden behind objective appearances:

> To the producers, (. . .), the social relations between their private labours appear as what they are, *i.e.* they do not appear as direct social relations between persons in their work, but rather as material relations between persons and social relations between things.
>
> (Marx, 166)

Our framework is now made explicit. Our field may be described as the *set of all quantitative relations (debts) and their settlement when mature, in a society where the market is the dominant form of organization.* The feeling of belonging to humanity takes (at least) the form of a common agreement for the quantification of some mutual obligations and, more generally, a common submission to the rules by which monetary relations are made effective.

Equivalence implies that individuals have the same prerogatives. Here, this means that they are all active:

Hypothesis 2

All individuals have access to the minting process

Market relations being clearly defined, it is worth inquiring into the specific form of the minting process associated with them. A fundamental result, namely the necessity of a non-private means of settlement called *legal money*, will be established below. Interestingly enough, this result is also valid for academic theory (even if no academic theoretician has shown an interest in it). For the sake of comparison between value and monetary analysis, we introduce commodities even if there is no presupposed commodity space in the monetary analysis. In our monetary analysis, a commodity is defined by its producer (commodity h is produced by individual h) and its quantity is the sum of the producer's voluntary payments ($q_h = \Sigma_k\, m_{hk}$). When academic theory is concerned, we keep the traditional notation: everybody knows which commodity is commodity i.

A question common to both approaches is: *how may the operations of exchange (or market relations) be carried out in accordance with the three basic specifications enunciated above?* Investigating that question leads to the result just mentioned: *a supra-individual device is absolutely necessary.* Private agreements are not sufficient to account for all the operations taking place. From the demonstration of that proposition, three basic features of money will be derived and three further propositions will emerge.

Market mechanism and payment systems: a critical examination

The demonstration proceeds in two steps. In the first one, the notion of a *market mechanism* is presented as a necessary consequence of the three basic specifications of any market economy. In the second, all possible payment systems are reviewed and scrutinized from the point of view of their accordance with the same three specifications.

A market mechanism

Due to decentralization the consequences of individual actions do not generally conform to the expectations which have induced them. Individual actions and market configurations are related – the latter are the consequences of the former – but the link is complex. A *market mechanism* is an algorithm which makes explicit that link and which allows one to determine, given all the individual actions, their effects on market prices and allocations. The presentation hereafter is such that it makes sense in both approaches, real and monetary.

Amongst all the possible market mechanisms, one has gained some fame. It is present in Chapter 7 of Smith's *Wealth of Nations*, in Chapter 10 of Keynes's *Treatise on Money* (Fundamental equations) and in the modern theory of strategic market games under the name of Shapley-Shubik's rule. As a matter of fact this rule can be traced back to Cantillon who enunciates it in his *Essai sur la nature du commerce en général*:

> les prix [se] fixent par la proportion des denrées qu'on y expose en vente et de l'argent qu'on y offre pour les acheter.
>
> (Cantillon, p. 7)

Hereafter we will refer it as Cantillon's rule.

Hypothesis 3

Cantillon's rule[3] is the market mechanism which governs the market

This rule is in accordance with the perfect competition hypothesis of academic economics: interactions amongst individuals take place through prices; individuals control only quantities. General competitive equilibrium (which supports the most fundamental theorems) is a special case of Cantillon's rule where expected prices (parametric prices), *i.e.* prices used by individuals when they make their *ex ante* calculations, are equal to *ex post* market prices. The three basic specifications of a market economy prevent us from restraining the study to that special case.

Cantillon's rule provides a general formula for the determination of market prices but there are many ways to apply it: in fact, as many ways as types of means of payment used. The question is thus: *are there some types of means of payment compatible with the three basic specifications of a market economy?* Given the postulates respectively of academic theory and of monetary analysis, only commodities in the former and only individual IOUs in the latter can be chosen as means of payment. In other words only *private means of payment* are considered at this stage. As we shall see, the interesting point is that *no private means of payment meets all three specifications.*

The different payment systems and their critique

Two types of systems are possible: either commodities or IOUs. Let us examine them successively and show how and why they fail to meet our criteria. The different modes of failure will, by contrast, sketch the characteristics of what kind of means of payment must exist in a market economy.

COMMODITIES AS MEANS OF PAYMENT

Three systems and only three may be dealt with: barter (any commodity against any other commodity), Shapley's window (a basket of commodities buys a commodity) and commodity-money (a commodity chosen as money buys any other commodity).

Barter: decentralization and non-consistency of prices   We follow here the presentation of Amir et al. (1987). In an l-commodity economy where any commodity may be a means of payment for any other, there are $l \, (l - 1)/2$ trading-posts. Individual h buys by putting on trading-post (i, j) some quantity of commodity i or j. Let b_{ji}^h be the action of h who intends to buy commodity i. There is no possibility of credit (*i.e.* to put more than one's endowment). The market price of i in commodity j is given, according to Cantillon's rule by the ratio of the total quantity of commodity j put on the trading-post (i, j) to the total quantity of commodity i put on the same trading post:

$$p_{ij} = \frac{\sum_h b^h_{ji}}{\sum_h b^h_{ij}} \tag{5-1}$$

Market prices[4] resulting from individual actions determine in turn the market allocations that individuals get from the market. The market allocation of individual h in commodity i is equal to his initial endowment e_{hi} *plus* the quantities of i got from the different trading-posts s *minus* those quantities of i he has given in order to get other commodities. Formally:

$$x_{hi} = e_{hi} + \sum_s b^h_{si} p_{si} - \sum_s b^h_{is} \forall h, i \tag{5-2}$$

In this regime market prices are the outcome of a decentralized process since rule (5–1) requires to apply to only what happens on trading-post (i, j) without any consideration for other trading-posts. This property is in accordance with decentralization.

The problem is that these market prices are not consistent: the direct evaluation of commodity i by commodity j will be generally different from the indirect evaluations using trading-post (i, s) and (j, s) Rule (5–1) does not guarantee that $p_{ij} p_{js} = p_{is} \forall i, j, s$. Barter does not provide a consistent system of prices giving either a common market evaluation of market allocations or of what each individual gives to or gets from other people. Consequently, it does not make sense to speak about equivalence (the third point of our specifications).

A simple way of getting consistent prices would be to express them in a common *numéraire*. Walras adopts that device in order to overcome the barbed problem of arbitrage. But to make a *numéraire* and a plurality of the means of payment (all commodities) co-exist is not that simple, as we shall see below.

In conclusion, *barter is not a possible system of payment for a market economy*. From developments above, it follows also that a common expression of prices seems to be highly desirable in that context. The fundamental postulate of a common unit of account finds here some rationale.

Barter with prices consistency: Shapley windows   The idea is to constrain barter to take place on l trading-posts only, instead of $l (l - 1)/2$ as above.[5] On these l trading-posts (or Shapley windows) individuals put baskets of commodities as a means of payment in view of acquiring quantities of commodity $1, \cdots, l$. If everybody buys, nobody sells. Selling commodity i means simply putting quantities of commodity i on all trading-posts except i.

Formally individual actions are described by a matrix B^h whose columns are the commodity baskets put respectively by h on windows $1, \cdots, l$. The ith row shows how h distributes his/her endowment of commodity i amongst the different windows. The economy is described by $B = \sum_h B^h$.

The problem here is the heterogeneity of the means of payment put on the different trading-posts. While with barter it is possible to buy a determinate commodity by using whatever other commodity – which leads to non-consistent prices in general – with Shapley windows heterogeneous composite means of payment are used so that it is no longer possible to calculate prices market by market, and to apply Cantillon's rule in a decentralized way.

The rule has to be changed to accommodate the heterogeneity of the means of payment. All markets (or Shapley windows) have to be *simultaneously* considered. In order that all the quantities put on markets be sold (as is the case with Cantillon's rule), one imposes that the value of the total composite means of payment put on market i (total "demand" for i) be equal to the total quantity of commodity i put on the different markets (the total "supply" of i).

Denoting $D(B)$ the diagonal matrix of the sums of rows of B, the market price vector p is solution of:

$$B'p = D(B)p \qquad (5\text{--}3)$$

The existence of a positive solution depends on the properties of matrix B (assumed to be irreducible which makes sure the existence of a solution). Market allocations are known as functions of the individual actions:

$$x_{hi} = e_{hi} + \left(\frac{p}{p_i}\right) B_i^h - B^{hi}e \ \forall h,i \qquad (5\text{--}4)$$

where $\left(\dfrac{p}{p_i}\right)$ is the market price vector expressed in commodity i, B_i^h is the ith column of B^h, B^{hi} is the ith row and e the unit vector. $\left(\dfrac{p}{p_i}\right)B_i^h$ is the quantity of commodity i bought by h thanks to the heterogeneous means of payment h has put on the different windows while $B^{hi}e$ is the quantity of commodity i h has sold, *i.e.* put on the different windows in view of buying other commodities.

Rule (5–3) respects the equivalence of exchange (by contrast with barter) but it violates the principle of decentralization. Instead of being fixed market by market, market prices are simultaneously determined as if a central institution could control, simultaneously, all markets. Prices are consistent precisely because they are centrally calculated.[6]

The failure to meet the specifications here is symmetric of that viewed for barter. Decentralization is lacking in the Shapley windows payment system but the consistency and equivalence of prices are ensured while equivalence is lacking in barter which, however, respects decentralization. Reconciling decentralization and price consistency would require an expression of prices in a common unit.

Commodity money: a self-contradiction   This last system of payment using commodities is a special case of Shapley window. Instead of placing baskets of commodities for backing their purchasing orders, individuals use a specific and same commodity g. As a consequence, only $l - 1$ trading-posts are available since it does not make sense to buy commodity g by means of commodity g. One could also say that the commodity system is a special case of barter where only one commodity is eligible for being a means of payment.

The commodity money system seems to meet perfectly the requirements of a market economy since barter prices are fixed market by market – which meets decentralization criterion – and, per Shapley windows, price consistency is ensured by the uniqueness of the means of payment.

Individual actions are described by the quantity of commodity g used for acquiring commodities b_{gi}^h and the quantities of other commodities put for sale on the $l - 1$ trading-posts, $b_{i \neq g}^h$. Cantillon's rule is thus:

$$p_i = \frac{\sum_h b_{gi \neq g}^h}{\sum_h b_i^h} \qquad i \neq g \tag{5-5}$$

Market allocations are accordingly:

$$x_{hi} = e_{hi} + \left(\frac{b_{gi}^h}{p_i} \right) - b_i^h \tag{5-6}$$

Decentralization and equivalence hold. There is, however, an asymmetry between commodities $i \neq g$ and commodity g. Does this asymmetry prevent one from thinking of commodity g as a means of payment, as money? The answer is: yes!

As a commodity, commodity g is produced and consumed exactly as any others. However, the fact that it is also a means of payment deprives it from having its own market and, by consequence, from having a market price. Commodity g is the only one which is not sold (and not bought) in the market (see Benetti, 1985). Cancelling this asymmetry would not make sense since it would lead to acknowledging a market for g where g be exchanged against itself. *Commodity g cannot be simultaneously commodity and the means of payment.* Such a proposition would be self-contradictory.

Consider the case of gold. Gold is clearly a commodity. When gold is used as the means of payment, in order to avoid the self-contradiction above, one should be able to distinguish between the two modes of existence of gold. This is achieved by *the minting of gold*. An institutional authority – the Mint – transforms gold-metal into gold-means of payment.[7] Legal coins of gold are no longer a commodity. In some observed cases in history it is forbidden to melt down or even to weigh them. Gold-metal is not a means of payment but a commodity while legal gold coins are not gold-metal but the means of payment.

A critical analysis of the so-called commodity money introduces an important idea: *commodities (or wealth in general) cannot be used as money unless an institutional procedure turns them into the means of payment.* Such a procedure – the minting process – is in fact very general.

NON-COMMODITIES (IOUs) AS MEANS OF PAYMENT

Having exhausted the payment system using commodities (which is relevant for a value analysis), a last possibility is a payment system with private IOUs (which is relevant for a monetary analysis).

Let us put aside the question of trust (very important indeed but beside the point here where individual behaviour is not taken into account) and concentrate on the question of the settlement of debts.

Debts are quantitative obligations by which the buyer promises to pay to the seller a determinate amount of the means of payment. Individual debt of a buyer h, corresponding to a spot transaction with k, is: m_{hk}. Each individual commits him/herself to pay some amount of units of account, say $\Sigma_k m_{hk}\$$, to others. But IOUs are private so that no common means of payment is available. Means of payment issued by h are different from those issued by k.

Clearly nothing can be said unless some link is established between these individual (private) means of payment. It is necessary to check whether the private estimations of individuals about their own means of payment are accepted by all the other individuals.[8]

Let t^h be the rates of exchange between units of account (unknown for the moment). Rates of exchange have to be determined in order to get a unified expression for individual actions (payments and receipts). We follow Sorin's (1996) presentation (avoiding the usual technicalities).

The quantities of commodities put for sale in the trading-post are $b_k^h = \Sigma_k m_{hk}t^h$ while the quantities of individual IOUs are $m_{kh}t^k$. Market prices are determined according to Cantillon's rule, which is:

$$p_h = \frac{\Sigma_k m_{kh}t^k}{\Sigma_k b_k^h} = \frac{\Sigma_k m_{kh}t^k}{\Sigma_k m_{hk}t^h} = \frac{receipts}{payments} \tag{5–7}$$

Here Cantillon's rule is not sufficient to get market prices since the t^h's are unknown. There are two possibilities: one is to take as given the rates of exchange, the other to determine them simultaneously with market prices. In the first case, differences will inevitably occur between receipts and payments for each individual. It would be only by fluke that arbitrary rates of exchange correspond to a strict equality between receipts and payments for all individuals. In the general case individuals would have to settle these imbalances, but this would be impossible. Individual IOUs cannot do the job since the imbalances are precisely due to the use of them. So far no other means of settlement has been introduced. Clearly, *a purely private system of payment with exogenous rates of exchange is unable to carry out the payments a market economy requires.*

Let's consider the second case now. Equivalence commands that payments and receipts are equal for all individuals (otherwise imbalances would appear and would not be settled). Consequently, rates of exchange cannot be determined but by imposing an equality constraint. The simultaneous cancellation of all settlement balances requires:

$$\sum_k m_{kh} t^k = t^h \sum_k m_{hk} \tag{5-8}$$

Only $H - 1$ conditions of (5–8) are independent (if $H - 1$ individuals have zero balances the Hth has also a zero balance). System (5–8) determines relative rates of exchange only, *i.e.* up to a scalar. Any private means of payment may be taken as *numéraire*. It is true also for relative market prices. This economy is analogous to a Shapley windows economy: market prices and rates of exchange are relative and centrally (simultaneously) determined up to a scalar. For the same reasons, it does not meet the specifications of a market economy.

Let us come again to the first case with exogenous rates of exchange $t^h = \overline{t}^h$. *This implies a presupposed unit of account.* Cantillon's rule applies as above except that it is sufficient to calculate market prices:

$$p_h = \frac{\sum_k m_{kh} \overline{t}^k}{\sum_k b_k^h} = \frac{\sum_k m_{kh} \overline{t}^k}{\sum_k m_{hk} \overline{t}^h} = \frac{receipts}{payments} \tag{5-9}$$

Market prices are now expressed in a common unit of account (they are thus consistent) and determined in a decentralized way.

Monetary imbalances are:

$$s_h = \sum_k m_{kh} \overline{t}^k - \sum_k m_{hk} \overline{t}^h \tag{5-10}$$

Whenever exogenous rates of exchange $\overline{t}^h$ differ from endogenous determined ones – which is the normal case – s_h differs from zero.

The mere assumption of fixed rates of exchange radically changes the properties of the payment system. The obligation to settle imbalances, which amounts to squaring the accounts, generates the need for *an institutional means of payment*. Imbalances remaining after compensation between IOUs cannot be settled by IOUs since, by construction, surplus individuals hold IOUs from deficit individuals.

The logical necessity of an institutional minting process issuing legal money, assumed above, is now proved.

Legal money

We can now enunciate a second proposition about money in a market economy.

Proposition 2

There is a non-private (*i.e.* institutional) ultimate means of payment: *legal money*; *monetary sovereignty* pervades the minting process.

Proposition 2 is not a postulate. It is the logical consequence of our three postulates and of the market organization of the economy. At this point nothing is known of its form, of its mode of issuance and cancellation, etc. What is sure is that implementing the unit of account requires that legal money be issued. Imbalances can be settled only by means of a superior means of payment issued by an institutional entity.[9] Here is the root of money hierarchy between money (or *money proper* in Keynes's terminology) and credit which is observed in most historical monetary systems. It is worth dealing a little bit with this basic issue.

Are money and credit complementary – how may money and credit co-exist in a complete monetary system? – or substitutable – is credit historically and logically prior to money or is it the reverse?

The latter issue is relevant for historians but certainly not for economic theory. It is misleading since it omits a preliminary and general question: how is it possible to organize transactions in a given economy? Starting from that interrogation obliges us to make precise the type of society for which the question is relevant. Relying on historical or anthropological arguments in favour of money or credit about societies completely different from ours brings more confusion than light. Decentralized economies are what economists most often deal with. Individuals in these economies are free to decide about their actions without the prerequisite of a general approbation. This is not the case in temple economies (Mesopotamia or ancient Egypt), nor in feudal systems.

As it has been recalled above, a very general proposition concerning decentralized economies is that individual decisions cannot take place but through a coordination *ex post*. The process by which individuals confront their decisions – the *market* – is the condition of sustainability of the economy. When economic relations are thought of as monetary – as is the case in a monetary analysis – the general concern above becomes: *what are the monetary forms of relations which ensure the mediation between individuals?* The pairing of money/credit cannot be meaningfully studied except in the precise context of a decentralized economy. Is a general system of transactions possible using only commodities? The answer is No! Is a general system of transactions possible using only private IOUs? The answer is No!

Proposition 2, above, is a little bit more general than introducing legal money. What Proposition 2 emphasizes is the necessity of "something above" individuals. A system of pure credit, *i.e.* with private IOUs, could be sustainable if for various reasons (ethical, religious or other) individuals would agree to renounce part of their freedom and to comply with a superior principle. This is perhaps what some authors call "trust" as a condition for credit, even if they do not make precise the content of that principle.

In our strict monetary framework, Proposition 2 states that whatever means of payment being used and whatever the modes of issuance making them circulate, there must exist a "monetary authority" which is an obliged complement of individual freedom. *Money and credit are two complementary components of any payment system in a decentralized economy.*

R. G. Hawtrey (1919) should be credited for having exposed that view with the greatest clarity in *Currency and Credit.* He does not empirically define money – as is too often the case with most authors – but theoretically: money is the means for stabilizing credit; this is as true for gold convertibility (even if inefficient) as it is for inconvertible paper money. It would make sense today to extend that view to rate of interest management. Perry Mehrling (2011) makes a further step in extending that view to financial markets: the "monetary view" emphasizes the role of the monetary authority as a "dealer of last resort".

Legal money (or money proper) is neither a special commodity nor a creation of the State but, first of all, an obliged complement of any credit system. Reference to Hawtrey may help the reader to acknowledge that legal money is not fiat money, the basic concept of academic theory. Legal money and fiat money only have in common that they are non-privately produced. What makes them radically different is that one belongs to a presupposed commodity space (fiat money) and will be consequently dealt with as a commodity (supply and demand apparatus) while the other (legal money) not only has nothing to do with commodities but is specific even with regard to ordinary private operations of purchases and sales. Issuance of legal and bank money is not a purchase/sale.

Legal money is not optional but the straightforward consequence of our postulates and of the features of a market economy. Legal money is the logical answer to the following question: how may a market economy be viable? How may individuals speaking the same language (dollars) engage in actions for their own account and agree to subject themselves to a common rule (equivalence and competition)? Legal money is a first element of the solution. *Legal money is the mediation through which individuals not only express their own actions but accept to be socially evaluated.*

Units of account combine with legal money in defining money. Conceptually distinct and functionally complementary, they are the basic elements of what may be called *money* or *payment system.* Unit of account and legal money are common knowledge: they make individuals capable of communicating between them. Private means of payment also have this property but to a lesser extent. Credit allows purchases and sales to take place but is not sufficient to make the transaction complete. The buyer and seller keep being related until credit comes to an end with the ultimate settlement. They are free from each other only after that final payment. *Legal money is the unique means of transferring definitely a monetary unit from an account to another.*

The important point here is that market relations (referred often to exchange relations in academic theory) are relations which make individuals free vis-à-vis each other once operations are complete. A perpetual debt would mean that debtor and creditor are not on the same level (the State, the zamindar, etc.).[10] Debts have to be paid, and this cannot be done but with legal money. Academic economics does not account for that fundamental property of the market (the very element of freedom indeed) because it deals only with equilibrium situations.

The issuance of means of payments in general and of legal money in particular is a strategic question since it commands the capacity of individuals to be present in the market. A monetary analysis excludes that the quantity of money be exogenous.[11] Academic theoreticians generally content themselves with treating the quantity of money as a parameter. Doing so avoids dealing with the sovereignty aspect of money issuance. A monetary analysis integrates that feature of legal money by making the minting process the core of the market.

Here enters sovereignty in our framework. Most authors are tempted to associate sovereignty and the State, a quite sensible position. We abstain from doing that not because we disagree but because we do not wish open a debate. Sovereignty is more general than the State – there are forms of sovereignty which imply neither a political organization nor the exercise of a legal violence. A monetary authority differs from the State (ECB, for instance); it has no military and no fiscal power.

Because they are non-privately produced, the way credit and legal money enter the economy has to be made explicit. Because of its exclusive role in squaring the accounts, legal money is of special interest. It is no surprise that the presentation of the minting process goes *pari passu* with the description of the working of a market economy. They are the two faces of the same coin.

The minting process in a market economy

In Chapter 4, a very abstract presentation of the notion of a minting process has been sketched. In the present chapter we have learnt that legal money (non-privately issued) was a necessary element of the minting process (Proposition 2). This allows for making more precise the working of the minting process and its fundamental role in a market economy (see also Bezemer (2009), Cartelier (2010) and Werner (2014)).

The Mint, a generic name for the institution responsible for the issuance of the means of payment, assesses whether or not individuals asking for new means of payment hold enough wealth as a counterpart. Wealth cannot be defined but as a component of the minting process. Being a minting basis, wealth's concrete contents depend directly on the institutional rules. The most famous one is the so-called Gold Standard. But any other rule may work as well in principle.

What matters is that the Mint and people asking for money agree to issue a determinate quantity of means of payment (expressed in $). Means of payment being not durable have to be cancelled at the end of the accounting period. The Mint's assessment of wealth is thus provisional. The quantity of $ issued for a given individual determines the extent of his/her capacity to intervene in the market. Means of payment in the hands of individuals at the opening of the accounts (of the market) are that part of their wealth socially recognized as performing a money mediation. Let's call them *legal money*.

Money mediation is realized by a circulation of legal money amongst individuals. A matrix of these voluntary payments is a convenient formal representation of that mediation.

Assume that besides legal money private promises of legal money at the end of the accounting period are accepted (they will have a major role in the dynamics of a market economy; see below). The cycle of the market is easy to describe. Wealth is a *stock*. Payments, *i e*. transfers of dollars, are *flows*. At the beginning of the accounting period, part or total of the wealth stock has to be transformed into legal money. Individuals voluntarily transfer dollars by means of legal money (and/or of private promises of it) in order to pay their debt (buyers to sellers, for instance). Everyone being both a buyer and a seller spends and gets some quantities and/or promises of legal money. The payments of one are the receipts for another. As we know, these voluntary transfers of dollars generally generate imbalances which, after partial compensation, have to be ultimately settled. The reasons why these unexpected payments may be called *constrained payments* have been mentioned in the preceding chapter. We have now to state explicitly how these payments may take place.

As said above, legal means of payment are made available by the Mint as a provisional *official* assessment of wealth. We may add that promises to pay legal money at the end of the market perform payments as *private* assessments of wealth (credit money). Imbalances measure the gap between these conditional evaluations and the one effected by the market. Means of payment are not durable. Excess individuals have to use them, deficit individuals have to get them. After compensation between all private promises imbalances have to be settled by means of legal money only. Hypothesis 1 (only viable economies are considered) means that no one fails to carry out his/her constrained payments. The procedure by which a constrained payment is done – and cancels legal money – is the reverse of the one by which legal money has been issued: money is turned into wealth.

Two general modes may be conceived. In the first one, excess individuals acquire those amounts of wealth deficit individuals are constrained to give up. In the second one, when private inter-individual constrained payments cannot take place (when excess individuals do not accept to spend toward deficit ones), the Mint intervenes, allowing excess individuals to acquire some rights to obtain legal money in the next minting process. Note that these rights are conditional to the future institutional rules of the minting process. It would be inappropriate to speak of a durability of legal money. It would be better to speak of *a perennial minting process*. As a counterpart of the conditional rights acquired by excess individuals, the Mint becomes creditor of the deficit individuals. In both modes, constrained payments perform a reassessment of the quantities of wealth.

A system of metallic currency may be convenient to illustrate what precedes. In such a system, legal coins are legal money and legal coins (and/or promises to pay with legal coins at the end of the market) are the unique means of payment. *Minting* is the operation through which monetary unit and a means of payment are related. Here, the monetary unit is defined by a weight of gold, say

$1\$ \equiv 1,5gr$ of gold, which is equivalent to fix a *legal* price for gold ($\frac{2}{3}\$\,pergr$).

Legal coins are issued by the *Mint*, which is a *legal institution*. Transfers of dollars are realized only by the moving of legal coins from one individual to another. These moves transfer dollars from one account to another and gold by the same token. But coins, not gold, are the means by which debts are discharged.

In a metallic minting process gold is wealth. *Gold is not wealth because it provides utility or pleasure to its holders (even if it may be the case) but because it allows them to intervene in the market.* Other forms of wealth are nothing but a private source of pleasure. They do not have an economic meaning and could remain hidden to others. It is not the case for gold, which gives to his/her holders a capability for social expression. In this sense, gold is not an item of whatever commodity space; *it is just the name of a rule of legal money issuance.* Gold is a standard, *i.e.* a form of wealth eligible to monetization with other forms of wealth. As such, gold as standard is even socially distinguishable from gold as a private good: its fineness and weighing unit are legally fixed. It is not thoughtless that the rule bears a natural appearance but what matters is the rule and its acceptance by individuals.

As individuals are defined by accounts, we may describe the cycle of the market by referring to accounting. A typical period is opened by the minting process and closed by a general cancellation of the means of payment (melting). The discrete interval between these two points of time is a period during which payments are observed. As a consequence: (a) means of payment are reckoned as *flows* and transfers of dollars have a *minus* one time dimension; they appear only in accrual accounts; (b) minting supports have a *zero* time dimension; they are to be observed only in balance-sheets. Coins in a chest observed at a certain point of time are gold, not a means of payment unless current legal rules make it so. A gold coin may transfer dollars only if it is recognized as legal money at the very point of time it is used. These conditions must hold at any point in the range of time between the issuance of the means of payment and the squaring of the accounts. What happens between these two points ($\tau = 0$ and $\tau = 1$) may be considered as belonging indistinctly to that discrete accounting period ($t = 1$).

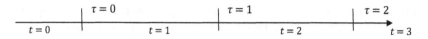

Table 5.1 Matrix of voluntary and constrained payments and mutual commitments to future payments

	Melting	Bank	1	2	...	H	Total
Minting			m_1^t	m_2^t	...	m_H^t	μ
Bank		0	m_{b1}^t	m_{b2}^t	...	m_{bH}^t	$m_b^t = ...$
1	$\mu_1^t + \tilde{\mu}_1^t$	μ_1^t	0	$m_{12}^t + \tilde{m}_{12}^t$	...	$m_{1H}^t + \tilde{m}_{1H}^t$	$m_1^t + \tilde{m}_1^t$
2	$\mu_2^t + \tilde{\mu}_2^t$	μ_2^t	$m_{21}^t + \tilde{m}_{21}^t$	0	...	$m_{2H}^t + \tilde{m}_{2H}^t$	$m_2^t + \tilde{m}_2^t$
...	...	...	...	...	...	...	...
H	$\mu_H^t + \tilde{\mu}_H^t$	μ_H^t	$m_{H1}^t + \tilde{m}_{H1}^t$	$m_{H2}^t + \tilde{m}_{H2}^t$	...	0	$m_H^t + \tilde{m}_H^t$
Total	μ	μ	$\mu_1^t + \tilde{\mu}_1^t$	$\mu_2^t + \tilde{\mu}_2^t$	...	$\mu_H^t + \tilde{\mu}_H^t$	

Let's consider individual h at $\tau = 0$. His or her wealth resulting from the squaring of accounts of period 0 (between $\tau = -1$ and $\tau = 0$), is ω_h^0 (to be read on his or her backward-looking balance-sheet). Taking into account his or her expectations and commitments to pay during period $t = 1$ (between $\tau = 0$ and $\tau = 1$) and the minting constraint, individual h decides to spend $\sum_k m_{hk}^1$. Individuals $k \neq h$ independently decide their expenses such that individual h receives $\sum_k m_{kh}^1 \neq \sum_k m_{hk}^1$. Individual h must settle his or her balance by a constrained minting of part of his or her wealth $\Delta \omega_h^1 = \sum_k m_{kh}^1 - \sum_k m_{hk}^1 = \pm \tilde{m}_h^1$. According to the current accounting rules, the settlement of his or her balance determines his or her new wealth ω_h^1 at $\tau = 1$. A similar sequence takes place at $\tau = 1$ and so on.

A complete description of the relations between individuals is given by the matrix of voluntary and constrained payments and mutual commitments to future payments.

The payment matrix is (omitting banks and the Mint):

$$M = \begin{pmatrix} 0 & m_{12} + \tilde{m}_{12} & \cdots & m_{1H} + \tilde{m}_{1H} \\ m_{21} + \tilde{m}_{21} & 0 & \cdots & m_{2H} + \tilde{m}_{2H} \\ \cdots & \cdots & \cdots & \cdots \\ m_{H1} + \tilde{m}_{H1} & m_{H2} + \tilde{m}_{H2} & \cdots & 0 \end{pmatrix} \tag{5-11}$$

Corresponding flows–of–funds are described in Schema 5.1.

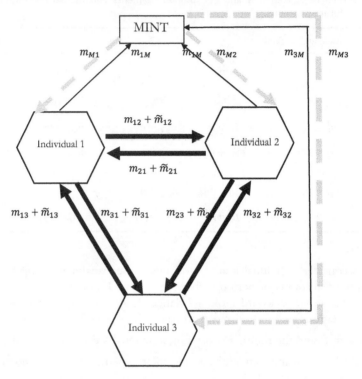

Schema 5.1 Money circulation in a market economy

Some propositions

The minting cycle is akin to the market defined by its three fundamental characteristics: (a) the access to the minting process, which makes individuals active ones, is the condition of decentralization, (b) the use of the means of payment, which is the substance of economic activity, allows for the payback of the debts, and (c) the melting, or the cancellation of the means of payment, makes clear what the market is about: the *restructuring of the social wealth*.

Individual wealth evaluation

An ultimate (legal) means of payment (Proposition 2, above) settles the payment balances, hence

Proposition 3

Constrained payments – by means of payment obtained against constrained transfers of minting basis – settle inter-individual balances;

distribution of the minting basis amongst individuals squares the accounts

Introducing constrained payments as a consequence of equivalence *and* decentralization is crucial. "Technically" this allows dealing with out-of-equilibrium situations. Theoretically this allows us to give an account of what an uncertainty inherent in the market means (and also to what Marx (1976) called the double character of labour embodied in commodities).

According to a correct and widely shared vision of a market economy, each individual able to choose by him/herself the type, the amount and the modalities of his/her activity will engage some efforts or some expenses in order to carry out his/her decisions independently from others. When labour is about, Marx speaks of concrete labour in order to describe how a private and independent producer behaves. That producer has in mind an "ideal price", *i.e.* an expected price at which his/her efforts would be correctly evaluated. When expenses are about – which is the case in a monetary analysis – the expenses incurred by the independent producer are what we have dubbed voluntary expenses.

Now, as Marx reminds the reader, concrete labour is not the end of the story. Other producers freely evaluate what our producer has brought to the market. This procedure is described at length by Marx under the heading "forms of value". Its result is a social evaluation of the commodity. In labour terms, that evaluation is called "social or abstract labour". The gap between the two evaluations, concrete and abstract labour, is reduced by a crisis, the commodity *"salto mortale"* in Marx's own terms. Marx was proud about his "discovery" that he named "double character of labour embodied in commodities". Unfortunately, that theory failed: concrete and abstract labours being not commensurable, no quantitative determination of values is available which would respect Marx's intuition.

In our monetary analysis, Marx's story has a happy end. Each producer freely chooses the amount of expenses he/she thinks will also be the amount he/she will get from others. But the effective evaluation by others is given by the sum of the voluntary expenses they address to the producer. This amount is given by the sum of the columns of the payment matrix. Each producer is now described by the amount of his/her voluntary expenses (their meaning is: concrete labour) and by the amount of his/her receipts (their meaning is: abstract labour). But, by contrast with Marx's attempt at solving the problem, the two evaluations are commensurable since they are both in money terms. The difference between the total amount of each row and the sum of each column – monetary imbalances – must be settled. Here enter the constrained operations which make explicit the procedure of the *"salto mortale"* Marx could not offer with his labour theory of value.

Philosophically, this allows us to distinguish between *possession* and *property*.

Proposition 4

Constrained payments transform possession into a legitimate property

Possession is what individuals may use in their actions – here: voluntary payments – property applies to what results from their actions – here the further possibility to intervene in the market. Property differs from possession in a market society: possession measures what active individuals (eligible for the minting process) may engage in the market, property measures what the market (society) recognizes and validates at the end of a period. Proposition 4 fits well with what is currently observable in our societies. However, it finds no room either in mainstream theory or in Classical theory (Benetti & Cartelier, 1987).

A very favourable interpretation of general equilibrium theory would credit it for distinguishing possession and property. Individuals would *possess* their initial endowments but they would *own* their market allocations. But academic theory tells only part of the story since it does not permit the co-existence of equivalence and decentralization: initial endowments and market allocations are necessarily equal in value as if a superior genius had the capacity to avoid any market sanctions. It sounds paradoxical to simultaneously maintain that (a) the composition of any individual property is given beforehand (initial endowments) and that (b) economic relations determine the value of another content, equilibrium allocations. It is, however, what most mainstream economists take for granted. This is twice incorrect. That belief (a) does not make sense since it implies that property rights are independent of the market and (b) does not allow market relations to affect the value of individual properties.

Proposition 4 is important. It draws attention to the capacity of a monetary analysis to deal with the crucial question of property in a self-contained way. The entire process of property determination is presented without resorting to disciplines other than economic theory. This does not mean that law and philosophical values have nothing to do with property but, on the contrary, that combining different disciplines does make sense only when their respective fields are well-defined. In the conclusion of the present essay more will be said on multidisciplinary research.

The schema above is not empirical but theoretical. In ordinary life, all payments, voluntary and constrained, take place simultaneously during the period and it is not easy to distinguish the former from the latter. Here, for the sake of intelligibility, they are supposed to take place at the beginning of the period for the former and at the end for the latter. This schema breaks away from academic economics as do the fundamental postulates and our specifications. What is shown as the normal outcome of a market session is nothing but an effective disequilibrium situation (not observable independently of constrained payments) and an observable structure of wealth different from the one expected by the individuals (but compatible with a viability of the economy by virtue of Hypothesis 1). There is room in a monetary analysis for market sanctions which cannot be provided by value theories. Instead of representing a market economy as a place where commodities permute amongst individuals leaving their relative wealth unchanged, monetary analysis shows a market economy as a place where *decentralized actions generate disequilibria, the resolution of which modifies individuals' relative wealth.*

Another point, related to what precedes, concerns money and wealth. Distinguishing between wealth (gold or any other minting basis) and means of payment (legal coins) contrasts with the common wisdom of economists, but *that* common wisdom is by no means wise. For academic theory money proper is a fraction of capital, the most liquid. This is the straightforward consequence of thinking of money proper as fiat money, maintaining that it is a durable commodity and ignoring sovereignty.

In a metallic system, this amounts to confusing gold and legal coins. Gold is durable, legal coins are not. Their validity as means of payment depends entirely on the law or on the decisions of the Mint. A decreed coin ceases to be legal and to be money proper (but does not cease to be gold!). Legal coins are legal tender only during the period that they are valid. At the end of each period they become gold. At the beginning of each period, following the current legal rules, all or part of gold holdings may be considered as means of payment since it will circulate as money proper under the form of legal coins. Transition at a point of time between two periods depends not only on individual reactions to what has happened during the last period but also on the stability of the legal framework of the economy in the period ahead. In order to avoid confusing money and capital – a confusion common to mainstream and most Keynesian theories – *legal money is conceived here as a set of rules whose validity over time may or may not be assumed.*

Legal money, the ultimate means of payment, may not be the most used. Credit, *i.e.* promises to pay with legal money at the end of the market, may take place between a seller and a buyer. Credit may also take place between a commercial bank and an individual. This generates an amount of bank money or credit money. Convertibility of credit into legal money is required for transactions to be complete, as we have seen above.

If the distinction between credit (debt) and legal money (currency) is conceptually clear, its application to concrete systems of payment is sometimes difficult. Convertibility is the keyword. Until 1833 in Gold Standard England, legal coins were legal tender and Bank of England banknotes were not. They had to be converted into legal coins in order to settle a transaction, meaning that both parties were free vis-à-vis of each other and that the transaction was complete. Today, checks and other means of circulating demand deposits must also be convertible into central money. Demand deposits are legally insured and banks protected by the adage "too big to fail". The convertibility of bank money into legal tender is quasi-guaranteed. We are tempted to not sharply distinguish between the two. But financial crises remind us that commercial banks are not monetary authorities; they are part of an organized system dominated by a central bank.

To make the story simple, we will hereafter consider money as being indifferently bank or legal money. This is acceptable since what matters is less the type of ultimate means of payment than to understand the difference between debt (or credit) and the means of payment of the debt.

For any individual needing credit, *i.e.* wishing to report the payment of whatever monetary obligation he/she must pay to another individual, whether he/she succeeds or not depends on circumstances: the rate of interest, a willingness to lend, etc. Individuals considered as a whole have the capacity to increase or decrease the absolute amount of reciprocal credits. They do not have the capacity to increase the quantity of legal money. Issuing money involves some degrees of sovereignty, which is precisely what is lacking in inter-individual relations. Here again, sovereignty is specific to economic relations; it does not engage a political position. Money issuance is a process where each individual faces society as a whole, either as a set of rules (it will be the case in a pure metallic system with free minting and melting of legal coins) or as a monetary authority ruling a hierarchical banking system (the central bank).

Assimilating market functioning and the minting process, as done in the schema above, leads to a special view about wealth. The transformation of wealth into a means of payment by an institutional process (minting and opening of the accounts) allows individuals to be present in the market. The transformation of a means of payment into wealth (melting and squaring of the accounts) determines the new structure of wealth.

It may be strange that something can be maintained about the nature of wealth prior to any definition of commodities. It is in fact not surprising. Neither credit nor gold are conceived of as commodities. Both are part of the complex combination of rules and elements shaping the monetary organization of the market. Legal money and "gold" belong to the field designed by our three postulates and have nothing to do with whatever pre-supposed commodity space.

Melting or squaring of accounts closes the period of the market; balance-sheets at the end of the period show the structure of wealth resulting from the market, *i.e.* of the minting basis. But, at the same time τ, a new period opens with the minting for market of $t + 1$. There are no *a priori* reasons for the minting of $t + 1$ being the same as that of t. Not only because unexpected wealth may change decisions individuals take for $t + 1$ but also because the general conditions of minting may have changed. For instance the Mint may have modified the legal price of gold or have introduced a new model for legal coins.

Contrary to the special case we have met in Kocherlakota's model, individuals are not in the same conditions at the end of period t and at the beginning of period $t + 1$, even if balance-sheets are established at the same date τ. Forward-looking and backward-looking balance-sheets are different. As a matter of fact:

Proposition 5

There is no objective relation between backward and forward-looking balance-sheets established at the same point of time

Proposition 5 is essential to understand why market dynamics cannot be modelled according to standard dynamics. Ordinary stock-flow representations of a decentralized economy (see Lavoie or Godley amongst the most notable) do not allow for the difference between backward- and forward-looking balance-sheets. They make readers believe that it makes sense to build a more or less mechanic dynamic model and to look for its specific dynamic properties. As we shall see below, usual methods of dynamic modelling are not well-suited for dealing with the evolution over time of a market economy.

Propositions 2 to 5 concern market relations only. Their validity cannot be extended, without discussion, to all monetary relations. The market is not the last word of the monetary analysis. The market is specific. Economic activity here may be described as repeated transformations of wealth into means of payment and of means of payment into wealth. In Marx's terms, market activity is characterized by Money – Commodity – Money and not by Commodity – Money – Commodity as Marx himself maintained. Minting and melting are the foundation of the market process which repeatedly challenges relative wealth by confronting individual decentralized monetary actions to each other.

We have taken above the voluntary payments as granted. There has been no attempt to explain how individuals behave. This is intentional. Even if it is reasonable to think that people behave rationally, *i.e.* maximize something under some constraints in a determinate setting, we don't wish to venture into that complex matter. No normative purpose is intended here. Individuals share the same prerogatives (they are all active); they are free, in the sense of Simmel, under the command of no individual in particular but of all in general (the principle of equivalence). They freely decide the level of their voluntary payments so that:

Proposition 6

The level of activity of all individuals in a market economy is constrained by the minting process only.

Proposition 6 is not important in itself but only because it ceases to be valid when wage-earners and entrepreneurs appear (see next chapter). The necessity of switching to a monetary analysis partly comes from the limit a real analysis meets when the level of economic activity is about.

Before embarking on a preliminary study of the dynamics of a market economy, it is worth dealing briefly with some basic questions: the measure of wealth, the nature of commodities and of assets.

Unit of account and measure: more on the minting process

Let us come back to Steuart's quotation about the nominal unit of account: money *measures* vendible things. The measure alluded to by Steuart differs from that commonly understood by value theoreticians. Let's see how and why.

In value theories, prices are interpreted as relative *values*, even when fiat money is the exclusive intermediary of transaction (recall that fiat money is an item of the commodity space). To deal with the price of wheat in fiat money or with the price of fiat money in wheat does not make any difference. What matters only, is the fact that wheat and fiat money are valued by individuals such that there is (or must be) some commensurability between them. When a quarter of wheat is exchanged at equilibrium against two quarters of oats we cannot say that one quarter of wheat is equal to two quarters of oats – a nonsensical proposition – but that their *values* are equal (an equivalence principle which is sometimes interpreted as if commodities had a common substance).

In a monetary analysis, measure is intended in an *absolute* sense, not in a relative one. Two points have to be made here:

1   Commodities, if not defined as monetary magnitudes, are not commensurable; however, some quantitative relations may be established between them.
2   There is no equivalence between the means of payment and what they allow one to buy.

Let's look at these two points separately.

Simmel offers an interesting idea of measure which does not imply any common essence between commodities:

> The two objects *m* and *n* may have some relationship that has nothing to do with qualitative identity, so that neither one can serve directly as a measure for the other. The relation may be of cause and effect, of symbolism, of common relationship to a third factor or anything else. Let us assume that an object *a* is known to be a quarter of *m*, and the object *b* is known to be some quantitative part of *n*. If a relation exists between *a* and *b*, corresponding to the relation *m* and *n*, it follows that *b* equals a quarter of *n*. In spite of a qualitative difference and the impossibility of any direct comparison between *a* and *b*, it is nevertheless possible to determine the quantity of one by the quantity of the other.
>
> (Simmel, p. 133)

Let's express Simmel's quotation in simple economic terms: if 100 dollars allows one to buy *n*, a mass of heterogeneous commodities, whereas 25 dollars allows one to buy *m*, another mass of heterogeneous commodities; then it makes sense to say that *m* is a quarter of *n*, which does not mean at all that *n* has a value which is four times that of *m* but that *in order to get n one must have four times more of dollars than to get m*. There is no commensurability between *m* and *n*. They only have in common that they may be obtained by means of 25 and 100 dollars respectively.

But the relation between 25 dollars and *m* or between 100 dollars and *n* is still left unexplained. In order to go further it is necessary to consider again the issuance of the means of payment which is the clue to the subject matter.

Value theoreticians think that 100 dollars buys *n* because 100 dollars and *n* have the same value (and through transitivity *n* as having four times the value of *m*). For them goods and fiat money have to be treated in the same way and on the same footing. However, these theoreticians admit at the same time that fiat money differs from commodities since it is not privately produced. To avoid further complications due to that basic heterogeneity between commodities and fiat money, they treat the quantity of fiat money as exogenously determined. In the best case, quantity of money is just a parameter.

The introduction of a minting process radically changes the deal. *The issuance of the means of payment is neither an exchange nor a purchase/sale.*

Consider again the pure metallic system. The individual who brings his or her gold to the Mint and gets legal coins has not sold his/her gold since he/she keeps it in the form of legal coins, and the Mint has not bought it either. Gold is transformed into a means of payment. Minting is neither an exchange nor a purchase/sale but a *sovereign act* which *takes place between an individual and the Mint which represents all of the individuals.*[12]

An analogous proposition holds valid for credit money. The individual who gets a credit of *x* dollars is recognized by a commercial bank as holding an amount *x* of wealth. He acquires a quantity *x* of dollars (demand deposits) against a new debt of *x* dollars. At the end of the period, if his receipts are equal to his payments, he pays back his debt to the bank and experiences no change in his balance-sheet: exactly as in the case of gold minting. Moreover, *the relation between the commercial bank and the individual is not a private one: the bank operates under the control and the authority of a central Bank.*

In both cases there co-exist two modes of regulation for the minting basis: one is an ordinary market (for gold or for financial assets) the other is the direct or indirect action of a monetary authority (the Mint fixes the legal price of gold, the central Bank regulates credit[13]). In the same way as gold contained in legal coins is not bought or sold in any market, new assets created by banks are not negotiable either. They must be transformed into ordinary financial assets through securitization in order to be sold in ordinary financial markets.

A full recognition that the means of payment are not privately produced and that their quantity is not a parameter but the outcome of a minting process combining private and sovereign actions prevents one from analyzing a purchase/sale operation as an exchange between two values, one being that of the commodity, the other that of the means of payment. Following Simmel's principle, a purchase/sale is *a sequence of purposes*, in which a means – the means of payment – is used in view of a certain end or purpose – the acquiring of the commodity. Means of payment (legal money and promises of legal money) are not bought or sold: establishing an equivalence between means of payment and commodities does not make sense. Value finds no room in a monetary analysis, even where market relations are concerned. *Equivalence, which means value equivalence in value theories, here only means that individuals are all active and have the same prerogatives and share the same condition.*

Commodities and assets in a market economy

To reject the commodity space postulate is not to exclude from theory those commodities the property rights of which are evaluated by the flow of the means of payment. It means that commodities are not considered as common knowledge amongst individuals. They are not a suitable language in the market. It means also that, deprived of any physical or "natural" support, their nomenclature is necessarily socially determined and endogenous to economic theory. They should be defined using only the elements already mentioned so far: (a) the monetary unit, (b) the minting process specified by its rules and (iii) the active individuals, *i.e.* the accounts.

The simplest view about commodities in a decentralized economy is to consider that each individual sells in the market the particular commodity which he/she chooses to specialize in. Consequently, there is a correspondence, one-to-one, between individuals and commodities. Any individual h produces a particular commodity in view of getting some means of payment from the others. All the commodities share that property so that the relevant distinction between commodities is between individuals. Individual h produces and sells in the market commodity h. Any commodity differs from any other by the index of the individual to whom its sale yields dollars. The quantity of commodity h is measured by the amount of voluntary payments individual h has performed in order to be able to receive flows of payment from other people. That quantity is perfectly defined when spontaneous receipts are equal to voluntary payments. We have adopted this view above when legal money has been introduced.

However, such a definition is not entirely convenient. It does not consider the durability of the commodity and leaves intertemporal operations undefined. In formal terms, we do not know how durable are the commodities bought by h – *i.e.* how m_{hk} affects h balance-sheet. The second point is easy to settle since the description of a commitment to pay some amounts of dollars in the future does not require any elements other than amounts of dollars, time and the involved individuals. The first point is more delicate since when expressed in ordinary terms it allows us to distinguish between consumption and investment. To make this description of a commodity complete we have to add the way in which it is amortized. This requires only amounts of dollars and time. We must thus associate to each flow a scheme of amortization. Purchases of consumption goods or of production goods used in one period do not affect balance-sheets but through constrained payments, while those of durable goods modify balance-sheets independently of the settlement of imbalances according to the scheme of amortization. For reasons which will become clear in the following chapter, we will abstract ourselves from that difficulty and will assume that all the m_{hk} are either consumption or amortization expenditures. Hence:

Definition 2

The *nature* of a commodity is defined by the individual who sells it in the market; its *quantity* is well-defined when the amount of sales in $ is equal to the voluntary expenses of the producer; its durability is defined by the inverse of the rate of amortization (supposed hereafter equal to 1).

No surplus product in a market economy

What seems more interesting about market relations is to show that *no surplus product can be observed*. By surplus we mean either what Ricardo-Sraffa's theory deals with (for any commodity the excess of the total quantity produced over the total quantity of it used as an input in all industries) – or what Neoclassical theory calls *net production* which is equal at equilibrium to the sum of remunerations of the factors of production. In both cases, observing a surplus requires that it is possible to distinguish between what is produced and what it is necessary to produce. When a commodity space is presupposed, it seems obvious that a surplus (in both senses of the term) may be known once the production technique is known. But this is misleading. It is an illusion due to a neglect of the social conditions of observation of a market economy. Let's look at that point, assuming a commodity space.[14]

What are the conditions that allow an external observer, capable of looking at physical reality only, to decide whether the observed economy generates a surplus or not? How is it possible for that "objective social scientist" to discriminate between necessary and non-necessary inputs? Let's consider a market economy and let's assume for the sake of simplicity that each industry is run by an independent producer only (or that individual h produces only commodity h). The "objective social scientist" observes a particular process of production, say a cabinet maker producing a table. Can the observer decide whether the commodities used by the producer, either in his workroom or at home, are or are not necessary for the production of the table? He has to decide, say, if an independent cabinet maker really needs to go to the theatre or to drink an excellent Burgundy wine. Neither moral nor common sense provide the relevant criteria for solving that problem. There is no objective criteria but market prices. If market prices are such that the cabinet maker can afford to drink Burgundy wine and go to theatre, then Burgundy wine and going to theatre must be considered as *objectively and socially necessary to the production* of tables. Society as a whole recognizes through the market process that the cabinet maker's consumption is economically necessary and well-founded. It would be nonsensical to ask: wouldn't the cabinet maker produce tables without drinking Burgundy wine but rather water? And to answer: yes he can! If this is not observed it must not be mentioned.

There is no sense in speaking of the existence of a positive surplus in such a market economy. The fact that surplus is identically equal to zero has nothing to do with any physical objectivity the "objective social scientist" could be capable of. This is just the effect of a social characteristic of the economy, *the fact that all individuals have the same social condition*: they are private persons specialized in production and freely working for their own account. In our terms, they are all *active* individuals having all access to the minting process. They are homogeneous from that point of view: they are all independent producers. What Sraffa calls "production for subsistence", with a strong physical and natural connotation, is in fact a simple market economy, the type of which Marx deals with in the first section of *Capital* before he introduces capitalists and surplus-value. There is nothing purely physical in it. That negative conclusion holds valid for Neoclassical theory also: there is hardly something which may be called "income of production factors".

Expressed in the terms of a monetary analysis, the proposition above simply means that, at equilibrium (to draw a parallel with real analysis), payments and receipts being equal for all active individuals, expectations are validated by the market. The economy as a whole validates the voluntary expenses individuals have freely decided. There is no possibility for the "objective social scientist" to state that it would have been better to spend less in order to get the same amount of receipts. Hence:

Proposition 7

No surplus can be observed in a market economy whenever a commodity's durability is equal to 1 (only accrual accounts are taken into consideration); in other terms, necessary and non-necessary inputs cannot be objectively distinguished.

When some commodities have a durability greater than one, even if it is still not possible to distinguish between necessary and non-necessary inputs, durable commodities showing up in balance-sheets (as amounts of dollars) become a component of wealth together with a minting base. Steuart has studied the effects of circulation on the "balance of wealth" with great care. Both components of wealth may, according to him, be monetized. Hence:

Proposition 8

A global increase of wealth can be objectively observed if and only if the durability of some commodities is greater than one (Steuart);

backward-looking balance-sheets and accrual accounts have to be considered to assess the effects of circulation on the distribution of wealth (durable commodities and/or a minting base).

We will see in the following chapter that observing a surplus in a monetary economy requires other social conditions for observation, namely that not all individuals will be active.[15]

The dynamics of market relations[16]

In value theory non-equilibrium situations are not to be found. By construction, the models provide only solutions which are equilibrium positions. Academic theoreticians nevertheless imagine these solutions as being the result of an asymptotic convergence of transient trajectories, solutions of a dynamical system associated with their static ones. The basic concern is about the asymptotic properties of the dynamical systems conceived as mimicking market adjustments. The rationale for that research program is the philosophy of a social contract: is exchange (in fact, the "law of supply and demand") sufficient to support a decentralized economy (and beyond, a decentralized society)? We know how this research program has failed.

As the developments above make it clear, minting processes are intrinsically dynamic. Imbalances generate variations of the composition of individual wealth which are observable by the active individuals who may react to these unexpected outcomes of the market. Asymptotic properties are not what concern us. We are not interested in the "Invisible Hand" question. What matters is not to justify a social vision of society but whether imbalances are not too important to prevent the economy from keeping working. As out-of-equilibrium situations are to be effective, the question is *their effect on the viability of the economy*. Traditional dynamics are not well-adapted to address that question. Viability theory is more appropriate. Although it is not the proper place to present what is a very complex mathematical theory (see Aubin, Bayen & Saint-Pierre, 2011), it is worth giving a brief indication about the basic principle which is at its root.

The two basic ingredients of a simple model of viability are:

• A dynamic model with *controls*.
• A *constraint set* of effective out-of-equilibrium situations which are viable (i.e. which do not put into question the survival of the economy).

The fundamental question is whether disequilibria are such that they prevent the economy from any possibility of survival or not. Formally, the problem boils down to the following: "does there exist a subset of the constraint set, such that from every point of this subset there starts at least one trajectory (subject to controls) which may remain in this subset forever?" The greater subset having such a property is called the *viability kernel*.

The philosophy behind that conception of dynamics has nothing to do with the myth of the social contract. Its main concern is not the possibility for an economy to automatically converge toward equilibrium but *the possibility for a managed economy to be sustainable*. The existence of a viability kernel does not guarantee that the economy will effectively survive (many trajectories may lead to a complete collapse of the economy) but only that a good management be found such that it will effectively be the case. That view is reminiscent of Steuart's statesman and of his conception of political economy as an art, not as a science.

Viability theory has developed in a very rich and diverse way. We will content ourselves with a simple illustration.

A simple model

Let there be a market economy where H individuals (or decision centres), indexed by $h = 1, \cdots, h, \cdots, H$, hold at (τ) an amount of wealth (expressed in monetary unit) $\omega_h(\tau)$. Wealth is defined as the quantity of gold, let's call it the *minting basis*, which allows for getting a means of payment from a special institution (the Mint). In a purely metallic monetary system, gold is the unique wealth and coins issued by the Mint are the exclusive legal money (read: which puts an end to transactions). When a dematerialized legal money circulates (say banknotes of the European Central Bank), wealth and legal money are synonymous (a simplifying assumption).

Now we suppose that some individuals may get a private means of payment from banks at (τ). They have to pay back these means of payment at the end of the market $(\tau + \varepsilon)$, out of their sales. Wealth allows the holder to get a determinate amount of the means of payment at (τ) and to finance his payments in the market during a period of length (ε). The maximum degree of monetization of the wealth is $\varphi_h(\tau)$. Variable $\varphi_h(\tau)$ indicates the importance of private or credit money. The $\varphi_h(\tau)$'s are supposed to be directly fixed by a monetary authority in order to avoid the complexity of the relations between banks and money authority.

The amount of means of payment an individual may get by monetization of his wealth is the simplest measure of his capacity to intervene in the market. A special case is $\varphi_h(\tau) = 0$ for all h and all (τ). It may be interpreted as describing a strict gold standard where gold is the unique wealth. When $\varphi_h(\tau) > 1$ individuals can spend more than their own wealth. This is the case in a general credit economy.

Let's consider a simple monetary economy where individuals voluntarily make payments to each other. A voluntary payment from h to k is denoted by m_{hk}. The receipts of any individual come from other individuals' payments

$\Sigma_k m_{kh}$ whereas the total payments of any individual is $\Sigma_k m_{kl}$. We have obviously: $\Sigma_h \Sigma_k m_{kh} \equiv \Sigma_h \Sigma_k m_{kh}$.

Payments matrix of period (ε) is:

$$
M(\varepsilon) = \begin{pmatrix} 0 & m_{12}(\varepsilon) & \cdots & m_{1H}(\varepsilon) \\ m_{21}(\varepsilon) & 0 & \cdots & m_{2H}(\varepsilon) \\ \cdots & \cdots & \cdots & \cdots \\ m_{H1}(\varepsilon) & m_{H2}(\varepsilon) & \cdots & 0 \end{pmatrix} \tag{5-12}
$$

At the end of each period (ε), each individual has to comply with the minting rules: his total payments $\Sigma_k m_{hk}$ must be equal to his total receipts $\Sigma_k m_{kh}$. When *voluntary* payments do not exhibit that property, *constrained* payments restore equivalence. Concrete forms of constrained payments depend on the type of monetary organization.

If gold were the specific socially recognized wealth, gold endowments would be the exclusive means to get legal means of payment from the Mint (to keep the story simple, monetization is supposed to be costless and free from any seignorage). The circulation of gold coins is the unique method for transferring dollars from one individual to another. In this system, quantities of gold and dollars are transferred at the same time even if gold and money (dollars) are not to be confused.

During period (ε), individual h cannot spend more than the amount of dollars corresponding to the coinage of his gold endowment. If a dollar is defined by a weight of α gr gold (which means that the legal price of gold is $\frac{1}{\alpha}$ per gr), individual h cannot spend more than $\frac{g_h}{\alpha} = \omega_h$ dollars which is the value in dollars of his gold endowment: $\Sigma_k m_{hk} \leq \frac{g_h}{\alpha}$. Let's suppose that h's voluntary payments are greater than his receipts. What will happen?

In such a system the answer is: nothing! The negative balance in dollars of individual h has been settled by the transfer of gold contained in the coins that h has paid in excess over his receipts. During this period voluntary payments have redistributed gold endowments. Excess individuals have gained some quantities of gold and deficit agents have lost what the others have gained. In a purely metallic system voluntary payments (in dollars) and constrained payments (in gold) take place at the same time. Monetary balances are *ipso facto* settled by the gold (monetizable wealth) represented in the coins (the legal means of payment). Conceptually (not necessarily concretely true), the coinage of gold (creation of money) opens circulation and the melting of coins (cancellation of money) closes it.

A remarkable feature of any purely metallic system (without seigniorage) is that no individual can run into bankruptcy. Even if an individual has no receipts, it cannot happen that his payments exceed his wealth.

Consider now the same economy with the following unique modification: instead of legal coins, individuals may finance their transactions using *promises to pay* with legal coins at the end of the period. We will check if viability holds true when the monetary system is based on credit. In such a system, individual h gets his private means of payment by borrowing from a bank. Take the simplest operation: h borrows at (τ), starting point of period (ε), an amount $m_h(\varepsilon)$ for financing part or all his voluntary operations during the period. The bank agrees to lend that sum if and only if (h) credibly promises to pay back the credit (we neglect the question of interest which is postponed to the next chapter). This means that at (τ) the bank recognizes that h holds some wealth and accepts to monetize it. This results from a private agreement. But, that agreement belongs to an institutional arrangement where a monetary authority (central bank) plays a role. In both cases, means of payment are issued along an institutional procedure. Individuals experiencing deficits are constrained to borrow from excess individuals if they will not go into bankruptcy. That constrained operation clearly means a loss of wealth for deficit individuals and a gain for the others.

A mixed monetary system

Suppose a mixed monetary system where credit allows individuals to get rid of gold endowments constraint. Let $(m_h + \varphi_h)(t)$ be the quantity at (τ) for market (ε) of means of payment that h may use for financing his desired transactions (legal coins *plus* promises to pay with legal coins at the end of the market). Now the payment constraint is $\Sigma_k m_{kh} \le (m_h + \varphi_h)$ (instead of $\Sigma_k m_{kh} \le m_h$ in a pure metallic system). Suppose for the sake of simplicity that all individuals use all the means of payment they get either toward other individuals or to themselves (hoarding), *i.e.* $\Sigma_k m_{kh} = m_h + \varphi_h$. It is straightforward that if h gets no receipts, his default payment is φ_h. More generally, his receipts must be greater than φ_h, in order to avoid going into bankruptcy. The property of being bankruptcy proof, specific to pure metallic systems, no longer holds as soon as credit is effective.

The payment matrix is now:

$$
M(\varepsilon) = \begin{bmatrix}
(m_{11} + \varphi_{11})(\varepsilon) & (m_{12} + \varphi_{12})(\varepsilon) & \cdots & (m_{1H} + \varphi_{1H})(\varepsilon) \\
(m_{21} + \varphi_{21})(\varepsilon) & (m_{22} + \varphi_{22})(\varepsilon) & \cdots & (m_{2H} + \varphi_{2H})(\varepsilon) \\
\cdots & \cdots & \cdots & \cdots \\
(m_{H1} + \varphi_{H1})(\varepsilon) & (m_{H2} + \varphi_{H2})(\varepsilon) & \cdots & (m_{HH} + \varphi_{HH})(\varepsilon)
\end{bmatrix} \quad (5\text{--}12)
$$

The payment matrix could be expressed also in the *minting basis* as $\alpha(\varepsilon)M(\varepsilon)$ to make precise the relation between current transactions and the redistribution of gold.

Let's suppose that proportions of payments from h to k during period (ε) are continuous and derivable functions of money endowments $0 \leq f_{hk}(m_h(\tau) + \varphi_h(\tau) \leq 1$. Current transactions of period (ε) modify h's wealth as follows:

$$\frac{m_h(\tau + \varphi) - m_h(\tau)}{\varepsilon} = \sum_{kh} f_{kh}(\cdot)\max\left(0,(m_k + \varphi_k)(\tau)\right)$$

$$- \sum_{kh} f_{kh}(\cdot)\max\left(0,(m_k + \varphi_k)(\tau)\right) \qquad (5\text{–}13)$$

The first member of RHS is the total receipts of h while the second member is his/her payments.

Making ε tend to zero and defining $[m_k(\tau) + \varphi_k(\tau)]^+ \equiv \max(0, (m_k + \varphi_k)(\tau))$ allows us to rewrite the system, giving the evolution of legal money endowments as:

$$\begin{pmatrix} m_1'(\tau) \\ \cdots \\ m_H'(\tau) \end{pmatrix} = \begin{pmatrix} f_{11}\left[m_1(\tau) + \varphi_1(\tau)\right]^+ - 1 & \cdots & f_{H1}\left[m_H(\tau) + \varphi_H(\tau)\right]^+ \\ & \cdots & \cdots & \cdots \\ f_{1H}\left[m_1(\tau) + \varphi_1(\tau)\right]^+ & \cdots & f_{HH}\left[m_H(\tau) + \varphi_H(\tau)\right]^+ - 1 \end{pmatrix}$$

$$\begin{pmatrix} \left[m_1(\tau) + \varphi_1(\tau)\right]^+ \\ \cdots \\ \left[m_H(\tau) + \varphi_H(\tau)\right]^+ \end{pmatrix} \qquad (5\text{–}14)$$

with $\Sigma_h m_h(\tau) = Cte = 1$, and $\Sigma_h m'_h(\tau) = 0$ for all (τ).

Let $F(\cdot)$ be the matrix of circulation coefficients, $m(\tau)$, $m'(\tau)$ and $\varphi(\tau)$ being the vector of $m_h(\tau)$, $m'_h(\tau)$ and $\varphi_h(\tau)$ respectively. The system above may be written as:

$$m'(\tau) = (F[m(\tau) + \varphi(\tau)]^+ - I)[m(\tau) + \varphi(\tau)]^+ \qquad (5\text{–}15)$$

System (5–15) has at least one stationary solution m^*. In the traditional approach the question is to determine global stability properties of that simple monetary economy, for constant φ_h. The intuition is that system (5–15) is self-regulated since any deficit individual loses and any excess individual gains some purchasing power. According to that story, the market punishes individuals who have spent too much and rewards the others allowing them to spend more in the future. That simple idea, very fashionable in the present time of financial crisis, is formally more or less the same as that of the so-called "law of supply and demand". We know that the latter has not the merits that the Vulgate of economists would make us believe. Theoreticians demonstrated at the beginning of the 1970s that Walrasian *tâtonnement* is not generally globally stable in Arrow-Debreu's model.

For analogous reasons, the spontaneous regulation of system (5–15) is less general than economists would have desired. The conditions under which that system is globally stable have no reason to be met in general.

Viability in a nutshell

Therefore it makes sense to abandon the traditional approach in terms of asymptotic global stability and to explore an alternative way less connected with a social liberal philosophy but more relevant, that of *viability*. Instead of researching the conditions under which system (5–15) converges toward a stationary equilibrium, it seems more sensible to determine a domain of viability, *i.e.* a set of situations of tolerable disequilibria. By tolerable disequilibria we mean any situation in which some fundamental constraints are not violated. For the sake of simplicity we admit that viability means a situation in which no individual goes bankrupt, that is:

$$(VC) \quad m_h(\tau) \geq z \quad \forall \ h, (\tau) \tag{5–16}$$
$$\Sigma_h \, m_h(\tau) = 1$$

where z is a meta-variable (see below).
The constraint set K is defined by

$$K := \{(m, z) \in R^H \ X \ R \text{ such that } m_h - z \geq 0, \Sigma_h m_h = 1\} \tag{5–17}$$

A viable situation is any $m(\tau) \ \varepsilon \ K$.

Let's consider a subset of K. If from each point of that subset starts at least at (0) a trajectory $m(\tau)$ such that $m(\tau) \ \varepsilon \ K$ for any (τ), we will say that the subset is a viability set. The greater viability set is the *viability kernel* $Viab(0)(K(0))$. It does not mean that the system is globally stable (a trajectory may converge toward equilibrium and be non-viable if it violates at some $[\tau > 0]$ the viability constraint (5–17)) but only that starting from $Viab(0)(K(0))$ there exists a manipulation of the controls $\varphi_h(\tau)$ keeping the economy in the constraint set for any $(\tau > 0)$. *The size of the viability kernel is a measure of the instability of the economy.*

Unfortunately, there is no general analytical solution for determining the viability kernel. Numerical simulations are the only method to evaluate the size and the form of the viability kernel.[17] Before embarking upon that task it is important to remind the reader of an important property of the model.

A fundamental property is the following:

Proposition 9

A system of pure legal money is viable

(If $\forall \ h, \varphi_h \equiv 0$, then from any initial position m(0) in k(0), the solution remains in k(0); in other words, $Viab(0)(K(0)) = $ k(0)

Whatever may be the dynamics of a market economy under a pure legal money system, the viability constraint is never violated. Such property is certainly responsible for the fascination that the Gold Standard has had and still has on some people. In terms of the model, the viability kernel is the simplex.

Starting from that proposition it seems reasonable to expect that the size of the viability kernel will be reduced as soon as a sufficient amount of credit money is added to legal money. As we shall see, this intuition needs some qualifications. Another intuition is that the size of the viability kernel depends negatively on the degree of harshness of the monetary constraint that is on z. In order to explore these questions, we first have to develop a numerical example.

A numerical example

Let's consider the following matrix of coefficients circulation:

$$F(\cdot) = \begin{pmatrix} -1 & 0.3(m_2 + \varphi_2) & 0.6(m_3 + \varphi_3) \\ 0.3(m_1 + \varphi_1) & -1 & 1 - 0.6(m_3 + \varphi_3) \\ 1 - 0.3(m_1 + \varphi_1) & (m_2 + \varphi_2) & -1 \end{pmatrix} \qquad (5-18)$$

In such an economy the relative size of individuals seems to crucially depend on the global amount of credit: when the φ_h's are important individual 1 benefits from the most part of the payments of individuals 2 and 3, individual 2 receiving the most part of individual 1's payments. It is the reverse when the φ_h's are close to zero. Individual 3 is then in a good situation and individual 2 gets an important fraction of individual 3's payments.

The model is now:

$$\begin{pmatrix} m_1'(\tau) \\ m_2'(\tau) \\ m_3'(\tau) \end{pmatrix} = \begin{pmatrix} -1 & \left[0.3(m_2 + \varphi_2)\right]^+ & \left[0.6(m_3 + \varphi_3)\right]^+ \\ \left[0.3(m_1 + \varphi_1)\right]^+ & -1 & \left[1 - 0.6(m_3 + \varphi_3)\right]^+ \\ \left[1 - 0.3(m_1 + \varphi_1)\right]^+ & \left[(m_2 + \varphi_2)\right]^+ & -1 \end{pmatrix}$$

$$\begin{pmatrix} \left[(m_1 + \varphi_1)(\tau)\right]^+ \\ \left[(m_2 + \varphi_2)(\tau)\right]^+ \\ \left[(m_3 + \varphi_3)(\tau)\right]^+ \end{pmatrix} \qquad (5-19)$$

$$z'(t) = \gamma(\cdot)$$

where $\gamma(\cdot)$ will be chosen depending what measurement we aim at.

The state constraints are given by (5–17).

The control constraints are:

$$U = \{\varphi \in R^H \text{ such that } \varphi_h \geq 0, \Sigma_h \varphi_h \leq c, \text{ and } \varphi_h = 0 \text{ if } m_h < 0\} \quad (5\text{--}20)$$

Viability and hardness of the monetary constraint

When it is about balances of payments, be that of an individual or of a country, a crucial point is the hardness of the monetary constraint imposed on the agents. It is possible to imagine, for instance, that the monetary authority accepts to cover any negative balance up to a certain amount. In terms of the definition of the constraint, set z denotes the hardness of the constraint.

Choosing $(z) = -z, z \in [-2, 0]$, which means that an individual with a quantity of legal money greater than -2 is considered as viable (think of a lender of last resort). Taking successive values for z and comparing the size of the viability kernel for these different values generates viability kernels with a decreasing size. When $z = 0$, the viability kernel is the simplex Σ in accordance with our proposition above.

In order to get an idea of the dynamics we show below a trajectory of our economy. At $(\tau = 0)$ individual 2 is in a bad position and would have been eliminated (and the economy would have violated the viability constraint), if the monetary constraint had been more severe (-1 for instance). But, thanks to the soft constraint, the economy eventually gets in a zone where all individuals have a positive wealth. The evolution of the controls is shown as well:

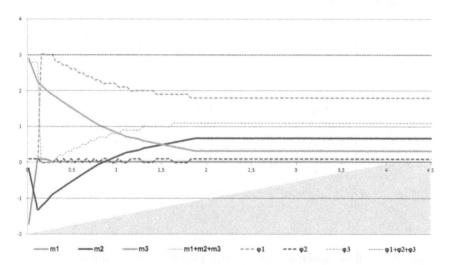

Figure 5.1 Trajectories with $z = -2$

An analogous result would be obtained if we had allowed for a progressive hardening of the constraint, as the figure below makes it clear:

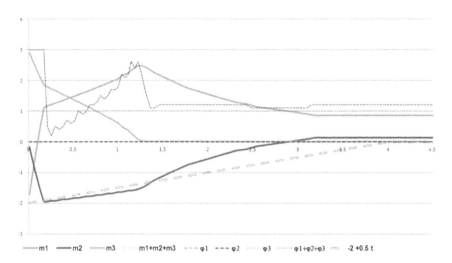

Figure 5.2 Progressive hardening of the constraint

Viability and credit

We have recalled above that a monetary economy where only legal money circulates, which means that nobody can spend more than his legal money endowment, would never experience viability violations. This proposition could make believe that if we introduce more and more credit money as a whole, the viability kernel should be reduced progressively. However, we should not forget that viability, which is in some sense a generalization of equilibrium, depends on *relative* wealth of individuals and not on absolute amounts of their spending. In other terms, if the constraint on the controls is not too strict, there are likely values of controls which ensure viability whatever the global quantity of credit C may be.

Our numerical simulations confirm this second intuition. The computation of the viability kernel gives:

$$Viab(K) = K = \Sigma \text{ X } [0, C] \tag{5-21}$$

But we have to interpret this result with caution. It means that for a high C there always exists some $\varphi_h(\tau)$ which allows the economy to remain in K. Now it could be asked: is the monetary authority capable of implementing such $\varphi_h(\tau)$?

A further inquiry has to be done with constraints on the velocities of the controls, that is on the $\varphi'_h(\tau)$.

Now we impose that φ the total amount of credit, allocated in equal parts $\dfrac{\varphi}{3}$ to each agent, cannot be modified but with a limited velocity u.

The control constraint is consequently:

$$U := \{u \in r \text{ such that } -0.2 \leq u \leq 0.2\} \tag{5–22}$$

Whereas K is now:

$$K := \{(m,z) \in R^H \times R \times R \text{ such that } \varphi > z,$$
$$\textstyle\sum_h m_h = 1, 0 \leq m_h + \varphi_h \leq c_h\} \tag{5–23}$$

Numerical simulation exhibits a very interesting phenomenon. The viability kernel is made of two unconnected parts corresponding to respectively low and high levels of overall credit, as the figure below makes clear:

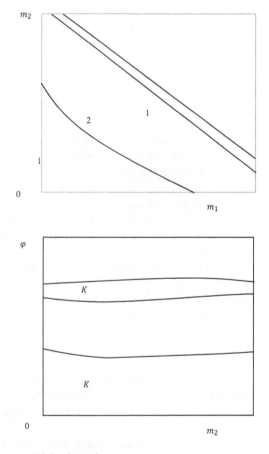

Figure 5.3 A two-part viability kernel

On the lower figure, a discontinuity of the viability kernel is clearly to be seen which would not appear if the constraint on *u* was not binding. On the high figure, the relative importance of individual 3 appears to be great when credit is low (1) and low when credit is important (2) but as the outer area proves there are also viable situations where individual 3 has a very low wealth (1).

It is not easy to interpret such a result at the present stage of the research but it is a strong incentive to explore further in this direction.

As suggested above, we have to check our intuition on the proportions. Namely, we have to examine whether or not an increase in credit money associated with a disproportion amongst the amounts of payments alters the size of the viability kernel.

The control constraint is now:

$$U = \{\varphi \in R^H \text{ such that } \varphi_h \geq 0, \Sigma\varphi_1 \geq z \text{ and } \varphi_2 = \varphi_3 = 0\} \quad (5\text{--}24)$$

And *K* is (here, $z = 0$):

$$K := \{m \in R^H \, XR \text{ such that } m_h \geq 0, \Sigma_h m_h = 1\} \quad (5\text{--}25)$$

Numerical simulations confirm that less than the absolute amount of credit, it is rather the disproportion between individual payments allowed by an important credit which matters for (in)stability. The figure below shows that two thresholds exist. Below the first (0.168), the viability kernel remains unchanged and equal to the simplex; above the second (0.339) the viability kernel is empty. The economy disappears or must change dramatically. In the range between the two thresholds the viability kernel is reduced but does not change:

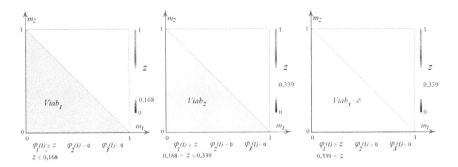

Figure 5.4 Viability and credit

This last result emphasizes the role of proportions between individual wealth and activity. The stress on proportions has a long story in economic thought. It is not without interest to meet again that tradition in our monetary analysis.

Notes

1 We will see later that the budgetary constraint for a non-active individual has to be interpreted differently.
2 The present state of the art is the result of (a) the failure of the theory of general competitive equilibrium to prove global stability and (b) the neglect of that question since the 1980s and the non-critical acceptance of rational expectations hypothesis.
3 See Benetti & Cartelier (2001) for more developments on this rule.
4 Prices are determined if an individual at least desires to sell a commodity and are positive if an individual at least desires to buy using the other commodity as a means of payment. In the following pages we will skip any technicality and stick to what is essential.
5 We follow Sahi & Yao's (1989) presentation but we skip many technicalities.
6 Market prices are determined up to a scalar; no idea of a common unit of account is to be found here.
7 This is the basis of Ricardo's proposal (see Deleplace, 2017).
8 I remember Hyman Minsky's saying that in a capitalist economy everybody is trying to issue and make accepted his/her own means of payment . . . .
9 Domestic payment systems differ from the international payment system: in the latter there is no ultimate or legal means of payment. The absence of any supra-national means of payment makes problematic the working of such a system.
10 See Graeber (2011) on this point.
11 Some Keynesians and Circuitists have already made that point, namely against Monetarists.
12 Marx was aware of that point: "In order to be able to buy without selling, he must have sold previously without buying. This operation (. . .) seems to involve a self-contradiction. But at the source of their production the precious metals are directly bartered against other commodities" (Marx, Capital, p. 228).
13 Rate(s) of interest are dealt with in Chapter 6 where capital is the minting basis.
14 See Cartelier (2014b) for more details.
15 When durability of commodities – *i.e.* partial amortization – is taken into account, it is possible to speak of an increase of wealth. This should not be confused with cost and profit. Mercantilists had perfectly understood the point: they did not speak about profit but about wealth conceived as durable commodities. The most durable was precious metals . . .
16 This section draws upon Cartelier & Saint-Pierre (2012)
17 For a complete view of that theory, see Aubin et al.

Chapter 6

Entrepreneurs, wage-earners and capitalists

A market economy is the economy in which most people and the quasi-unanimity of academic economists – not only the academic ones – believe to belong to. Consequently, we tend to interpret our economic actions (and also a lot of others) by referring to moral values ordinarily attached to the market: individuals are free to decide what they do; they are thus responsible for their actions and should accept all their possible consequences: wealth or poverty, success or failure. Since we are mutually linked by exchange relations, we have just to accept and respect the corresponding ethic: self-enforcement of contracts, respect of property rights, individual as the highest moral value (individual utilities should not be compared), etc.

Some people are critical of that ethic and more generally of the way market principles govern our society. They are pessimistic about stability of such an economy, following Sismondi, Marx and to some extent Keynes, to name the "great forebears". They condemn the greediness inherent in market economies, the lack of concern for society as a whole, etc. Others are optimistic. The market generally ensures global stability and is the best way to manage a peaceful coordination between individuals. We have just to abstain from troubling its smooth working with arbitrary interventions. *In spite of this fundamental dissent amongst economists and amongst lay people, both camps agree to consider that a market economy is what economics is about.*

That belief or that conviction is the stumbling-block which prevents us from conceiving our economies as having specific properties not to be found in pure market economies, namely to experience involuntary employment equilibria (radically distinct from under-employment equilibria) and, more generally, to be subject to forces and motives beyond those associated with simple permutations of commodities amongst individuals looking to their own welfare. Removing that obstacle is one of the purposes of this chapter.

We will proceed in three steps. As a first step we have to account for the fact that individuals may be divided, and are indeed, in two groups or classes according to their prerogatives when they are in the market. Amongst many possible divisions into groups, the one between entrepreneurs and wage-earners is of special interest for studying our economies but also for understanding many aspects of economic theory. That division in classes has something to do with the rights of property. It gives birth to an entrepreneur economy. As a second step we will examine some specific properties of an *entrepreneur economy*; cost and profit, notions foreign to a simple market economy, will be defined. A third step will give us the opportunity of comparing our monetary analysis with a class of Post-Keynesian models (SFC models) about the determination of the level of activity.

The rationale for the differentiation of entrepreneurs and wage-earners

Exchange and wage relations: homogeneity or heterogeneity of conditions

Voluntary exchange defines market economies. Now, the question is whether or not economic relations other than voluntary exchange may take place in our societies, making them different. As most people take part in production not as independent producers but as wage-earners, what is crucial is the way relations between wages-earners and entrepreneurs are conceived of: as voluntary exchange or as something else? Not being capable of dealing with economic relations other than exchanges – even hierarchy is thought of as being the outcome of a special voluntary exchange – academic theory is deprived of any possibility to explore an alternative. Whatever may be the qualifications to the proposition that wage-earners exchange something (labour force, labour services, etc.) against real wages – information asymmetry, differences of initial endowments, etc. – they do not allow academic theoreticians to grasp what makes a wage relationship radically distinct from a voluntary exchange. They may console themselves by believing that a wage relationship is *effectively* a voluntary exchange ruled by equivalence but, in any case, even if they have philosophical or political doubts about it, they are intellectually constrained, *as economic theoreticians*, to adopt that position.

Classical economists, Marx and some others have developed a different view, grounding the division between wage-earners and entrepreneurs on the ownership of the means of production. However, this view is not very convincing either. It is putting the cart before the horse: the concentration of the ownership of the means of production in the hands of a fraction of people has to be explained and should not be taken as a given.

Our claim is that, *being open to a variety of economic relations, a monetary analysis has a decisive advantage over value theories*. It rationally accounts for the division between entrepreneurs and wage-earners, by using only the specific concepts and notions associated with money and already presented above. These notions are valid and useful far beyond the sole exchange relations and the sole pure market economy. Different versions of the minting process can be imagined, and various forms of circulation may be associated to these versions. As a result, an alternative view about our economies and societies is possible, in which exchange relations co-exist with other ones, namely the wage relationship which will appear a *sui generis* one. Even if intrinsically identical individuals (in mainstream terms: having the same preferences) are assumed, a sharp differentiation between entrepreneurs and wage-earners may be the consequence of the monetary organization of the economy. *At the root of the division between classes is the minting process.*

This view is not radically new but, instead of being founded on non-economic arguments, it will be entirely developed inside economic theory, a way of attacking the "citadel", as Keynes called the academic theory of his time, from inside.

After a brief reminder of the two basic stories told by economic theoreticians on that point, we will proceed in successive steps, the first one being to introduce hierarchy in such a way that it co-exists with exchange in an integrated economy more complex and more relevant for our societies than a pure market economy. It will then be possible to define some basic notions as cost, surplus and profit which are irrelevant in a pure exchange economy as we have seen above. Finally we will show some important properties of an *entrepreneur economy*, a short appellation for an exchange economy embedded into a wage relationship. These properties cannot show up in a pure market economy. Keynes's conjecture about involuntary equilibrium unemployment is one of them.

The two basic stories

A major "stylized fact" about entrepreneurs and wage-earners in our economies is that both categories of people *are in the same qualitative position in the markets for commodities* (academic theoreticians would say that both maximize utility under a budgetary constraint) but *they are in a qualitative opposed position in the "market for labour" and in production* (wage-earners do not decide what, how much, how and when to produce). The co-existence of these two aspects of the wage relationship, one being interpreted in terms of equivalence (in the market for commodities), the other of subordination (in production), correlates with the failure of Marxian (or Sraffian) and mainstream theories to give an appropriate synthetic view of it. In Ricardian (Sraffian) theory a wage-earner, a slave, an engine or a horse are treated on the same footing and are hardly distinguished, which is not compatible with the "stylized fact" above. In academic theory, wage-earners and entrepreneurs are supposed to share the same status in spite of the capacity to decide about production being exclusively on the side of entrepreneurs. Should wage-earners and entrepreneurs be treated as homogeneous agents (differing only *quantitatively* in their market allocations) or as heterogeneous agents (differing *qualitatively* in their capacity to intervene in the market)? The answer to these questions has to do with the story told of the way that differentiation occurs.

Two global views may be contrasted. Smith is typical of the one which links the differentiation of individuals into two classes with a difference in saving and capital accumulation; Schumpeter is representative of the other which links the differentiation into classes with their relation to the minting process. Making explicit the process through which an *a priori* homogeneous population became split into two groups or classes: entrepreneurs and wage-earners generate two different stories. These stories are complementary in the sense that each one explains part of what is observed. They are, however, difficult to reconcile since they rely on radically different approaches.

THE TRADITIONAL STORY

According to Classical and Marxian traditions, what makes entrepreneurs (capitalists) and wage-earners different is the ownership of the means of production.[1] The former are responsible for all economic decisions whereas the latter are almost passive. Even if Ricardo-Sraffa and Marx do not present exactly the same version of the story, it remains that in both versions only entrepreneurs decide what, how and how much to produce, and wage-earners most often comply with a biologically (and historically) determined consumption.

Ownership of means of production may be accepted as a *definition* of entrepreneurs (at large) but not as an *explanation* of the co-existence of the two classes. Ownership of commodities in general and of means of production in particular is an *outcome* of the market, not a presupposition. What is at stake with the market and the circulation of commodities (and possibly money) is the social justification of property rights over commodities (see Proposition 3 above). This is true for Ricardo, Marx and Walras as well. Rather than postulating the existence of entrepreneurs-owners of means of production, it is better to show how some people become these happy owners while others do not. Smith – his great merit amongst others – gives the first consistent theory of such a process of differentiation of agents according to their preferences. Later, Matsuyama has given a rigorous version of Smith's theory.

Two basic oppositions allow Smith to elaborate his version: one is between productive and non-productive labour, and the other is between saving and prodigality. The former is independent of the intrinsic qualities of individuals, while the latter is not.

The first one has been the subject of many discussions and debates. At first glance, the durability of the product of the labour is the right criterion: productive labour

> fixes and realizes itself in some particular subject or vendible commodity, which lasts for some time at least after that the labour is past. It is, as it were, a certain quantity of labour stocked and stored up to be employed, if necessary, upon some other occasion. (. . .) The labour of the menial servant, on the contrary, does not fix or realize itself in any particular subject or vendible commodity.
>
> (Smith, I, p. 330)

Durability is in any case a condition for accumulation. In this sense, productive labour is a necessary component of Smith's scenario. But durability is not the most interesting criterion, according to Smith himself. This appears clearly when Smith's text is more carefully read. Productive labour is also, and over all, exchanged against capital while non-productive labour is exchanged against income.

> Whatever part of his stock a man employs as a capital, he always expects is to be replaced to him with a profit. He employs it, therefore, in maintaining productive hands only; and after having served in the function of a capital to him, it constitutes a revenue to them. Whenever he employs any part of it in maintaining unproductive hands of any kind, that part is, from that moment, withdrawn from his capital, and placed in his stock reserved for his immediate consumption.
>
> (Smith, I, p. 332)

For Smith, "capital" is the name of the means of production when they yield an income proportional to their value. Capital and uniformity of the rate of profit is one and the same thing.[2] Maintaining that productive labour is exchanged against capital amounts to saying not only that some accumulation of capital will take place (durability) but also that this accumulation will generate a proportional profit. In Smith's terms, a given capital, spent as an amount of productive (commanded) labour, reproduces itself and generates an additional profit which opens the possibility to employ later a greater quantity of commanded labour. The rate of profit measures that increase. Neglecting rent, one may say that the maximum rate of growth is given by the rate of profit.

But, whether the rate of growth is low or high, for a given rate of profit, depends on the thrift of those who receive profits (entrepreneurs). Here enters the second opposition stressed by Smith.

> Parsimony, and not industry, is the immediate cause of the increase of capital.
>
> (p. 337)

Fortunately, adds Smith, frugality dominates over prodigality since most people's aim is to make their condition better off.

Mixing the two criteria suggested by Smith allows for giving an account of how parsimony and industry may turn some into rich people becoming entrepreneurs and others into poor people becoming wage-earners.

As it often appears in such type of storytelling, what has really happened in history does not matter. What counts is the meaning of the parable. This explains why Smith's story may be rationalized with ahistorical models where equilibrium or steady-states characteristics are important and where there is no effective evolution over time.

This is the case with Matsuyama (2006), who proposed a dynamic model of Smith's version. His paper is an outstanding one. At the heart of it is the evolution of the distribution of wealth. Two conditions must be fulfilled in order to become an entrepreneur: (a) the entrepreneurial position must yield an *income* greater than that of wage-earner (profitability condition) and (b) *wealth* must reach a certain investment threshold thanks to some borrowing (indebtedness constraint). At a given moment, an agent's wealth depends on his/her wealth at the preceding moment (inter-periodic transfer of wealth). The wage level is determined by the labour market equilibrium and depends on the proportion of entrepreneurs (demand) and wage-earners (supply).

> It depends on their relative positions in the distribution of wealth within this society. That is, the agents who inherited relatively large wealth become employers, while those who inherited relatively little become workers. The threshold level of inherited wealth, which divides the agents between the workers and the employers, is determined endogenously to keep the balance between the labour supply and labour demand. Thus, the vertical division of labour, or the employer-worker relation, always emerges endogenously in this model, for any distribution of wealth. The question is then whether this vertical division of labour evolves into the class structure in steady state.
>
> (Matsuyama, p. 2)

The answer to that question – the main result of the model – is that two steady-states exist depending on the level of the wage. For values lower than a critical threshold, two classes exist, entrepreneurs being the richer of the two. For the critical value, all agents could be entrepreneurs since they fulfil the profitability condition and the indebtedness constraint. Not all will actually be entrepreneurs but it does not matter for Matsuyama since all have the same wealth whatever position they may have.[3]

Matsuyama's model fits with the story told by Adam Smith. It is the difference amongst individuals in the progressive accumulation of wealth (saving being a virtue) which generates the division between entrepreneurs and wage-earners.

THE MONETARY STORY

Another story may be told. The name of Schumpeter is representative of it. That the richer become entrepreneurs, and the poorer become wage-earners, is not the intuition at the root of that story. Even if such an intuition seems to make good sense, it does not help much in understanding the logic of an economy where production is due to wage-earners working for entrepreneurs. Our intuition would be the reverse of Matsuyama's: *it is precisely because some individuals become entrepreneurs that they become richer and, concurrently, because others become wage-earners that they are poorer.* From a logical point of view (rather than an historical one), wealth inequality is a *consequence* of the differentiation into classes rather than its cause. We need to explain how some people become entrepreneurs (and others do not) *independently of their current wealth (and even of their utility functions)*.

According to Schumpeter it is the ability to benefit from money creation through bank credit which is the distinctive feature of entrepreneurs (who can finance innovations thanks to credit). In *The Theory of Economic Development*, Schumpeter maintains that entrepreneurs are the only ones being specifically debtors. As Morishima rightly remarks:

> Since the beginning of his academic career, he [Schumpeter] was a mon-etarist economist rather than a specialist of industrial economics. He saw that the entrepreneur needs to get purchasing power "in order to pro-duce at all, to be able to carry out his new combinations, to become an entrepreneur. He can only become an entrepreneur by previously being a debtor".
>
> (Morishima, p. 41)

An exclusive access to new means of payment allows a would-be entrepreneur to modify the equilibrium allocation of the means of production (and the prop-erty rights) to achieve innovation, and ultimately, profits. The entrepreneur's position is provisional and is not guaranteed by any level of wealth.

A modern version of that scenario is available (Cartelier, 2016). In an econ-omy where different modes of production of commodities are open to identi-cal individuals (autarky, specialization and association under the control of an entrepreneur), different types of equilibrium may exist under diverse condi-tions. The condition for the existence of an equilibrium where two classes (entrepreneurs and wage-earners) co-participate in production inside firms are reasonable: an efficient monetary system, a sufficient gap between the produc-tivity of mass production compared to other types, and a possibility to induce wage-earners to work significantly more than they would as free producers. For a large range of value of these parameters, *a selective access to the minting process is a necessary and sufficient condition for the co-existence of entrepreneurs and wage-earners*. Individuals not eligible for the minting process prefer to be wage-earners rather than autarky producers (as a consequence of a high productivity which may compensate for low relative wages) while the others prefer to be entrepreneurs rather than independent producers (thanks to the availability of people not allowed to initiate their own productions).

Even if Smith and Schumpeter scenarios may be taken as complementary for understanding what has really taken place in *history*, they are opposed and substitutable from a *logical* point of view. Given the general spirit of this book we will adopt a Schumpeterian attitude. The access to new means of payment will be considered as more important than the level of wealth. *It is more the het-erogeneity of conditions than the difference in wealth which matters.*

At this point of our presentation it may be useful to briefly make clear why a logical genesis of economic classes is relevant while a logical genesis of money is not. We have seen in the first part of this book and in the preceding chapters of Part II that the question of money cannot be elucidated in a real analysis. Even when the existence of monetary equilibria is demonstrated, what these models show is not the existence of money (which is presupposed as fiat money) but the conditions of its effective utilization for exchange. Money existence in real analysis is never a demonstrated proposition but an interrogation on the composition of the commodity-space. Real analysis fails not because theoreticians postulate fiat money (instead of making it emerge from nowhere) but because fiat money does not fit the commodity space, which is the fundamental postulate of mainstream economics. It is why postulating a nominal unit of account, tantamount to accepting the impossibility of a logical genesis of money, is the foundation of a monetary analysis.

Once this first step is over, it is quite possible to derive from that postulate many propositions. Amongst these propositions, the conditions for the co-existence of two groups of individuals, entrepreneurs and wage-earners, perfectly make sense. They are not postulated but logically derived as we shall see below.

We have now to check how that Schumpeterian story fits into the general framework presented in the Chapter 5.

Two forms of money circulation

In Chapter 5, devoted to pure market relations, all individuals have been supposed to have an equal access to the minting process. An unequal access would not have *qualitatively* changed the picture. Different initial endowments would not alter the basic properties of general competitive equilibria either. What matters is that, in both cases, nobody is excluded from that process and that everybody has a positive capacity to act in the market. All individuals in a pure market economy are active. Things dramatically change when an access to the minting process is denied to a fraction of individuals, whatever the reasons may be.

Hypothesis 4: (alternative to Hypothesis 2 supra)

Some individuals have access to the minting process (they are active); some do not (they are non-active)

Non-orthodox economists often criticize mainstream economists for not leaving a role for power and violence besides reciprocity. In short, exchange and predation should be simultaneously considered to give a realistic account of what happens in our societies. Following that line of reasoning is probably not the most convenient approach, contrary to what may appear at first sight. Piccione & Rubinstein's paper (2007) is convincing on that point. We will put aside this opposition and tackle the problem of multiplicity of economic relations, keeping our framework based on money mediation.

We will stick to our basic principle: only mediations can account for inter-individual relations. In fact, individuals and mediations are so strongly linked that an individual without any mediation is no more an individual than a mediation without individuals is a mediation. Any individual in our society is a combination of simultaneous mediations: he/she is a part of a family or of a kinship relationship, a citizen, a member of some associations, an account with a bank, etc. The fact that these various mediations – familial, political, economic, etc. – happen simultaneously in the ordinary life is the main problem faced by "social sciences". Their specialization has something to do with the complexity generated by it. Individuals, as conceived by economics, are not conceptually those studied by sociology, politics or anthropology. Economics is specific amongst these disciplines: it deals with money mediation only. This restriction seems to be a handicap but it gives an advantage – the relation of economic theory to other "social sciences", although not easy to assess, is made more clear (see Conclusion below). In any case, studying society from the point of view of economics makes sense. Our three postulates (Chapter 4) provide a precise framework for that.

In a monetary economy richer individuals have an advantage over poorer ones, a very general proposition indeed! In our monetary framework, this is true only because wealth is defined as being made of minting supports. If wealth were conceived of as an accumulation of durable commodities only (precious paintings, luxuries, castles and so on) rich people would certainly enjoy life more than poor people but they would not dominate them economically speaking. What creates that domination is the advantage due to an exclusive access to the means of payment. Only wealth owners are free to take initiatives in the market. *It is only if the Mint and banks acknowledge that you hold wealth that they will issue means of payment for you.*

It is true, however, that the mere fact that the Mint or banks recognize that some individuals hold wealth does not ensure that the market will validate that expectation. It may happen that people having access to the minting process fail to sell what they propose to other people. Let us suppose for the sake of simplicity that someone does not sell anything. In that case his/her deficit is such that the totality of his/her wealth will be used to settle his/her deficit. In that simple example, market will make valid neither the bank's expectations nor the individual's action. This reminds us that wealth in not a physical data or a set of means of production but a social construction.

In what follows, for the sake of clarity, individuals are supposed to differ not by the amount of wealth they possess but by their condition, *i.e.* whether *they are or are not eligible for the minting process.* Means of payment are the way individuals make known their actions to others. To get means of payment from the minting process is the condition for being active. What would be the consequence of a difference between individuals, namely to be active or non-active?

Note that only individuals eligible for the minting process – *i.e. active* ones – may experience market relations amongst themselves. Reciprocity and equivalence hold only for them. But the fact that other individuals, although unable to entertain market relations, may be members of that society needs to be elucidated; it is desirable, in the same way, to assess whether, when market relations are no longer the exclusive economic relations, the economy is or is not still a market economy.

Proposition 10

Hierarchical relations derive from the different situations in which individuals are vis-à-vis of the minting process: to be or not to be active

Individuals, when not eligible for the minting process, cannot take any initiative in the market. Lacking the social language they cannot make known – through their payments – the activity they have chosen; they are condemned to live outside the market. They can, however, be present in the market, *i.e. as buyers but not as sellers*, if they get some means of payment from active individuals.

How and why would active people agree to transfer dollars toward non-active people? Two indirect relations to the market are conceivable giving birth to two completely different forms of circulation: active people transfer dollars to non-active people either for reasons having nothing to do with the market (which leaves open a lot of possibilities, not evoked in this essay), on the one hand, or for associating them to their own market activities, on the other. The first case corresponds to what Smith calls non-productive labour (menial servants), the second one to the productive labour – an "exchange" of labour against income and capital respectively.

The first relation may be called *domestic relationship*. It is represented by Schema 6.2 below. Payments of active individuals are directed toward non-active individuals independent of the activity the former runs in the market. The latter may be called domestic people: what they do for active individuals is not intended to be sold in the market. Active individuals do not expect any direct receipts from the activity of domestic people. Smith reminds us that the latter are paid out of income and not out of capital. Domestic activities, even if they are more important than their denomination may suggest (they encompass public administration, justice, etc.), will not be dealt with hereafter. When non-active people are involved in circulation, the relation they bear with active people cannot be assessed without studying the form of that circulation.

The form of domestic relation is shown in the schema below.

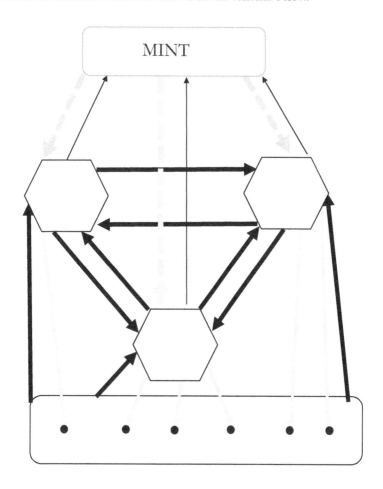

Active individual Non-active individual Market relations Minting and melting Domestic relations

Schema 6.1 "money domestic circulation"

The economy appears to be made of two subsets: a market economy (amongst active people represented as hexagons), on the one hand, and a loose group of non-active people (represented by black circles) existing only as an appendix to the market economy. They have no relation amongst them;

they exist in the market only thanks to their special relation to active people; since they receive transfers of dollars from active people, they are able to be economically present as buyers. *They do not participate, however, in any activity oriented toward the market.*

By contrast, in the second form of circulation, non-active individuals are associated with the market activity of active individuals. That second form of circulation is as follows:

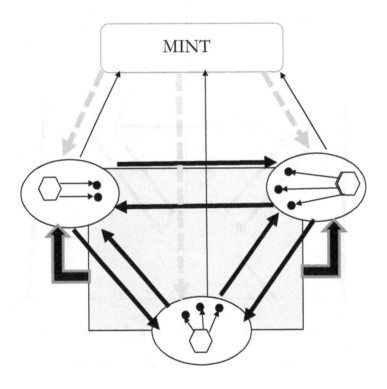

Schema 6.2 Money circulation in an entrepreneur economy

Now non-active individuals are integrated into the activity run by active people. Non-active and active individuals acting together constitute a new entity. In accordance with our second postulate (individuals or economic entities are accounts in which dollars are written down), we have now to introduce new accounts. Let us call these new entities *firms*.

Proposition 11

A *firm* is an entity composed by an active individual and non-active individuals; firms are run by the former for his or her own account; active people have accounts distinct from the accounts of the firms they run

Payments amongst firms follow the schema of exchange relations ruled by equivalence. Firms (run by an entrepreneur) are economically responsible in that they decide privately their activities (their payments) and they accept to be evaluated by the expenses other people address to them. But payments inside firms (from entrepreneurs to wage-earners) follow a totally different schema. They are totally asymmetric: non-active people are integrated into firms but bear no economic responsibility. Non-active people do not decide the payments they get from the entrepreneur; they do not decide the payments firms perform amongst them; what they do inside firms depends on the active people who run them. They are subject to two dominations, not only one. The first one is direct; it comes from the one who transfers dollars to them – it is also the case in a domestic relationship – the second is indirect; it comes through the economic responsibility of the firm vis-à-vis the market. Non-active people have no active relation with the market – they spend but do not decide what they earn. If firms do not succeed – if their deficit is too high – they would go bankrupt but non-active people do not. They simply leave the market. They do not exist any longer from the point of view of economics.

Such a schema of circulation reproduces the major "stylized fact" mentioned above about the wage relationship. Consequently, let us call *wage-earners* these non-active people while active people who run the firms are called *entrepreneurs*.

Proposition 12

Wage-earners and entrepreneurs are such only in that specific form of circulation involving firms; wage-earners are economically submitted to entrepreneurs

Heterogeneity between active and non-active people is too radical for equivalence between them to make sense: *entrepreneurs are economically responsible, wage-earners are not*. Here is the basis for the hierarchical character of the wage relationship which takes place inside firms only but not outside, *i.e.* in the market for commodities.

The two *schemas of circulation differ independently of any concrete content of the activity*. A music lesson may take place as a market relation (between independent professional musicians), a wage relation (the teacher gets a wage from the entrepreneur who runs a private music school) or a domestic one (Haydn and Esterhazy). What matters is *the logic of social relations which depends on the form of money mediation and not the material aspect of it.* The fact that immaterial services tend to dominate material production in our modern economies does not affect *per se* the social way economic activity is run.

A firm is distinct from its wage-earners and from the entrepreneur who runs it; a firm encompasses both of them. Note that firms are not institutions. Institutions are defined as pre-determined sets of rules, which means that there is no sense in trying to micro-found them. Here, a firm is a set of relations between individuals (active and non-active) but firms are not pre-supposed: they are the consequence of a difference of position of individuals vis-à-vis of the minting process and of other considerations. *Firms are a result of the analysis, not a logically prior assumption.*

In order to account for the different roles played by wage-earners and entrepreneurs inside firms, we will consider separately what firms spend (in order to run their activities) and get on the one hand, and what entrepreneurs spend (out of their income), which is what they get from firms, on the other hand. Both are consequences of their access to the minting process. Wage-earners spend what they get from firms.

While firms' mutual relations are formally pure market relations (similar to those presented in Chapter 5), firms' existence implies a generalized wage relationship. Such an economy, taken *as a whole*, is no longer a market economy. Against the many prejudices academic theory strongly reinforces, we assert that we do not live in a market economy but in an economy where exchange relations are embedded in a generalized wage relationship, in short an entrepreneur economy.

When economic activity is mainly run by firms and not by individual producers, it makes sense to consider that exchanges amongst firms are embedded in a wage relationship and not the other way round. It is not easy to historically fix the period at which the transition occurs, but the distinction between a market economy and an entrepreneur economy is theoretically clear. That embeddedness of exchange in a generalized wage relationship radically changes the properties attributed to exchange economies.

Specific properties of an entrepreneur economy

Surplus, cost and profit

We have shown so far that a differentiation between entrepreneurs and wage-earners may be conceived of as an effect of a different position *vis-à-vis* of the minting process, a concentration of property of means of production being a consequence and not the origin of the existence of two classes of individuals. As the schema of circulation makes it clear, relations amongst entrepreneurs are exchange ones – ruled by equivalence – whereas those between wage-earners and entrepreneurs are hierarchical in a specific way and are not ruled by equivalence. The combination of both types of relations is responsible for the specific *qualitative* properties evoked hereafter.

Having introduced a differentiation between wage-earners and entrepreneurs, we have now a first complete although very simple description of the type of economy we are living in. It will provide a convenient framework for introducing the basic notions of *cost*, *surplus*, and *profit* which do not make sense in a pure market economy.

For the sake of simplicity we assume:

Hypothesis 5

Entrepreneurs own the firms they run

Hypothesis 5 allows for clarifying the presentation. It will be relaxed in the next chapter.

The outstanding characteristic of the circulation when entrepreneurs and wage-earners are differentiated is that both are components of the specific entity called firm. This creates the possibility of observing the *cost* of economic activities.

Defining costs implies distinguishing between payments which are necessary to the activity of the firms and those which are not. In a pure market economy, the cost undergone by individual h cannot be distinguished from the evaluation of his/her activity: both are defined by $\Sigma_k m_{hk}$ and socially validated (see Chapter 5, Proposition 7). When a wage relationship is added to a pure market economy, a qualitative mutation occurs. Activities are run by firms under the responsibility of entrepreneurs. The differentiation between entrepreneurs and wage-earners introduces a wedge between the necessary payments (wages m_{hW}) and the amount produced ($\Sigma_k m_{hk}$). For the latter it is beyond any doubt that the payments to wage-earners are a cost, the only expenditure which can be said necessary to their activity. The notion of cost emerges, not as an empirical phenomenon but as a theoretical concept, once the duality of firms' components shows up. Entrepreneurs, as active individuals, run activities in view of the market ($\Sigma_k m_{hk}$); they do that with the help of non-active individuals, the wage-earners, to whom they have to transfer dollars (m_{hW}). Wages are the unique cost. For the other expenditures, as we have seen above, it is not possible so far to state whether they are necessary or not, whether they are a cost or not.

As a consequence, the difference $\Sigma_k m_{hk} - m_{hW}$ may be called *gross profits* (more precisely, *expected* gross profits since $\Sigma_k m_{hk}$ and m_{hW} result from voluntary decisions not yet validated by the market). Gross profits – the outcome – are compared to wages – the cost undergone for that outcome. Consequently come all the various and complex variations about "how to get the best from a resource".

Wage-earners have not sold anything because they cannot produce anything by themselves (they are wage-earners precisely because they cannot sell anything), and they are subordinate to entrepreneurs, who manage the activities for themselves. Entrepreneurs have to make wage-earners participate efficiently in activities they have not chosen and they are not responsible for. History teaches that the ways to obtain good results are diverse and do not depend only on economic factors as the history of industrial relations testifies. We do not comment on that well-documented story and content ourselves with disqualifying the story told by the mainstream invariably based on an assumed equality of condition between wage-earners and entrepreneurs.

The wedge between expected receipts and wages potentially generates gross profits. Here is the main theoretical point. It is well-known that distinguishing between gross and net profits – which requires a distinction between gross and net investment – is difficult as Keynes reminds us in *General Theory* Chapter 6. Here, we assume that payments amongst firms represent amortization of the whole engaged capital (circulating capital *plus* amortization of fixed capital) so that gross profit boils down to the difference between sales and wages; net profits are equal to gross profits minus expenditures addressed to other firms. Consequently, firms' net profits of firm (entrepreneur) h are:

$$\pi_h = \sum_k m_{kh} - \sum_k m_{hk} - m_{hW} = \sum_k \check{m}_{hk} \tag{6–1}$$

Proposition 13

Wage relationship makes it possible to objectively distinguish *necessary and non-necessary inputs*; consequently *a surplus may be observed in an entrepreneur economy*; gross profits are equal to entrepreneurs' total receipts *minus* total wages; net profits are equal to gross profits *minus* firms' payments (including amortization when durability of commodities is greater than one)

A preliminary table of payments may be arrayed. Payments amongst enterprises and entrepreneurs are of the same type as viewed above: they express market relations subject to equivalence and voluntary exchange. Thanks to the separation between entrepreneurs' and firms' accounts, it is possible to distinguish m_{hk} (amortization of circulating and fixed capital) and $\check{m}_{hk}$ (expenses of net profits).

They are written down into the grey area. Payments between entrepreneurs and wage-earners show the *monetary subordination* of the latter to the former since wage-earners work not for their own account but for that of firms. They are written in the dark area; nothing is implied here except that *for wage-earners, payments are constrained by wages*. The area left uncoloured shows wage-earners' payments to firms. They are ordinary purchases. They may be as complex as the other ones (consumption commodities, financial assets, etc.).

Table 6.1 Payment matrix 1

	1	2	⋯	H	Total firms	Wage-earners	Total
1	0	m_{12} $\check{m}_{12}$	⋯	m_{1H} $\check{m}_{1H}$	m_{1F} $\check{m}_{1F}$	m_{1W}	m_1 $\check{m}_1$
2	m_{21} $\check{m}_{21}$	0	⋯	m_{2H} $\check{m}_{2H}$	m_{2F} $\check{m}_{2F}$	m_{2W}	m_2 $\check{m}_2$
⋯	⋯	⋯	⋯	⋯	⋯	⋯	⋯
H	m_{H1} $\check{m}_{H1}$	m_{H2} $\check{m}_{H2}$	⋯	0	m_{HF} $\check{m}_{HF}$	m_{HW}	m_H $\check{m}_H$
Total firms	m_{F1} $\check{m}_{F1}$	m_{F2} $\check{m}_{F2}$	⋯	m_{FH} $\check{m}_{FH}$	m_{FF} $\check{m}_{FF}$	m_{FW}	m_F
Wage-earners	m_{W1}	m_{W2}	⋯	m_{WH}	m_{WF}	0	m_{WF}
Total	m^1	m^2	⋯	m^H	m^F	m_{FW}	μ

Note that payments m_{hk} and $\check{m}_{hk}$ are distinguished but they merge into receipts m^H without being separated.

The (simplified) payment matrix is now:

$$M_w = \begin{pmatrix} 0 & m_{12}+\check{m}_{12} & \cdots & m_{1H}+\check{m}_{1H} & m_{1W} \\ m_{21}+\check{m}_{21} & 0 & \cdots & m_{2H}+\check{m}_{2H} & m_{2W} \\ \cdots & \cdots & \cdots & \cdots \cdots \\ m_{H1}+\check{m}_{H1} & m_{H2}+\check{m}_{H2} & \cdots & 0 & m_{HW} \\ m_{W1} & m_{W2} & \cdots & m_{WH} & \mu \end{pmatrix} \qquad (6\text{--}2)$$

Production technique, consumption and investment

Payments amongst enterprises are relative to *circulating capital* and to the amortization of fixed capital reflecting *purchases/sales of inputs*. Commodities being defined by the producer who spends money to bring it in the market in order to get payments from others, it makes sense to use inter-enterprises payments (m_{hk}) for calculating input-output coefficients. The absence of any commodity space postulate is not an obstacle to deal with what economists call a production technique.[4]

Let's consider the payment matrix and select the submatrix of the m_{hk} after imbalances have been settled, *i.e.* when the sum of each column is equal to that of each corresponding row, which means that the quantity of all commodities is uniquely determined by this common amount. We may then proceed as if a commodity space were postulated, which is not the case, and derive a "production technique" from the payment matrix. It is even possible to develop a theory along a Neoricardian view, where commodities, production technique, natural prices and rate of profit appear. Such a metaphor may make a Sraffian economist feel comfortable but does not allow us to get any information or result in addition to what is already known from a monetary analysis. The Sraffian model of simple production appears to be just an illusory and truncated representation of a money economy (see Appendix).

The flow of payment m_{hk} means that the producer of commodity h has bought a quantity $\dfrac{m_{hk}}{m_k}$ of commodity k in order to bring in the market a unit of commodity h. Coefficients $a_{hk} = \dfrac{m_{hk}}{m_k}$ show the quantity of commodity k used to produce one unit of commodity h. To get the quantities of "labour" (in fact *units of employment* in the sense of Keynes) we have just to divide each amount of wages of the branch by the total amount of wages: $l_h = \dfrac{m_{hW}}{\Sigma_h m_{hW}} = \dfrac{m_{hW}}{m_{FW}}$.

Table 6.2 Production technique, consumption and investment

	1	2	H	"Labour"	Total
1	0	$a_{12} = \dfrac{m_{12}}{m_2}$	$a_{1H} = \dfrac{m_{1H}}{m_H}$	$l_1 = \dfrac{m_{1W}}{m_{FW}}$	1 unit of 1
2	$a_{21} = \dfrac{m_{21}}{m_1}$	0	$a_{2H} = \dfrac{m_{2H}}{m_H}$	$l_2 = \dfrac{m_{2W}}{m_{FW}}$	1 unit of 2
...	...	...	...	...	...	...
H	$a_{H1} = \dfrac{m_{H1}}{m_1}$	$a_{H2} = \dfrac{m_{H2}}{m_2}$	0	$l_H = \dfrac{m_{HW}}{m_{FW}}$	1 unit of H

Flows of payment from firms to wage-earners are *wages* while those from wage-earners to firms are *consumption* payments. Even if entrepreneurs are supposed to own entirely the firm they run, entrepreneurs and firms have distinct accounts. What a firm pays to its owner (entrepreneur) is *profits* while what entrepreneurs spend toward firms is real assets or *investment*. The sum of circulating capital payments *plus* wages payments is the *cost* (Keynes dubbed it *factor cost*).

It is therefore possible to express the "technique of production" of our economy in the usual terms of input–output analysis (adding a constant return assumption) or according to the Ricardo-Sraffa tradition:

$$A = \begin{pmatrix} 0 & a_{12} & \cdots & a_{1H} \\ a_{21} & 0 & \cdots & a_{2H} \\ \cdots & \cdots & \cdots & \cdots \\ a_{H1} & a_{H2} & \cdots & 0 \end{pmatrix} \blacksquare \begin{pmatrix} l_1 \\ l_2 \\ \cdots \\ l_H \end{pmatrix} \rightarrow \begin{pmatrix} 1 & 0 & \cdots & 0 \\ 0 & 1 & \cdots & 0 \\ \cdots & \cdots & \cdots & \cdots \\ 0 & 0 & \cdots & 1 \end{pmatrix} = I \qquad (6\text{--}3)$$

From the matrix of payments it is also possible to distinguish between investment and consumption payments. This is due to the exclusion of a fraction of people from the minting process which generates a division between entrepreneurs on the one hand, and wage-earners, on the other. That special configuration of circulation did allow Keynes to distinguish between *investment goods* and *consumption goods* independently of any physical characteristic: consumption goods are those which are counterpart of flows of dollars spent by wage-earners toward entrepreneurs while investment goods are the counterpart of entrepreneurs' expenditures amongst themselves (see Chapter 6 of *General Theory*). In the payment matrix above, consumption payments are made out of the m_{hW}'s (the other part being *saving*, if financial assets are concerned).

Let's consider firms as a whole. The economy is now described by Schema 6.3.

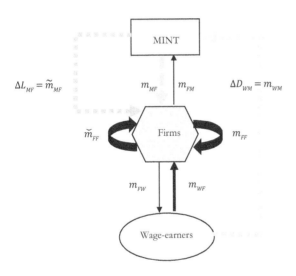

Schema 6.3 Global money circulation in an entrepreneur economy

The level of activity: a crucial point

In a pure market economy the level of activity is the outcome of decentralized decisions taken by all individuals subject only to their expected budgetary constraints and to the additional minting constraint (Proposition 6). In that context, the basic problem is the capacity of monetary organization to make individuals responsible for the level of activity they desire. The shortage of means of payment is a traditional topic in money theory (limited quantity of precious metals, credit crunch, lack of confidence in the credit mediations, etc.). When receipts are equal to payments (*i.e.* expected receipts) for each individual, the equilibrium level of activity is voluntary. There would be no point speaking of any kind of "involuntary under-activity". The differentiation of individuals in entrepreneurs and wage-earners changes the deal.

Keynes's conjecture and its vicissitudes

In an entrepreneur economy, the question of the level of activity is qualitatively different. The level of activity is determined by the decentralized decisions of a *fraction* of individuals only – those who are eligible for the minting process – the others being subordinate to the decisions of the former. Only entrepreneurs are endowed with that prerogative which make them economically responsible for what they do. As a consequence they are subject to constrained operations which is the mere manifestation of their (economic) freedom and responsibility. Wage-earners do not share that condition. From that basic characteristic of an entrepreneur economy stems the possibility that, even if all entrepreneurs would experience equilibrium, some individuals – the wage-earners – may be obliged to content themselves with a level of receipts different from what they desire. They do not decide the level of their activity as they do not decide the amount of their wages. *Equilibrium makes sense for entrepreneurs only, not for wage-earners.* This is the straight consequence of their non-eligibility for the minting process. Wage-earners cannot make known their situation since they cannot initiate payments. In other words, when entrepreneurs are all at equilibrium nothing can be said about wage-earners. Wage-earners' involuntary unemployment is not observable unless some payments (unemployment benefits, for instance) make it appear. But there are no economic reasons for that involuntary unemployment to be zero. It could happen only by fluke. In the terms of academic economic theory, involuntary unemployment equilibria are the rule.

Proposition 14

The level of activity of entrepreneurs is constrained by their expected budgetary constraints and the minting process; the level of activity of wage-earners is constrained by the level of activity of the entrepreneurs; even when there are no constrained payments (*i.e.* at

equilibrium) wage-earners may wish to have a higher level of employ-ment (involuntary unemployment equilibrium à la Keynes)

The tenets of academic theory deny the possibility of such involuntary unem-ployment equilibria. A "market for labour" is supposed to take place which ensures a co-ordination between entrepreneurs' and wage-earners' decisions such that full-employment equilibria are the rule. Academic theory deals with labour (or "labour services") as if labour were a commodity and as if wage-earners would exchange their services against a real wage in the same way as a corn producer exchanges his/her product against iron. We have seen above that wage-earners and entrepreneurs do not share the same prerogatives. Wage-earners are not subject to the same constraints as entrepreneurs since they do not have a direct access to the minting process. Even if it is true that the level of wages is the outcome of a negotiation between entrepreneurs and wage-earners, the amount of total wages (*i.e.* the number of employed wage-earners) is decided by entrepreneurs only. Wage-earners' monetary subordination, responsible for the hierarchy inside firms, makes totally irrelevant a representation of a "market for labour" with supply and demand curves.

In other words, the question *whether involuntary unemployment equilibria are or are not conceivable entirely depends on the way economic theory deals with labour and wage-earners.* That fundamental point has been forgotten in the literature, even by most of those economists claiming they are Keynesian.

It is a pity since Keynes may be credited for having introduced the possibility of involuntary unemployment equilibria. Understanding how Keynes did it is therefore important. Let's remind the reader with the argumentation of *General Theory.*

Expressed in terms of the "citadel", Keynes's conjecture is that *general competi-tive equilibria with flexible prices and wage and involuntary unemployment are the rule, zero involuntary unemployment a special case.* Keynes's basic idea is both simple and deep. The argumentation destined to his colleagues runs as follows.

Let's accept the "first Classical postulate" which is nothing but the stan-dard condition of profit maximization by entrepreneurs. The consequence is a (Neo)classical curve of demand for labour and the decreasing function of marginal productivity of labour (and real wage) in relation with the amount of production. But let's refuse the "second Classical postulate" which is the stan-dard maximization of utility of households. Why? For two reasons: one of less importance (it is the nominal and not the real wage which matters), the other more important:

> For there may be no method available to labour as a whole whereby it can bring the wage-goods equivalent of the general level of money-wages into conformity with the marginal disutility of the current volume of employment.

> (*General Theory*, p. 13)

Wage-earners have not the possibility to adapt their efforts or the supply of labour to the level of the real wage. In usual words, the demand for commodities is disconnected from the labour supply. One can show that this happens for all wage rates above the equilibrium rate. For that range of wage rates the denial of the "second Classical postulate" is tantamount to assuming that wage-earners are subject to a budgetary constraint different from the usual one (Walrasian): their demand for commodity is constrained by the value of the *demand* for labour instead of by the value of the labour supply. The consequence is that Walras's law – which is the sum of all (Walrasian) budgetary constraints – ceases to hold. The supply of labour no longer enters that constraint (for all wage rates above equilibrium) so that the sum of all budgetary constraints (Walrasian and non-Walrasian) leaves the market for labour outside its domain.

This is the key point since Walras's law excludes involuntary unemployment at equilibrium. It cannot happen that only one market ("market for labour") be in excess supply while all others clear. But if the so-called "market for labour" does not enter Walras's law, it could well happen that it be in excess supply while all others are in equilibrium.[5] The refusal of the "second Classical postulate" is a necessary (but not sufficient) condition for the existence of Keynes's equilibria. It has to be completed by effective demand theory (the entrepreneurs' expectations about their receipts). But effective demand theory without a specific budgetary constraint for wage-earners does not generate involuntary unemployment equilibria: either we get full-employment or disequilibria.

Keynes's conjecture has been demonstrated later as a theorem in an Arrow-Debreu setting where wage-earners do not master a part of their budgetary constraint.[6] A more simple expression for Keynes's argument is given by the idea of a Restricted Walras's law (Cartelier, 1996) opposed to Full Walras's law, the difference being due to the respective positions of entrepreneurs and wage-earners (more details are given below when SFC models are discussed).

Walras's law is the core of mainstream theory when general equilibria are about. In spite of the obvious fact that Walras's law is incompatible with Keynes's conjecture, the reader may be bewildered by our affirmation that involuntary unemployment equilibria have no room in mainstream economic theory. The reason is that two well-known models belonging to a real analysis seem to invalidate it since they exhibit such equilibria. The first one, due to Hicks (1937), is ISLM (investment-savings, liquidity-money) which can be found in any macroeconomic textbook, the second is due to Clower in his 1965 model. This last example is even more striking since Clower explicitly denies that Walras's law applies to his model and that this denial is the condition for his result:

> Walras' law is not, after all, an independent postulate of orthodox analysis; it is a theorem which is susceptible to direct proof on the premises which are typically taken as given in contemporary as well as classical price theory. The conclusion which I draw from all this may be put in one phrase:

> either Walras' law is incompatible with Keynesian economics, or Keynes had nothing fundamentally new to add to orthodox economic theory.
>
> (Clower, 1965, p. 41)

The reader should not be surprised, however, by our claim that only a monetary theory may host involuntary unemployment equilibria. Commentators of ISLM and of Clower's (1965) article, have failed, to my knowledge, to identify what explains the possibility of involuntary unemployment equilibria in these models. We maintain that the necessary condition is neither an insufficient demand for commodities (as it seems to be in ISLM) nor the monetary character of transaction (as assumed by Clower) but the *special treatment of wage-earners* (as it is the case for Keynes). More precisely, that special treatment of wage-earners is hidden in ISLM and misinterpreted in Clower (1965).

Let's prove that claim by considering these two models successively.

The most meaningful difference between ISLM and a standard general equilibrium model with three markets (unique commodity, labour and money) is neither sticky prices and/or wages nor a special treatment of money (liquidity preference and all that); it is rather the assumption that the demand for commodity has for argument the effective income and not the value of labour supply. This seemingly innocuous assumption is in fact responsible for the generality of involuntary unemployment equilibria exhibited by ISLM. Most commentators, when they did not take rigidities as the unique source of that, have emphasized the exogenous character of investment (animal spirits). They have not realized that the consumption function had the property of breaking from Walras's law since it introduces a wedge between the supply for labour and the demand for commodity. In others terms, ISLM was true to Keynes's argumentation although the users of ISLM were not conscious of it.[7] This has probably something to do with the fact that Hicks's original version of ISLM did not address the question of unemployment but that of monetary policy . . .

Whatever the reason may be, the decisive role of the consumption function was not perceived as the consequence of treating wage-earners on a different footing from other agents but as providing the multiplier mechanism associating exogenous demand for commodity (investment *plus* public expenses) to the level of total income and employment. It should have been clear, however, that if wage-earners' consumption were dependent on their labour supply, that an insufficient effective demand would lead not to an involuntary unemployment equilibrium but to a double disequilibrium, the value of the excess supply in the labour market being strictly equal to the value of the negative excess demand in the market for commodity, in conformity with Walras's law. *An insufficient effective demand leads to involuntary unemployment equilibria only if the budgetary constraint of wage-earners does not depend on the labour supply.*

That most commentators fail to discover what precise feature of ISLM was responsible for its main result partly explains why "academic Keynesianism" (an oxymoron!) has turned into "mainstream theory with rigidities and frictions".

Instead of searching to remedy unemployment through a non-market regulation, these "academic Keynesians" could not logically propose anything but fighting against rigidities and frictions, a neoliberal plea in favour of "more market"!

Clower's model is even more difficult to analyze. Walras's law is explicitly denied but not in relation with a specific condition of wage-earners but with the monetary character of transactions. Agents are not constrained by their notional resources (the value of their commodity or labour supply) but by the amount of the sales they can realize for the given level of prices (the value of the demand facing their supply). As a result, involuntary unemployment equilibrium rightly is the consequence of wage-earners not being rationed by the value of their labour supply but by the demand for labour entrepreneurs address to them. The constraint Clower assumes for the wage-earners is exactly that one Keynes assumed in *General Theory* and also that we have admitted above. Such a constraint entails a non-validity of Walras's law and is responsible for the existence of involuntary unemployment equilibria. But, instead of attributing this restriction to a characteristic of wage-earners making them different from other people in the market, Clower makes it the effect of the monetary character of transactions. In the 1965 article, it is impossible to distinguish the two because only wage-earners are considered in this very simple model. That ambiguity of Clower's model has misled commentators and followers. Things become clear, however, when that constraint is generalized. As all agents use money for their transactions (and not wage-earners only), Clower's constraint concerns all agents and not only the wage-earners. The consequence is straightforward: such a generalization rehabilitates Walras's law as Patinkin (1987) did notice:

> In brief, a sufficient condition for the validity of Walras' Law is that the individual's demand and supply functions on which it is ultimately based are *all* derived from the same budget constraint whatever quantity-constrained or not.
>
> (Patinkin, pp. 335–336)

Fixed-prices models (infelicitously and misleadingly dubbed "disequilibrium approach") consequently exhibit under-employment but no involuntary unemployment equilibria. Walras's law prevents them from illustrating Keynes's conjecture.

Keynes's conjecture and SFC models

So far nothing has been said about modern authors working along a monetary analysis. This does not mean that monetary analysis ends with Keynes. This is obviously not the case. Even if the authors working today in a monetary analysis spirit are not well-recognized in academic circles they exist and they have produced a lot of interesting works. They affirm often to build an alternative theory to mainstream economics even if it is not always clear what should be understood by that claim. They are convinced also to be true to Keynes and Kalecki. Most of them manifest, however, a moderate interest for the very foundations of Keynes's economics, no more, no less than for a careful study of mainstream theory. They content themselves with criticizing the latter for the lack of realism of its assumptions and to pay lip services to the former. Post-Keynesian economists – a global appellation which encircles most of them – seem to be more interested by adding new considerations (money, uncertainty) to macroeconomic models or by contesting some typical assumptions (rationality, perfect competition, etc.) than by elaborating an alternative analysis to value theory, starting from new foundations.

It would certainly be worth drawing a general map showing the diverse paths followed by them, with their interrelations and filiations. The story of the various attempts at developing a monetary analysis – which could not be limited to Keynes and his disciples – is still to be written. Augusto Graziani in Italy, Bernard Schmitt in France, Hyman Minsky in the USA would certainly be the heroes of that history. They have paved the way for the new generations and we all have a debt to them. But the purpose of the present book is not to provide such a general view (it may be found in Lavoie, 2014). As mentioned in the introduction, we attempt at sketching the foundations of a monetary analysis at a level of abstraction comparable to that of general competitive equilibrium theory. Too ambitious and immodest as it may be, this project seems to be the only one capable of making crystal-clear the opposition between a value approach and a monetary analysis, the main cleavage in economic theory according to Schumpeter but not exactly the one he had identified. The strategic importance of the stake may excuse the arid quasi-axiomatic presentation of Chapters 4 and 5.

Such a purpose requires a short book and, consequently, an unjust silence about many promising works. An exception has to be made, however, for a class of models whose methodology seems so closed to the one adopted in this book that it would be astonishing not to mention it: the so-called stock-flows consistent models. An excellent general survey has been recently supplied by Caverzasi & Godin (2013).

These models (SFC hereafter) rely on an accounting approach, and their authors emphasize the consistency of the framework they have adopted. Copeland (1949) is the great ancestor here. Cohen has also to be mentioned. Amongst all the models presented during the ten last years, one may be worth considering. They are in the book by Godley & Lavoie published in 2007, "the main reference work on the methodology" according to Caverzasi & Godin. Even if Godley & Lavoie's work belongs to applied economics, it contains frequent allusions at a filiation from Keynes and Kalecki. A reader familiar with Steuart's *Inquiry* may even feel to be at home when reading some pages of Godley & Lavoie's book.

The main purpose of Godley & Lavoie is not, however, to elaborate an abstract theory in the monetary analysis spirit. They try rather to exhibit how capitalist economies are working in our time. Their book is incredibly pedagogic both in presentation and in progression. At each step the reader is invited to proceed himself to numerical simulations and to analyze and comment on the results. On the whole the book is very impressive. It is surely a reference for any study in applied macroeconomics. If Godley & Lavoie do not devote themselves to present a pure theory, it is certainly because they think that this has been done somewhere, at least in the works of Keynes and Kalecki.

In what follows, we only consider the link claimed to exist between Keynes's economics and the Godley & Lavoie SFC models. Our conclusion is that link is more apparent than real. A systematically proclaimed preference for "realism" misleads the authors and prevents them from inquiring carefully and critically into the theoretical foundations of mainstream theory and of Keynes's economics as well. The "realism" invoked by the authors eventually appears neither a critique of mainstream nor a sensible way of joining Keynes's economics. Reluctant to be involved in a discussion of mainstream themes (for instance, Walras's law) Godley & Lavoie underestimate the strength of the mental habits mainstream theory has inculcated to the profession, themselves included. They share with mainstream economists the naïve conviction that they are doing science. This was not Keynes's view about economics but his scepticism did not impede him from attacking the "citadel" directly at its theoretical foundations.

The double interrogation we raise is the following: Are the theoretical foundations of the Godley & Lavoie models firm and sound? Are these models really a critique of mainstream? A double negative answer is given. This explains why we evoke these models after and not before the presentation of our basic postulates. The reader may judge now whether our quasi-axiomatic presentation does or does not make sense.

The mere fact of reasoning with the help of a consistent accounting framework – which is the less a theoretician is expected to do, be she "orthodox" or "heterodox" – is not sufficient to generate an original approach being critical of mainstream. Beyond the accounting framework what counts is the theory itself which does not boil down to behavioural assumptions.

We shall proceed taking *Keynes's conjecture* as a fundamental criterion. Keynes's conjecture is certainly the most decisive attack ever made against general competitive equilibrium, which is still the basecamp of mainstream theory even if it is no longer in favour in academic circles due to its complexity and limits. If game theory has replaced general competitive equilibrium as a current tool of analysis, the latter is still the intellectual reference since it has provided the profession with the most important theorems. Two of these theorems are well-known. The first one says that a general competitive equilibrium exists (under precise assumptions), which means that an individualist society based on voluntary exchange only is intellectually conceivable. The second theorem concerns welfare; it says that any general competitive equilibrium is Pareto-optimal, which means that an individualistic society is at its best from the point of view of its members.

We have seen in the first part of this book that the validity of welfare theorem is suspended to the existence of a decentralized process of transactions realization, which is not guaranteed unless a general means of payment is presupposed. Moreover the relevance of both theorems is doubtful due to the negative results of global stability analysis (Sonnenschein and Saari). Keynes's attack is different but no less radical; it consists in affirming the possibility of *involuntary unemployment general equilibria under perfect competition with flexible prices and wage*. This proposition has been called above *Keynes's conjecture*.

Keynes's conjecture and underemployment equilibria: a reminder

In the three first chapters of *General Theory* Keynes claims to have established the possibility of *involuntary unemployment* equilibria as the general case, the traditional *voluntary unemployment* (or full-employment) equilibrium being a special one. His basic argument is to be found in these three chapters forming the introductory first part of the book. The place and the nature of the argument (about postulates) clearly show the importance Keynes accorded to his conjecture. The title of the book, a *General Theory*, is also an indication in the same sense.

Curiously enough the point appears to have been underestimated by those theoreticians who should have emphasized it as the true departing step from the "citadel". It is strange, more than eighty years after, to feel the need to remind modern readers of the devastating power of Keynes's conjecture. But, as an examination of SFC models shows it, even "heterodox" economists seem to forget it.

To begin with, the radical difference between Keynes's conjecture and any proposition about underemployment equilibria has to be recalled. No *involuntary unemployment* characterizes the latter; underemployment equilibria exhibit equilibrium in the labour market. It is true that the level at which the labour market clears is below the level of perfect competition equilibrium (full-employment) but that unemployment is not involuntary but *voluntary*. It is due to frictions and imperfections in the working of the market (monopolistic competition, for instance). The remedy to such sub-optimality is to get rid of these frictions (anti-monopolistic laws, weakening of trade unions, restoring flexibility in the markets, etc.). The motto is: *make the market work smoothly again!* Keynes's involuntary unemployment general equilibria need another cure. No improvement of the working of the market can remedy the situation. Markets are working smoothly and the *possibility* of involuntary unemployment equilibria (what allows effective demand to play the villain) comes from something else, merely from the fact that *the wage relationship differs from an exchange relation.* What matters here is not the more or perfect working of market relations but the *extension* of their field of application. We have seen above why waged labour should not be dealt with as if it were an exchanged commodity. We pretend that Keynes's conjecture entirely relies on this proposition, as Chapter 2 of *General Theory* makes it clear.

Godley & Lavoie's models do not exhibit involuntary unemployment equilibria but voluntary unemployment only. In the two models in which labour market is explicitly described (models SIM and BMW), equilibrium condition in that market determines (with other equations) equilibrium values (level of employment included). By their very construction these models cannot exhibit anything but equilibrium in the labour market, exactly as is the case with any mainstream model. The fact that perfect competition is no longer supposed and that economic agents do not proceed to optimal calculation (for the sake of "realism") is responsible for the underemployment. Such a conclusion is perfectly sensible for a mainstream theoretician. It is a direct implication of the welfare theorem and, in a sense, an indirect confirmation of it. We are far away from an attack against the foundations of the mainstream. The attack concerns its empirical application only, *i.e.* the form of behavioural equations and the numerical value of the parameters, not the logical structure of the model.

Godley & Lavoie are certainly right when they assume imperfect competition and non-optimal behaviour of economic agents. But being empirically plausible does not guarantee to be theoretically relevant (as being theoretically coherent does not guarantee to be empirically relevant either). Fighting against mainstream models for their empirically doubtful assumptions is certainly well-founded but this should not be considered as a decisive attack against mainstream theory. By contrast, giving a precise account of Keynes's conjecture and demonstrating the existence of competitive involuntary unemployment equilibria – an expression impossible to stomach for a mainstream economist – put into danger the very foundations of mainstream theory. We will show that *a too low level of effective demand is not a sufficient condition* for Keynes's conjecture to be valid. A necessary one is required which is not to be found in Godley & Lavoie. In Godley & Lavoie's models a too low level of effective demand, consequence of imperfect competition, produces underemployment equilibria only.

Market for labour equilibrium in Godley & Lavoie's models

Let's consider the first model (SIM). The authors carefully present the transaction matrix with wages paid by firms and received by wage-earners. Coming to the formalization, the authors add suffixes to these variables to indicate whether they denote supply or demand.

In this simplified model, the wage level is taken as exogenous. The authors note that payment matrices do not describe what is *expected* by the various agents but what is *observed* at the time of transactions. These magnitudes, which are written down in the accounts, measure *effective transactions*. Here no ambiguity is possible (by contrast with balance-sheets as we will see). Godley & Lavoie rightly take their time to fully making explicit the interpretation they adopt, which applies to commodity markets and labour market as well. The question is the following: how do supply and demand, which differ ex ante, turn into an equality between sales and purchases?

They present four adjustment mechanisms and discard three of them (quantity adjustment by prices, quantity rationing and stocks variations). The one they retain is qualified Keynesian or Kaleckian:

> The equality between demand and supply, the latter being here defined as production, is achieved by an instantaneous quantity adjustment process, as is always the case in standard Kaleckian and Keynesian models.
>
> (Godley and Lavoie, p. 65)

In the service economy of SIM model (no commodity production), that process seems adequate.

The demand for labour is determined by the ratio of the product by the exogenous rate of wage. Given the simplifying assumptions of the SIM model, this is also sensible. Besides, the supply for labour is assumed to be infinitely elastic. As a consequence, the level of employment depends upon the demand for labour, independently of the wage level. The condition for labour market equilibrium is given by equation (3.4), p. 91. Special assumptions apart, there is no doubt for Godley & Lavoie that wages are generally determined in the labour market. Such a proposition is tantamount to renouncing to Keynes's economic logic according to which it is the commodity markets and not the labour market which determine the real wage.

The fact that labour demand depends on the level of effective demand (which in turn depends on some exogenous expenditure) gives a Keynesian flavour, if we content ourselves with interpreting any demand-led equilibrium as Keynesian. But this is misleading: doing that we get the flavour only but not the substance. The mere fact of introducing an equilibrium condition in the labour market absolutely excludes any involuntary unemployment equilibrium and condemns the model to exhibit under-employment equilibria only, far away from Keynes's conjecture.

The second model which explicitly describes the labour market is the BMW model. The BMW model is more complex than the SIM model. It leaves room for a monetary system with banks, commodity production, stocks, etc. But the market for labour is treated in the same way as in the SIM model with the addition of productivity. Here also, the equilibrium condition for the labour market (equation (7.3) p. 222) is an element of the model and partly determines its solution. For the same reason as in the SIM model, the BMW model cannot generate involuntary unemployment equilibria. *Keynes's conjecture finds no room in Godley & Lavoie's models.*

That negative conclusion would not be altered if supply for labour were assumed to depend on the wage rate or on whatever other endogenous variable.

What prevents Keynes's conjecture from being a possible outcome of Godley & Lavoie's models is not the form of the labour supply but the way in which "labour market" is integrated into SFC models. *Considering the labour market on the same footing as the commodity market is absolutely incompatible with Keynes's conjecture.*

The reader may realize how crucial and delicate is the question dealt with here. It does not concern "realism" or any empirical convenience but theory only. In Chapters 4 and 5 above, we have followed a completely different path. A decisive step in this difficult route is facing Walras's law. Walras's law is not an empirical statement but a theoretical one. We have to face it and understand it as it is: not a purely accounting identity but a fundamental proposition full of social implications.

Walras's law and SFC models

Godley & Lavoie insist on the importance of adopting a consistent account-ing framework where all rows and columns sum to zero. This affirmation is repeated at each chapter with the purpose of emphasizing the coherence of the models. The authors realize that such a coherence has something to do with Walras's law. But they avoid the expression which is not mentioned with one exception, by way of an allusion to Tobin:

> Finally, there is [a] feature, which says that agents must respect their bud-get constraint, both in regard to their expectations and when they assess realized results. In the case of expected results, this is sometimes referred to as Walras' Law, as does Tobin in his Nobel lecture, but we would rather refer to a budget constraint or to a system-wide consistency requirement. In a water-tight accounting framework, the transaction flows of the ulti-mate sector are entirely determined by the transaction flows of the other sectors.
>
> (Godley and Lavoie, p. 14)

Godley & Lavoie's reluctance to explicitly tackle Walras's law – a fear of tres-passing in the Neoclassical field? – makes them miss the radical critique Keynes addressed to the "citadel" in his *General Theory*. Reading *General Theory* Chap-ter 2 clearly shows Keynes's target: the *Neoclassical postulates* (dubbed Classical postulates), not the lack of empirical "realism".

Walras's law may be stated according to different formulations. The more general is: the algebraic sum of all budgetary constraints is identically zero, a formulation which holds at and out of equilibrium. A corollary is that it is impossible that all markets but one be in equilibrium, the last (say the mar-ket for labour) being in excess supply. *Walras's law is incompatible with Keynes's conjecture.*

If SFC models' coherence relies on Walras's law, as Godley& Lavoie's quota-tion above makes it clear, the following conclusion ensues: SFC models cannot host Keynes's conjecture. We have no choice here: we have to deal with Walras's law and to face the challenge proposed by Keynes against the "citadel":

- Either all markets, the market for labour excepted, are in equilibrium; following Walras's law the market for labour must also be in equilibrium; the level of employment equilibrium may be lower than the competitive equilibrium revealing some underemployment; that equilibrium unemployment is *voluntary*, unemployment being measured by the difference between full-employment (competitive equilibrium) and underemployment
- Or there is an excess supply in the market for labour (involuntary unemployment) but another market at least must be in excess demand (typically the market for commodity); there is *no equilibrium* and consequently *no involuntary unemployment equilibrium*; such a disequilibrium situation may be durable if market adjustments are not efficient (a major point in old debates made obsolete since the 1970s); a *disequilibrium* with involuntary unemployment is not what Keynes intended to show in *General Theory*.

Both cases differ from Keynes's conjecture. The mere enunciation of that conjecture is sufficient to express its devastating effect on the welfare theorem, a sacred cow of general competitive equilibrium theory. In order to be able to adopt that potentially decisive critique against the mainstream we have no choice but to frontally address Walras's law. Dispensing themselves from such a task, Post-Keynesian authors have been led *to drift from competitive involuntary unemployment equilibria to realistic under-employment equilibria*.

It is a pity since the first three chapters of *General Theory* are crystal-clear in showing where the critical point lies. While Keynes accepts what he dubs the "first Classical postulate" – in fact the standard profit maximization of entrepreneurs – he insists in rejecting the "second Classical postulate" – in fact the standard utility maximization of the wage-earners.[8]

The refusal of the "second Classical postulate" entails a radical transformation of the so-called "market for labour". Wage-earners do not have the possibility to make effective a correspondence between the marginal utility of the real wage and the disutility of their labour, as Keynes's quotation already mentioned above reminds *General Theory*'s readers:

> For there may be no method available to labour as a whole whereby it can bring the wage-goods equivalent of the general level of money-wages into conformity with the marginal disutility of the current volume of employment.
>
> (*General Theory*, p. 13)

Wage-earners' budgetary constraint does not consist in forbidding them to spend more than *the value of their labour supply* but more than *the value of the demand for labour* (this is true only when the wage rate is above its equilibrium level; see annex).

The consequence is straightforward. The *value of labour demand* now appears in two different budgetary constraints, on the expenses side for the entrepreneurs and on the resources side of wage-earners (where it takes the place of the value of the labour supply). The *aggregation of budgetary constraints of all economic agents makes disappear the value of labour demand and, by the same token, the market for labour.* Instead of getting a full Walras's law, that aggregation gives a Walras's law amputated from the labour market. Let's call *Restricted Walras's law* (RWL hereafter) such a modified Walras's law. While Walras's law is incompatible with Keynes's conjecture, RWL does not forbid a full competitive equilibrium in every market except for a labour market in excess supply. *RWL and Keynes's conjecture are to sides of a same coin* (Cartelier, 1996).

Treating entrepreneurs and wage-earners as subject to different budgetary constraints is the key of any rehabilitation of Keynes's conjecture.[9] It is true that RWL is not a sufficient cause of involuntary unemployment equilibrium: a too low effective demand must be added. But, *in the absence of RWL a too low effective demand does not produce any involuntary unemployment equilibrium.* In *General Theory*, effective demand theory (Chapter 3) logically comes *after* the refusal of the "second Classical postulate" (Chapter 2). Forgetting about Chapter 2, *i.e.* forgetting about Walras's law and insisting on demand-led models, as it is the case in Godley& Lavoie' book, allows to getting underemployment equilibria only. Claiming being true to Keynes is not sufficient. We must understand exactly why general competitive equilibrium and Keynes' economics produce so radically different outcomes. Contrary to what is too often said, the crucial point is neither imperfect competition nor uncertainty but the attitude toward the division between entrepreneurs and wage-earners. Whenever the wage relationship is treated as an exchange between labour and wage (*i. e.* between wage-earners and entrepreneurs), Keynes' conjecture is made out of reach. It is only by considering that the wage relationship is irreducible to exchange that Walras's law may be turned into RWL making Keynes' conjecture a possible outcome of economic theory.

Godley & Lavoie avoid a serious discussion of Walras's law, contenting themselves with the coherence of their accounting framework. Consequently, they end up with results opposed in nature to those they were pretending to get: instead of the devastating *competitive involuntary unemployment equilibria* – impossible to be found in mainstream economics – they get *imperfect competitive voluntary unemployment equilibria* – perfectly compatible with welfare theorem.

SFC models' drift away from Keynes' economics comes from a too superficial critique of mainstream. Reproaching mainstream economists for their lack of realism only amounts to forgetting that the strength of mainstream theory does not come from its capacity to predict the level of economic activity and its fluctuations but from its capacity to offer a coherent (even if not relevant) intellectual framework which is widely used to interpret economic and social life. The performance of the "citadel" should be appreciated less by the realism of its applied models (which may always be improved by *ad hoc* tricks) than by its general principles and their possible transformation into a political philosophy (toward which tends any serious economic theory at its higher level of abstraction). Neglecting this deeper aspect of economics and retaining only its apparent empirical relevance is tantamount to deserting the main battlefield and to accept without discussion the hegemony of mainstream economics.

We have recalled above that RWL (not Walras's law) is a necessary condition for Keynes' conjecture to hold valid. But this is not the end of the route. We have now to make appear the relation between that point and the adoption of a monetary analysis against a real one. It is perfectly possible to prove Keynes' conjecture in a very simple mainstream model without money, uncertainty and all so-called Keynesian ingredients by changing the budgetary constraint of wage-earners only (see Appendix). It is also possible to prove Keynes's conjecture within an Arrow-Debreu model modifying adequately wage-earners' position (see Glustoff, 1968). If so, why bother with pleading for a monetary analysis?

SFC framework and monetary analysis

SFC models and our monetary analysis share a common representation of economic activity under the form of an accounting framework. Succession of flows-of-funds accounts is rhythmed by an evolution of balance-sheets registering how wealth of people evolves over time.

That view of wealth as a conventionally built quantitative representation has been opposed to value theory according to which wealth is not nominal but real. We have adopted and defended a monetary analysis following Steuart and Keynes to cite the two most eminent theoreticians belonging to that tradition. Elaborating a monetary analysis does not go without difficulties. Many questions have been raised in the preceding chapters; some have been solved, some are still pending. It may be useful to examine how SFC authors address these questions.

Why prefer a flows-of-funds matrix to a market excess-demand matrix?

This is a technical formulation of a larger interrogation about monetary versus real analysis.

Mainstream theory, in spite of its great diversity, is built according to a common robust and efficient schema. Economic agents are defined as initial endowments and preferences, both referring to a common commodity space. Demand and supply functions (individual and/or aggregated) are derived from a maximizing behaviour subject to budgetary constraints in a context of perfect competition. This allows us to get a matrix of excess-demand. A fundamental problem is whether a vector of real prices exists which equates the functions to zero (existence problem).

Why prefer a flows-of-funds presentation to the mainstream one? Such an interrogation is inescapable since it is always possible to derive a flows-of-funds schema (in *numéraire*) from an equilibrium situation characterized by a simultaneous equilibrium in every market. A real analysis seems to perform better than a monetary one since it includes the latter and offers an explanation in terms of goods and individual happiness.

This is not true. We have seen in the first part of this book (see Ostroy & Starr, 1974) that no decentralized process of transaction realizations exists in absence of money. Postulating money (unit of account *plus* means of payment) cannot be dispensed with when decentralized economies are about. Godley & Lavoie do not mention that argument. They prefer to invoke once again realism and fidelity to a Post-Keynesian tradition. This is not very illuminating. They do not see that choosing to deal with economic activity only nominally is not an empirical choice but a theoretical one. Not resorting to value theory and its postulated commodity space should not be but a conscious and motivated choice.

Godley & Lavoie do not seem aware of that since they proceed as if they simultaneously postulate both money *and* commodity space. They are concerned by prices and *real* variables. They assume that economic agents calculate their actions in real terms. Consequently they resort to price deflators.

From a practical point of view this is perfectly acceptable but there is no theoretical foundation for that. Keynes is well-aware of that difficulty. He avoids dealing with prices when he selects the relevant variables for his theory. The only variables he accepts to consider are monetary or ratios between monetary magnitudes (unit of employment):

> In dealing with the theory of employment I propose, therefore, to make use of only two fundamental units of quantity, namely, quantities of money-value and quantities of employment.
>
> (*General Theory*, p. 41)

In the present book we are true to Keynes's position contrary to Godley & Lavoie. Adopting that position is not well-accepted today, even amongst the hard-liner Keynesians. Keynes justifies it in this well-known passage:

> To say that net output to-day is greater, but the price-level lower, than ten years ago or one year ago, is a proposition of a similar character to the statement that Queen Victoria was a better queen but not a happier woman than Queen Elizabeth – a proposition not without meaning and not without interest, but unsuitable as material for the differential calculus.
>
> (*General Theory*, p. 40)

Empirical attitudes are not deprived of merits but they do not favour rationally founded propositions. It is a pity to leave to mainstream economists the apparent privilege of being both rational and conforming to common sense. The commodity space postulate does not need any justification since it is taken as natural: is it not obvious that goods and services do exist? Is it not an extravagance to deny it?

An instant of reflection may suffice to raise a doubt about that evidence. The role effectively played in mainstream theory by the commodity space postulate is not that of Nature but that of language. Once this language is adopted it is almost impossible to introduce money in that framework, as we have seen in the first part. If integration of money in value theory has failed – a diagnosis accepted by most of Keynesians – why keep doing as if it had been successful? Either postulate a commodity space without bother about money or postulate money without a commodity space. That is the choice any theoretician respecting parsimony of hypotheses is confronted with.

Commodity space is no more and no less natural than money. Both are socially determined. Starting from money right from the beginning leads to the conclusion that payments are the basic economic relation amongst people. Commodities, instead of being postulated, become a result of social activity, not of Nature. Computers, drugs and movies are not to be found in nature.

In short, it makes no sense to postulate a money *and* a commodity space. Parsimony principle leads to choose either one or the other. It is precisely how Keynes proceeds when he decides to resort to monetary variables only (which does not prevent him from distinguishing consumption and investment in *General Theory* Chapter 6 as endogenous).

Godley & Lavoie are more concerned by empirical evidence than by theory; they do not follow Keynes's attitude. They have to pay the price for that. Not having seriously got rid of mainstream theoretical background, they are exposed to get outcomes already obtained by it. This is the case as noted above with the imperfect competitive voluntary unemployment equilibria far away from the competitive involuntary unemployment equilibria of Keynes's conjecture.

What kind of data in the SFC framework?

An SFC framework characterizes a monetary analysis. Now we know the reason for that congruence. A further point is to decide the type of data to inscribe in the accounts. Accounting practitioners provide useful answers to most usual questions. But they do not solve theoretical problems.

It is worth noting, to begin with, that in spite of the formal coherence of the framework, the data registered in flows-of-funds qualitatively differ from those registered in balance-sheets. Payments are the very substance of economic relations; they are the raw material of a monetary analysis. Assets and liabilities evaluation is conventional. It depends on rules which are derived from theoretical foundations. Godley & Lavoie are well aware of that problem but they are not troubled by it. They note the opposition between an historical and a market evaluation, they decide in favour of the latter (which avoids re-evaluation) but do not care about a theoretical justification except for the internal coherence of accounting framework. This amounts to imposing an equality between value of total net assets and value of total equities (Tobin's $q = 1$), *i.e.* a full equilibrium in the capital market. Unless adhering to mainstream economics, there is no reason for being subject to that condition.

In the next chapter, we will admit that evaluation rules of assets are conventional whatever they may be; they are an ingredient of the economy. Being an institutional element they are socially objective but not as fundamental as payments. The reference to accounts has to be made precise: it does not mean that accounting is the "true real economy". Only payments, *i.e.* flows-of-funds accounts, can be said to be the substance of economic relations. The organization of the accounts *inside* each economic agent is purely conventional. As such they matter but not at the same level as payments. Accounts too should be taken *cum grano salis* and theoretically considered.

In any case, a problem remains to solve: how are payments figures to be interpreted? What do they reveal?

Godley & Lavoie give a clear and logical solution with an important implication. Reasoning on the example of commodity transactions (firms' receipts and total agents' expenses in the market for commodities) they rightly emphasize that payments denote *realized* not expected transactions. Being aware that individual actions are not mutually compatible in a decentralized economy, they interpret the fact that transactions are effective and observable as the outcome of an unobserved adjustment process making mutually compatible the expected transactions. In other terms, following the logic of the mainstream, they admit that observable and effective transactions must be thought as taking place at some equilibrium. An adjustment process drives the economy to equilibrium *before* the realization of transaction; this process is the condition of observation.

> The first mechanism is mainly associated with mainstream theory, that is, neoclassical theory: variations in prices clear the market. (. . .). The second mechanism is associated with the so-called rationing theory, also called constrained equilibrium theory. Despite being based on an essentially neo-classical view of markets, this approach eschews market clearing prices, by imposing some rigid prices. (. . .). The third mechanism is linked to the existence of inventories. Firms hold a buffer of finished goods, which can be called upon whenever demand exceeds production. Sales are always equal to demand because it is assumed that inventories are always large enough to absorb any discrepancy between production and demand. (. . .). Finally, there is a fourth mechanism, the so-called Keynesian, or Kaleckian, quantity adjustment mechanism. This is the mechanism that is being called upon in the present model. (. . .). The equality between demand and supply, the latter being here defined as production, is achieved by an instantaneous quantity adjustment process, as is always the case in standard Kaleckian and Keynesian models.
>
> (Godley and Lavoie, pp. 63–65)

That long quotation shows how important for economic theorizing are the interpretations of observed payments. It is clearly not a purely empirical question but a theoretical one.

The four processes alluded to by Godley & Lavoie have a common property: they make the observed payments the outcome of an *unobservable process* leading to an equilibrium (temporary, transitory or stationary depending on the model). Mainstream economists think that way. It is difficult to think different. Keynes did the same in *General Theory*, perhaps because

> [t]his book is chiefly addressed to my fellows economists
>
> (*General Theory*, p. xxi)

a condition for a critique to be internal or immanent.

Considering that effective transactions in a decentralized economy necessarily take place at equilibrium seems unavoidable. There seems to be no alternative. Although logical and well-admitted that position is marred by a terrible drawback. It puts under the rug the most fundamental characteristic of a market economy which is the contradiction between decentralization of individual decisions (freedom of choice) and necessary validation of these decisions by the market (acceptation of a social sanction as a counterpart of individual freedom). Marx more than anyone else did stress that contradiction as the "double character of labour embodied in commodities": a contradiction between private (or concrete) and social (abstract) labour. General competitive equilibrium theory has dealt with that point under the heading of global stability of general equilibrium. Its failure has been acknowledged by the profession at the beginning of the seventies (Debreu, Sonnenschein and Saari). This should have made theoreticians think about it, be they Keynesian or Neoclassical.

Is it true that no alternative may be found? A negative answer has been suggested above. It does not consist in inscribing individuals' expectations in the accounts (Godley & Lavoie rightly discard that trick) but in distinguishing amongst observable payments the *voluntary* and the *constrained* ones. The idea is to interpret market sanctions as constrained payment, the other being the socially observable outcome of the private decision processes (voluntary payments). That distinction would make the adjustment process observable in principle. Realized transactions could be conceived of as out-of-equilibrium phenomena. An outstanding achievement indeed not to be obtained in a value approach.

There is no doubt that distinguishing between voluntary and constrained payments is theoretically relevant since it is the straightforward consequence of the combination of freedom and responsibility. Individual freedom (voluntary payments) and social validation (constrained payments) are the two sides of the same coin (market economy). But there is no doubt too that distinguishing voluntary and constrained payments is empirically problematic. If one of the pitfalls of Godley & Lavoie's book is a misleading obsession about realism, as we have seen above, the reader may think that the drawback of the present book is the opposed characteristic, an obsession about theorizing without looking at economic reality. Why bother about voluntary *versus* constrained payments if it is not possible to empirically distinguish them? There is a good reason for that. There is no symmetry between empirical and theoretical problems. Uncertain and shaky theoretical notions not only lead to uncertain and vague theorizing but they do not allow one to conduct meaningful empirical studies; uncertain and ambiguous data are not an obstacle to elaborate a theoretical knowledge which in turn may shed light on empirical data and may allow for interpreting them more accurately. In sum, it is easier and more sensible to remedy drawbacks in applied economics than to try to interpret empirical data without a coherent and relevant theory. Applied studies may tolerate some approximations while economic theory does not (Keynes's refusal of deflators is a good example).

There is no doubt that the distinction between voluntary and constrained payments has an empirical correspondent in economic reality. Nobody would deny that an independent producer who has engaged into some trade by *voluntarily* acquiring raw material and various tools may experience unexpectedly low sales and may be *constrained* to borrow on unfavourable conditions in order to avoid bankruptcy. The problem is that observed situations in real economic life are not so crystal-clear. Further empirical analysis, guided by that theoretically well-founded distinction, will hopefully illustrate the strategic importance of the theoretical distinction.

SFC framework and dynamical analysis

Above, we have reminded the reader that balance-sheets are affected by conventional rules of evaluation. None of these rules may be theoretically founded; marked to market is no better than historical cost: why retain a market evaluation resulting from the sale of a fraction only of an asset? Why retain a value observed in the past and no longer valid now? In the absence of any incontestable evaluation rule, why consider, as Godley & Lavoie suggest, that the balance-sheet which closes period (t) is the same as the one which opens period ($t + 1$)?

Although "realist" and conforming to accounting rules, that point of view is theoretically too restrictive. The break existing between two successive periods is given its full importance when backward-looking and forward-looking balance-sheets are distinguished and made possibly to differ. The former shows the consequences of what happened during period (t), the latter gives a sense to the voluntary payments realized in period ($t + 1$). That break between the two balance-sheets is at the heart of dynamics.

Using the vocabulary we have proposed in the preceding chapters, we may say that backward-looking balances derive from voluntary and constrained payments of period (t) while forward-looking balance-sheets are evaluated at the same time voluntary payments of period ($t + 1$) are decided. It is true that the latter is not empirically observable but it makes intelligible what is observable, namely the voluntary payments of period ($t + 1$).

Godley & Lavoie do in fact the same without discussing the point. In the model BMW, the entrepreneur is supposed to adopt a determinate objective and decide about his current operations of the period by reference to that objective:

> [P]roduction firms target a certain capital stock KT. This targeted capital stock depends on the sales achieved in the previous period. The implicit assumption made here is that entrepreneurs, when they decide on their orders of investment goods, see overall sales of the previous period as the indicator of the overall sales in the coming period, and attempt to maintain a normal rate of utilization of their capacity.
>
> (Godley and Lavoie, p. 226)

But they do it as if the succession of periods would proceed in a mechanical and automatic way. As soon as we are aware of that break between successive periods, nothing prevents us from adopting a more open and less deterministic dynamics. For the same reasons that distinguishing voluntary and constrained payments emphasizes a fundamental characteristic of a market economy, distinguishing between backward- and forward-looking balance-sheets opens to a different and more adequate dynamics.

Godley & Lavoie's dynamics is traditional even if they choose behavioural assumptions which are not. Their models share some drawbacks with most mainstream ones. These dynamical models are generally not very robust to the parameters and to the kind of mathematical functions adopted. But, more than that, there is something of scientism in that more or less Laplacian method. By contrast, Steuart's idea about economic evolution or Keynes's point of view are different. Both latter authors express doubts about dynamics. They are not very much confident in the scientific character of economic knowledge. Dynamics associated with monetary analysis does not go along such a mechanistic and determinist view.

Emphasizing the difference between backward- and forward-looking balance-sheets amounts to acknowledging that no mechanical link exists between them. Taking for granted that some indeterminacy is inherent in the economic evolution over time leads to raising original questions about dynamics. The method of viability, referred to at the end of the preceding chapter, is an example of such a new approach.

In a few words, viability theory deals with correspondences rather than functions (*i.e.* differential inclusions rather than differential equations). This leaves some room for indeterminacy and, most significantly, raises and solves different problems. Leaving aside asymptotic stability properties, viability theory tackles a fundamental question: whether or not the authority (Steuart's statesman, Keynes's government) has the possibility to keep the economy on a sustainable trajectory; a positive answer does not imply that it will effectively succeed (while a negative makes sure that it will not unless a deep structural change happens).

This idea cannot be developed further due to a lack of competence. We nevertheless allude to viability to remind the reader that deeply different philosophical stances are hidden behind technical tools. This is especially true about dynamics.

SFC models: general remarks

In the conclusion of their book Godley & Lavoie give a synthetic view of what they have done. In spite of a reference to "an alternative monetary theory", the authors seem far from self-conscious of what is engaged by the opposition between real and monetary analysis. They are incredibly timid by comparison with Keynes. Amongst the ten points they list in the belief that they give a fair account of their book, four are relative to economic theory properly speaking. All of them are in fact incompatible with a monetary analysis. As we have seen above, their main results are those mainstream applied authors would get if they were realistic in the choice of their parameters and behavioural assumptions.

Our critique should not be ill-understood. The authors have produced an amazing work in realist applied macroeconomics. We have no reluctance toward such an objective. What we wish to contest is their claim to being true to Keynes and to the tradition of monetary analysis. It is not a question about labelling, which has no interest at all, but about the way economic theory is conceived of. Showing, as we have tried to do, that SFC models do not owe much to Keynes's economics does not mean that they are not useful but only that their impact on economic theory is not the one the authors believe. Godley & Lavoie have not wished to commit themselves in a careful (and empathic) study of mainstream theory, as exemplified by their abstention about Walras's law. They have preferred to reject it for empirical reasons (maybe also for their implicit ideology). As a result they succeed in getting better empirical results only, but these better results are compatible with the theory Godley & Lavoie claim to reject (something like a *"retour du refoulé"*). It is why we have not put these models in the centre of our presentation.

Caverzasi & Godin borrow from Cohen and Jacob an interesting sentence which felicitously grasps the nature of the difficulty met by economists working along SFC models:

> As observed after twenty-five years by Cohen (1972), the work of Cope-land certainly had a great influence on economics – mainly as a source of financial data – but its potential disruptive impact on the study and model-ing of the interdependences between real and financial flows failed to occur (at least until the time in which Cohen was writing). As to the possible causes of this missed evolution of economics, Cohen indicates "the lack of a so-called 'organizing theory,'" or in other words, "they lack their Keynes".
> (Jacob, 1972, p. 13). Quoted by Caverzasi & Godin (pp. 5–6)

No "new Keynes" has showed up since; a careful reading of the "old one" would have made clear, however, that Keynes's economics is not only a jolly piece of an empirically relevant economic theory but also an outstanding achievement in fundamental economic theory. *General theory* is really a strong blow against the mainstream and if, contrary to Keynes's expectations, mainstream economics is more than ever alive it is amongst other things due to the incapacity of Keynesians to understand the message and to formulate it in renewed terms. Keynesians have done a lot of good stuff but not being aware of what was really at stake – namely what Schumpeter called "the main cleavage in economic analysis" – they have not addressed their critiques at the right level of economic theory.

A reflection about history of economic analysis could have suggested that Keynes had rejuvenated (being conscious of it or not is another problem) an old tradition Adam Smith had strongly contributed to putting at the margins. Nine years before *Wealth of Nations* was published, our profession had been provided by Steuart with a full-fledged framework where flows-of-funds and "balances of wealth" were systematically linked together. This went along with an insistence on the statesman and a conception of economics as an art rather than a science. Moreover, Steuart's theory of money, partly inspired by John Law, was oriented toward the question of issuance of money very remote from later preoccupations about integration of money into value theory.

Such a reflection about the past could have convinced modern "heterodox" economists that a subterranean stream of thought had permanently flowed in spite of the hegemony of value theory. It would have helped Quesnay and Marx readers to interpret them differently from what has been too often done. It would have also allowed Wicksell, Hawtrey and Schumpeter to be better recognized than has been the case. At the same time, the necessity to give clear and sound theoretical foundations to that old tradition would have been manifest. It is a feeling of that necessity which is at the root of the present book.

Let's briefly sketch some points at stake here.

Mainstream theoreticians have a basecamp in which they feel sure: the general competitive equilibrium theory. Even if that basecamp is rarely mentioned, it provides the profession with the most fundamental notions and with a basic view about what a good economic theory should be like. A rigorous axiomatic presentation of that theory makes it respectable and respected (critiques about its lack of realism notwithstanding). Whether that axiomatic presentation is judged adequate or not is debatable. We have shown in the first part of this book that it is not relevant for money. We have known since the beginning of the 1970s that it does not allow us to deal successively with global stability. These two examples are worth noticing. It is precisely because such an axiomatic presentation does exist that it is possible to discuss, confirm or invalidate theoretical propositions. If not, debates remain superficial.

Out-of-mainstream theoreticians cannot benefit from that kind of debate. No axiom is available for an alternative economic theory. To my knowledge few isolated works are devoted to that kind of reflection (let us mention Benetti & Cartelier's *Marchands, salariat et capitalistes* as a first attempt). It is a pity because the extent of the domain of validity of theoretical propositions highly depends on the initial assumptions. Moreover, giving a quasi-axiomatic character to the theory helps a lot in checking its internal coherence.

Mainstream theory assumes that individuals are endowed with a full rational behaviour. That postulate makes it extendable to every field of social life. There is no a *priori* reasons for refusing an application of that postulate to marriage, crime, entertainment and so on. Criticizing the rationality postulate or substituting limited rationality makes sense from an empirical point of view but does not change anything to the soft power of mainstream theory or to the imperialism of economics over social sciences.

By contrast, a monetary analysis does not need any assumption about individual behaviour. Its domain of validity does not depend on behavioural assumptions. That domain is strictly limited to the relations mediated by money, *i.e.* flow of payments between accounts. That substantial conception of economics not only makes economics imperialism difficult but radically changes the way a multidisciplinary study may be conceived of (see more in the conclusion of the book).

A more difficult interrogation is in order. The reader may raise a legitimate question: is it not contradictory to maintain, as done above, on the one hand, that Keynes's conjecture can be demonstrated in a very simple model of real analysis and, on the other hand, that Keynes's conjecture belongs to a monetary analysis?

There is no contradiction. There are, however, two different levels of interpretation, the deeper making clear that Keynes's conjecture may be logically founded in a monetary analysis only. In the minimalist version of a mainstream model (see Appendix to this chapter), Keynes's conjecture is demonstrated by changing the budgetary constraint of the wage-earner, in accordance with Keynes's refusal of the "second Classical postulate". This specific treatment of wage-earners is the *necessary condition* for Keynes's conjecture to be valid. In the resulting framework, it is easy to establish the possibility of involuntary unemployment equilibria. This possibility becomes effective if the state of expectations is such that investment and any other exogenously determined expenditures are sufficiently low.

So far so good. But we need to go deeper in order to understand why it is legitimate to refuse the "second Classical postulate". Why are wage-earners, and wage-earners only, subject to that special budgetary constraint? While we keep reasoning in the mainstream framework there is no justification. In that framework, as we know, only voluntary transactions ruled by equivalence are to be seen. There is no available argument against the attribution of a Walrasian budgetary constraint to everybody (hence Walras's law and the incongruity of Keynes's conjecture). As noted above, Hicks avoided facing that problem by assuming a consumption function in which labour supply plays no role but without discussing the point (labour supply and unemployment are not mentioned in the article!). Clower in 1965 justified the special treatment which allowed him to get Keynes's conjecture by the fact that wage-earners may be short in money; this will prevent them from spending as much as they desire. This ingenious argument invalidates Walras's law. Ingenious as it is, that argument is by no means specific to wage-earners. If it is generalized Walras's law becomes valid and, consequently, Keynes's conjecture ceases to be valid.

There is no escape here. Getting Keynes's conjecture as the possible outcome of a model requires that wage-earners not be treated on the same footing as other agents. This special treatment has to be justified. This is possible only within a monetary analysis as we have shown above. The decisive advantage of a monetary analysis is that it may host different types of economic relations while the mainstream deals with equivalence only. This is not due to the adoption of an SFC framework but to the consideration of the means of payment issuance.

Appendix: Keynes's conjecture: a minimalist formalization

Let there be a competitive economy with a unique commodity serving for consumption and investment (corn) and a unique production factor, labour. Production technique is given by a Cobb-Douglas production function:

(1) $\quad q = \left(\frac{1}{a}\right) N^a$

where q is the quantity of product and N the quantity of labour. There are two agents. Agent 1 owns the unique firm. She maximizes the profit under the constraint of the production function (Keynes's "first Classical postulate"). This gives labour demand and commodity supply functions:

(2) $\quad N^d = \left(\frac{w}{p}\right)^{\frac{1}{a-1}}$

(3) $\quad q^s = \left(\frac{1}{a}\right) \left(\frac{w}{p}\right)^{\frac{a}{a-1}}$

The firm owner gets the totality of the profit $q^s - \left(\frac{w}{p}\right) N^d$. She spends all the profit by purchasing corn (there is no alternative use). Let D denote that expenditure. Agent 1's budgetary constraint is:

(4) $\quad D = q^s - \left(\frac{w}{p}\right) N^d$

Agent 2 (the wage-earner) is endowed with all the available labour N; we assume without any loss of generality that she supplies a constant fraction of N,

$N^s = bN$ whatever the real wage may be (maximization of a Cobb–Douglas utility function under the usual constraint). Agent 2's demand for corn is:

$$(5) \quad C = \left(\frac{w}{p}\right) N^s$$

Which is also her budgetary constraint.

It is easy to check that the sum of the constraints (4) and (5) gives Walras's law:

$$(6) \quad C + D - q^s + \left(\frac{w}{p}\right)\left(N^d - N^s\right) \equiv 0$$

The unique equilibrium is $\left(\dfrac{w}{p}\right)* = \left(bN\right)^{a-1}$. Consequently: $N* = bN$ (no involuntary unemployment) and $D* = \left(\dfrac{1-a}{a}\right)\left(bN\right)^a$.

Let us modify that model by refusing the "second Classical postulate" and stating the wage-earner budgetary constraint as follows:

$$(7) \quad for \ \left(\frac{w}{p}\right) \geq \left(\frac{w}{p}\right)* \rightarrow C = \left(\frac{w}{p}\right) N^d \ for \ \left(\frac{w}{p}\right) < \left(\frac{w}{p}\right)* \rightarrow C = \left(\frac{w}{p}\right) N^s$$

The sum of the constraints (4) and (7) gives $\left(\dfrac{w}{p}\right) \geq \left(\dfrac{w}{p}\right)*$:

$$(8) \quad C + D - q^s \equiv 0$$

The market for labour is now excluded from Walras's law; expression (8) is RWL, the restricted Walras's law.

Now, for all situations $\left(\dfrac{w}{p}\right) \geq \left(\dfrac{w}{p}\right)*$ the economy is in equilibrium with an excess supply in the market for labour, the Keynes conjecture. This justifies Keynes's affirmation which according to Neoclassical theory is a

> special case only and not the general case, the situation which it assumes being a limiting point of the possible positions of equilibrium.
>
> (*General Theory*, p. 3)

The fact that Keynesian equilibria are parametered by the real wage may make people think that they occur only in case of real wage rigidity. It is true that, when $\left(\dfrac{w}{p}\right) = \left(\dfrac{w}{p}\right)*$ there is no involuntary unemployment. Does it mean that wage rigidity is responsible for Keynesian equilibria? Not at all, maintains Keynes. The labour market is not the place where the real wage is determined!

Equilibrium selection amongst the continuum $\left(\dfrac{w}{p}\right) \geq \left(\dfrac{w}{p}\right)*$ takes place by the level of effective demand. In a temporary equilibrium model (Walras and Keynes's reason in that framework), expenses depend upon the state of expectations.

In our elementary model, this amounts to determining agent 1's expenses by an exogenous element. Keynes calls this type of expenses investment. D depends upon exogenous elements (animal spirits) and is noted $\underline{D}$. Wage-earner gets (and spends) a fraction a of the product while firm owner spends $\underline{D}$. Equilibrium in the commodity market becomes:

$$(9) \quad q = aq + \underline{D} \rightarrow q = \frac{1}{1-a}\underline{D}$$

which is the Keynesian multiplier.

Note that the real wage corresponding to that level of involuntary unemployment, far from being rigid, is an endogenous variable: $\left(\dfrac{w}{p}\right) = \left(\dfrac{1}{1-a}\underline{D}\right)^{\frac{1}{a}}$. A positive variation of $\underline{D}$ causes an increase of q; this increases stops when $\underline{D} = D*$. Employment is no longer elastic, which is the definition Keynes proposes for the absence of involuntary unemployment (*General Theory*, Chapter 3). Note also that introducing $\underline{D} < D*$ in the Neoclassical version of the model does not lead to involuntary unemployment equilibria but to a disequilibrium in both markets (opposite sign and equal value: Walras's law in majesty).

Notes

1 Marx (1976) devoted the long section VIII of Capital (Book I) to the historical genesis of the division between capitalists and wage-earners. Primitive accumulation is the basic notion Marx resorts to.

2 "The profits of stock, it may perhaps be thought, are only a different name for the wages of a particular sort of labour, the labour of inspection and direction. They are, however, altogether different, are regulated by quite different principles, and bear no proportion to the quantity, the hardship, or the ingenuity of this supposed labour of inspection and direction. They are regulated altogether by the value of stock employed, and are greater or smaller in proportion to the extent of this stock" (Smith (1996), I, p. 66).

3 Jean-François Jacques & Antoine Rebeyrol also propose a logical genesis of classes. They start from a Solow model in which a fraction of people experience an evolution leading to a complete destruction of their capital (see Jacques & Rebeyrol, 2009). As for Matsuyama, a basic point is that inequality of wealth is the origin of the division in classes.

4 Actual input-output tables are mainly based on enterprises accounts and not on engineering considerations. The way economists deal with production techniques is largely metaphoric: they believe they are speaking about technique but they are dealing in fact with costs given by monetary quantities drawn out of accounts.

5 Keynes should have remarked that his involuntary unemployment is not observable since the relevant part of the labour supply curve is not active (for the same reasons that

involuntary under-activity of wage-earners is not observable in our framework except for unemployment benefits payments).

6 See Glustoff (1968) and Cartelier (1996) for a simplified version. Due to common prejudices, Keynesians have turned a blind eye to Glustoff's demonstration, probably because it took place in an Arrow-Debreu context and was published in a prestigious academic review. As a consequence, Keynes's main analytical contribution to a critique of economic theory – the consequences of treating wage-earners on a different footing as attested by his refusal of the "second Classical postulate" – was unnoticed by those who should have put the focus on it. They have chosen to insist on other features: expectations, imperfect competition, incertitude, all topics common in mainstream economics.

7 Ironically, the most fervent Keynesians have criticized ISLM for being a Neoclassical model. They would have better tried to understand the analytical origin of the ISLM main proposition.

8 For the sake of clarity and fidelity to Keynes, wage-earners are identified with households and entrepreneurs with non-wage-earners (see Appendix to this chapter).

9 A different treatment of entrepreneurs and wage-earners is characteristic of Keynes's economics. In the *Treatise on Money* entrepreneurs and wage-earners are not put on the same footing. The notion of a normal income (normal profit) concerns entrepreneurs only. Any difference between normal and effective profit triggers a dynamic adjustment. No mention of a normal wage and no capacity for wage-earners to generate any adjustment are to be found in the *Treatise*.

Chapter 7

Some specific properties of a capitalist economy

The existence of involuntary unemployment equilibria relies on a qualitative difference of condition between entrepreneurs and wage-earners as abundantly illustrated in Chapter 6. But there is much to be said. For the sake of comparison with mainstream theory we have considered equilibrium situations only. But, as we know, a monetary analysis is not limited to these special situations. An important general property characterizing any economy is the *primacy of expenses*. In a capitalist economy that property has been independently unravelled by Keynes in his *Treatise on Money* (the widow's cruse) and by Kalecki. Let us call that property according to the latter: *Kalecki's principle*. Kalecki's principle is not an equilibrium condition. It does not state that profits are equal to investment minus wage-earners' saving. Kalecki claims that profits are *determined* by investment, wage-earners' saving coming as some kind of leakage from the circulation. *The primacy of expenses introduces a causality where mainstream economists see only a principle of mutual interdependence.*

Kalecki's principle

Kalecki's principle results from our postulates, from the role of the minting process and more generally from the general spirit of a monetary analysis. It is easily deduced from the matrix of payments and the primacy of expenses. Entrepreneurs, if they desire, can spend as much as the minting process allows them to do so. What they cannot decide is the level of their receipts. But, what they spend toward other entrepreneurs generates gross profit by definition. Any expenditure of an entrepreneur to another increases the profit of entrepreneurs taken as a whole. As the matrix of payments makes it clear, the total expenditures of entrepreneurs to entrepreneurs are *ipso facto* their profits, unless wage-earners save all or part of their wages. Wage-earners' saving prevents firms from recuperating their expenses by means of sales; they have to get them by means of increasing indebtedness. Hence:

Proposition 15

Entrepreneurs earn what they spend; wage-earners spend what they earn (Kalecki's principle)

Formally, Kalecki's principle is, in our framework:

$$\pi = \check{m}_{FF} - \left(m_{BW} - m_{WF}\right) \tag{7-1}$$

where π are profits, $\check{m}_{FF} = \sum_h \check{m}_h$, $m_{BW} - m_{WF}$ the saving out of wages (total wages minus consumption); total income (profits plus wages) is

$$y = \underbrace{\check{m}_{FF}}_{investment} + \underbrace{\widetilde{m_{WF}}}_{consumption} = \overbrace{\check{m}_{FF} - \left(m_{BW} - m_{WF}\right)}^{profit} + \underbrace{\widetilde{m_{BW}}}_{wages}. \tag{7-2}$$

Keynes's proposition about involuntary unemployment and Kalecki's principle are two different expressions for the same idea: the *primacy of expenses*: individuals having the capacity to give the first move to money circulation – entrepreneurs eligible for the minting process – determine the nature of economic relations, either pure market, domestic or wage relationship.

A dynamic extension of the principles of primacy of expenditure and Kalecki is worth studying. It will allow us to rehabilitate Harrod's razor-edge idea and explore some dynamic properties of an entrepreneur economy; these properties are different from those of a pure market economy, presented in Chapter 5. Harrod's views will be found again but without the confusions typical of mainstream economists who inappropriately interpret Keynes's and Harrod's results as special cases (fixity of prices, production functions with fixed coefficients, and so on).

Involuntary unemployment steady-states: Solow as a special case of a monetary analysis

It is now possible to proceed rather quickly since the basic idea is clear: when wage-earners are treated on a different footing from entrepreneurs the main claims of mainstream economic theory about equilibrium and optimal properties cease to be generally valid; they hold only in special cases. That claim can be shown while resorting only to the variables written down in the payment matrix. But, in order to make easier a comparison between mainstream and a monetary analysis, we will use a traditional notation. The table below allows the passing from one notation to another. There is an exception, however. As Solow and others mention the total capital, which is absent so far from our developments, we will use the variable K and $v = \dfrac{K}{y}$ without any further explanation (see below).

Following Solow, let's accept that profits are a constant fraction α of income, wage-earners getting a fraction $1 - \alpha$ of it. Due to the Cobb-Douglas parable in Solow's model, the rate of profit is $r = \dfrac{\alpha k}{1-\alpha}$ where k is the capital per capita.

Elementary manipulations bring the first fundamental relation

$$r \equiv \frac{\alpha}{v} \leftrightarrow v \equiv \frac{\alpha}{r} \tag{7-3}$$

where v is the capital coefficient.

Assume that entrepreneurs only invest (they do not consume and do not save) and that wage-earners save a fraction s of their income. Entrepreneurs are satisfied (equilibrium in the market for commodities) if their receipts, coming from the sales of investment and consumption goods, are equal to their expenses, or, alternatively if global saving is equal to global investment. Elementary manipulations bring our second fundamental relation where g_K is the equilibrium rate of growth:

$$\left(\alpha + (1-\alpha)s\right)y = \overset{\vee}{m}_{FF} \leftrightarrow g_K^* = \frac{\left(\alpha + (1-\alpha)s\right)}{v} = \frac{\left(\alpha + (1-\alpha)s\right)r}{\alpha} \tag{7-4}$$

Table 7.1 Correspondence between standard notation and matrix payment

$y = \overset{\vee}{m}_{FF} - \left(m_{FW} - m_{WF}\right) + m_{FW} = \overset{\vee}{m}_{FF} + m_{WF}$

Income = profits plus wages = investment + consumption

$\dfrac{\pi}{y} = \alpha = \dfrac{\overset{\vee}{m}_{FF} - \left(m_{FW} - m_{WF}\right)}{\overset{\vee}{m}_{FF} + m_{WF}}$

$1 - \alpha = \dfrac{m_{FW}}{\overset{\vee}{m}_{FF} + m_{WF}}$

$(1-\alpha)s = \dfrac{m_{FW} - m_{WF}}{\overset{\vee}{m}_{FF} + m_{WF}}$

$\dfrac{y}{K} = \dfrac{1}{v} = \dfrac{\overset{\vee}{m}_{FF} + m_{WF}}{K}$

$g_K^* = \dfrac{\alpha + (1-\alpha)s}{v} \rightarrow g_K^* = \dfrac{\overset{*}{m}_{FF}}{K^*}$

$r \equiv g - \dfrac{(1-\alpha)s}{v} \rightarrow r \equiv \dfrac{\overset{\vee}{m}_{FF}}{K} - \dfrac{m_{FW} - m_{WF}}{K}$

Kalecki's principle

Kalecki's principle, distinct from an equilibrium condition, is our third fundamental relation:

$$r = g_K - \frac{(1-\alpha)s}{v} = g_K - \frac{(1-\alpha)sr}{\alpha} \equiv \frac{\mathring{m}_{FF}}{K} - \frac{m_{HW} - m_{WF}}{K} \qquad (7\text{--}5)$$

where g_k is the rate of growth of capital which is the consequence of entrepreneurs' decisions and generally will differ from g_K^*. Solow's assumptions about
profit and wages are the consequence of assuming a Cobb-Douglas production
function. But nothing prevents us from sharing the same assumptions for the
sake of comparison even if there is no such Cobb-Douglas production function in our approach. Starting from this common environment let's see how
the story told by Solow and that adopted by our monetary analysis completely
diverge.

Solow takes for granted the existence of a "market for labour". Wage-earners
are assumed to have the same prerogatives as entrepreneurs except that they
supply labour services and demand commodities while entrepreneurs do the
reverse. Walras's Law rules the roost; condition of equilibrium in the labour
market is:

$$n = g_K = \frac{(\alpha + (1-\alpha)s)}{v} = \frac{(\alpha + (1-\alpha)s)r}{\alpha} \qquad (7\text{--}6S)$$

where n is the exogenous rate of growth of the labour supply.

The dynamic general equilibrium (steady-state) is unique: $g_K^* = n$, $v^* \equiv \frac{\alpha}{r^*}$.
No involuntary unemployment is possible. Moreover, if the rate of accumulation
of capital g_k would be different from g_K^*, this would trigger a process of adjustment such that g_k would go back to g_K^* and v to v^*. If $g_k > g_K^*$ (resp. $g_k < g_k^*$)
capital grows faster (less) than income so that v increases (decreases) and r
decreases (increases) consequently. In both cases $g_k \rightarrow g_K^*$ and $v \rightarrow v^*$ when
$(t) \rightarrow \infty$.

Our monetary analysis tells a different story. Instead of adding to relations
(7–2) to (7–4) an equilibrium condition in the (non-existent) market for labour,
$g_K^* = n$, condition (7–6S) becomes, due to Restricted Walras's Law (RWL):

$$0 \le g_K^* \le n \qquad (7\text{--}6K)$$

Consequently, there is a continuum of general equilibria $g_K^* \in [0, n]$ satisfying
condition:

$$g_K^* = \frac{(\alpha + (1-\alpha)s)}{v} = \frac{(\alpha + (1-\alpha)s)r}{\alpha} \qquad (7\text{--}7)$$

All equilibria are characterized by involuntary unemployment steady-states
$g_u = n - g_K^*$, full-employment being the exception.

Proposition 16

Steady-states with involuntary unemployment are the rule; full-employment steady-state is a special case

The aforementioned is the transposition to steady-states of the reasoning presented above in the static case. Here also the absence of any "market for labour" – wage relationship precludes the existence of such a market – is the necessary condition for Proposition 16 but not a sufficient one. As effective demand theory is an additional (and sufficient) condition for Keynes (Proposition 14), here what is needed is a determination of the effective rate of growth g_k. The rate of growth of capital rules the roost, not the exogenous rate of growth of labour as for Solow's version.

Selection of an equilibrium in the continuum $g_K^* \in [0, n]$ depends on the rate of growth of capital g_k which determines the rate of profit. To keep the story simple, we adopt a basic idea: the amount of investment depends positively on the expected profits (Keynes's animal spirits) and negatively on an exogenous constant G which may be interpreted as a public investment:

$$\check{m}_{FF} = \varpi \pi^e - G \tag{7–8}$$

Dividing (7–8) by K gives:

$$g_K = \varpi r^e - \overline{g} \leftrightarrow r^e = \frac{g_K + \overline{g}}{\varpi} \tag{7–9}$$

The rate of growth of capital g_k is decided by entrepreneurs on the basis of the expected rate of profit r^e such that for $r^e \leq \dfrac{\overline{g}}{\varpi}$ entrepreneurs do not invest.

Equilibrium is obtained for $r = r^e$, at the intersection of the two curves of (7–7) rewritten as:

$$r = \frac{\alpha}{\alpha + (1-\alpha)s} g$$

and (7.9)

$$r^e = \frac{1}{\varpi} g_K + \frac{1}{\varpi} \overline{g}$$

Equilibrium values are respectively:

$$g_K^* = \frac{\alpha + (1-\alpha)s}{\alpha \varpi - (\alpha + (1-\alpha)s)} \overline{g}$$

$$r^* = \frac{\alpha}{\alpha \varpi - (\alpha + (1-\alpha)s)} \overline{g}$$

It is easy to get the conditions on $\bar{g}$ and ϖ:

$$0 \le g_K^* \le n \leftrightarrow g \ge 0 \quad \frac{\alpha + (1-\alpha)s}{\alpha} \le \varpi \le \left(\frac{\alpha + (1-\alpha)s}{\alpha}\right)\left(\frac{\bar{g}+n}{n}\right)$$

Figure 7.1 illustrates the point.

What is worth noticing here is the difference between the stories respectively told by Solow and by a monetary analysis. In our approach, the exogenous rate of growth of (wage-earners) population no longer determines the steady-state rate of growth (the equilibrium condition $g_K^* = n$ is irrelevant due to the wage-earners' special constraint). The steady-state rate of growth is fixed instead by the rate of accumulation of capital (which depends on entrepreneurs' animal spirits amongst other variables). If this rate of accumulation is less than n involuntary unemployment grows at an equilibrium rate $g_u = n - g_K^*$. This result is by no means due to a special assumption about technique (as it is too commonly maintained in textbooks). It comes only from the causality implicit in the model: the rate of growth of capital (instead of n) is an independent variable which rules the roost. Steady-state rates of growth of employment and output must be adjusted to g_k and not to n so that $\frac{K}{N}$ appears to be constant (and $\frac{K}{Y}$ as well). Capital output ratio and capital per capita are, however, flexible: at each level of steady-state rate of growth of involuntary unemployment

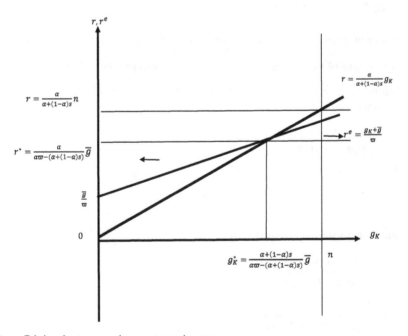

Figure 7.1 Involuntary employment steady-states

corresponds a determined $\dfrac{K}{N}$ and $\dfrac{K}{Y}$, respectively greater and lower than their full-employment steady-state values.

Not only full-employment equilibrium is a special case but all equilibria may be unstable as Harrod taught us long ago.

Disequilibrium dynamics: Harrod's razor-edge

From Kalecki's principle (Proposition 15 above) and monetary subordination of wage-earners it is possible to derive Harrod's razor-edge argument conditional to our assumption about ϖ.

Entrepreneurs' decisions about capital accumulation are the independent variable. They take the lead as a consequence of their exclusive eligibility for the minting process. Keep assuming that their decisions are governed by their animal spirits, another way of saying that they require or expect a given level of the rate of profit. The level of the effective rate of growth of capital is given by (7–9) $g_k k = \varpi r^e - \bar{g}$.

If, by accident, $g_k k$ coincides with the equilibrium rate of growth of capital g_K^*, we have $r = r^e$ and we get a steady-state rate of growth with a steady-state of growth of involuntary unemployment:

$$g_{IU} = n - g_K^* = n - \frac{\alpha + (1-\alpha)s}{\alpha\varpi - (\alpha + (1-\alpha)s)}\bar{g} \qquad (7\text{–}10)$$

If, for any reason, $g_k k(t)$ is greater (respectively smaller) than g_K^*, we have, following Kalecki's principle: $r - r^e > 0$ (respectively $r - r^e < 0$). It seems reasonable to assume that $g_K'(t)$ will be positive (respectively negative). If windfall profits generate optimistic views about the future, entrepreneurs will accelerate (decelerate) accumulation when the effective rate of profit is greater (smaller) than expected.

More precisely, we have:

$$r(t) - r^e(t) = \frac{\alpha\varpi - [\alpha + (1-\alpha)s]}{\varpi[\alpha + (1-\alpha)s]}g_K - \frac{\bar{g}}{\varpi} \qquad (7\text{–}11)$$

Let's assume that entrepreneurs modify their rate of accumulation according to:

$$g_K'(t) = \lambda[r(t) - r^e(t)] = \lambda\frac{\alpha\varpi - [\alpha + (1-\alpha)s]}{\varpi[\alpha + (1-\alpha)s]}g_K - \frac{\lambda}{\varpi}\bar{g} \quad \lambda > 0 \quad (7\text{–}12)$$

We have thus:

$$g_K'(t) = \lambda A g_K(t) - \frac{\lambda}{\varpi}\bar{g} \qquad \lambda A > 0 \qquad (7\text{–}13)$$

with $A = \dfrac{\alpha\varpi - \left[\alpha + (1-\alpha)s\right]}{\varpi\left[\alpha + (1-\alpha)s\right]}$; $g_K^* = \dfrac{1}{A\varpi}\,\overline{g}$.

The general solution is:

$$g_K(t) = \left(\frac{g_K(0) - g_K^*}{g_K(0)}\right)e^{\lambda A t}g_K(0) + g_K^* \qquad (7\text{--}14)$$

The equation (7–14) generates unstable trajectories. Any initial disequilibrium tends to increase explosively. In Figure 7.1, the arrows show the direction of the evolution of the rate of growth of capital according to the sign of the disequilibrium. Equilibrium is clearly unstable. The steady-state g_K^* exhibits a razor-edge property as Harrod explained it eighty years ago.

If an exogenous shock at $t = 0$ changes entrepreneurs' animal spirits such that $(g_K(0) - g_K^*) > 0$ (resp. $(g_K(0) - g_K^*) < 0$) the economy will never return to an equilibrium position and would grow (decrease) exponentially without economic limits. The equations above express a very fundamental property of a monetary economy with entrepreneurs and wage-earners. The reason for that razor-edge property is very simple. Having the ability to decide their expenses, entrepreneurs as a whole indirectly decide their receipts since for them investment ($\overset{\smile}{m}_{FF}$) is at the same time an expense and a receipt.

Kalecki's principle, as we know, is the straightforward consequence of the monetary subordination of wage-earners. It does not mean that entrepreneur h has the capacity to increase his/her own profit by spending more. By spending more, entrepreneur h increases profits of entrepreneur k instead. Decentralization (and competition associated to it) excludes that entrepreneurs may be able to act as a unique centre of decision. The diverse amounts of dollars spent by entrepreneurs are determined by their own and particular expectations (under the constraint of the minting process). But it may also happen that the expectations of all entrepreneurs may move together from pessimism to optimism (or the other way round).

That strong instability of a monetary economy with entrepreneurs raises many problems. The most obvious we have to address is: why is it that such economies do not disappear in the real world? What are the "laws of regulation" which prevent real economies from exploding or from shrinking to zero?

No clear and wide accepted answer is so far available from economic theory. Common sense, however, suggests that our economies keep working not thanks to a providential self-regulating social mechanism called "the market" or "the law of supply and demand" but more likely thanks to conscious efforts in finding appropriate reactions through a process of trials and errors. In this process many kinds of factors intervene which are not all economic in their principle. It would be beyond the scope of this essay to discuss this very complex matter further. We will content ourselves with a quick application of the viability approach to that question.

Economists are often interested in asymptotic global stability. This is an immediate consequence of a philosophical stance: what matters is to demonstrate that market forces drive society toward the greatest happiness, *i.e.* that a Pareto-optimal equilibrium or steady-state is "around the corner". Two reasons at least make this view rather uninteresting. The first one is that asymptotic global stability will remain for long an unsettled problem in economic theory. The second one is that this problem is not relevant. Capitalist economies are not generally in equilibrium and the concern is less about the long term but about what is going on *hic et nunc*. Moreover, the fact that they are not in equilibrium does not necessarily put their existence into danger. Capitalist economies exist and evolve thanks to their institutional setting which provides many possibilities of adjustment and corrections to disequilibrium. The problem is less to tend toward Pareto situations in the very long run than to overcome the many problems which appear at any time due to the decentralized organization of our economies. We have maintained above that the monetary system and constrained payments have a very important role to play. Clearly monetary authorities are more interested to keep economies smoothly working than to look after an improbable Heaven. For these reasons economists should change their mind and try a viability approach to their problems of dynamics.

The point is not whether economy is in equilibrium but whether evolution away from equilibrium is compatible with the fundamental requirements and ordinary rules of the economy. It then becomes natural to specify the minimal conditions under which an economy can work and check if the dynamic evolution of the economy does not violate these conditions. Given the very elementary model we refer to, these conditions here are a little bit arbitrary. For the sake of simplicity (more than of relevance) we assume that the rate of growth must not be negative but not higher than the rate of growth of population (in order to avoid recourse to too much foreign labour). Formally, the constraint is: $0 \leq g_k(t) \leq n$.

As an economy evolves according to a determinate institutional setting, it is possible to specify a control variable which may influence evolution of $g_k(t)$ over time. Let $\gamma = \dfrac{\lambda}{\varpi} \bar{g}$ be the control which can be moved by the authority or regulator taking into account the value of the state variable. Modifications of γ are assumed to be subject to constraints. For institutional reasons there is some viscosity in the changes of γ. Formally, we assume limited speeds of variation: $-c \leq \gamma'(t) \leq c$. Following Aubin (1997, pp. 46–48), we have the system:

$$g_K'(t) = bg_K(t) - \gamma \qquad \lambda A = b > 0$$
$$-c \leq \gamma'(t) \leq c$$

(7–15)

subject to:

$$0 \leq g_K(t) \leq n$$

Note that instead of a unique equilibrium, the economy exhibits a locus of managed equilibria $g^{K^{**}} = g^{K^*} + \dfrac{\gamma}{b}$ where the economy is in equilibrium although entrepreneurs have not found the right rate of growth of investment. Thanks to the action of the authority – Steuart would have said the statesman – a steady-state exists for any admissible level of γ.

The system above may be written as:

$$g'_K(t) = -\gamma$$
$$-c \leq \gamma'(t) \leq c$$

(7–16)

subject to:

$$0 \leq g_K(t) \leq n$$

with $g_K^{**} = g_K + \dfrac{\gamma}{b}$.

The problem viability theory deals with is to find viable subsets S of the constraint set $\aleph$ defined by $0 \leq g_K(t) \leq n$ where a viable evolution is always possible, i.e., subsets S satisfying the following viability property: for all $(g_K(0), \gamma(0)) \in S$ there exists a state-control solution $(g_K(t), \gamma(t))$ of control system above starting at $(g_K(0), \gamma(0)) \in S$ and satisfying $0 \leq g_K(t) \leq n$ for any $(t) > 0$.

In plain terms, we are looking for all the pairs $(g_K(0), \gamma(0))$ from which it is possible through an appropriate action on γ (satisfying constraints imposed on the speed of change) to keep over time the economy into the constraint set $\aleph$. If there exists such a non–empty subset S of $\aleph$ it does not mean that the economy will always survive for all (t) but only that it is always possible to keep a chance to survive.

The figure below, borrowed from Aubin,[1] shows the viability kernel of our simple economy, i.e. the greatest S satisfying viability property. It is delimited by curves H and L which are such that at each point maximum variation of γ allows the economy to keep evolving inside $\aleph$.

Directions of the trajectories without any change of γ are shown by the arrows which exhibit the intrinsic instability of the system (razor-edge). Instability may be mitigated by an active policy of the authority but there is no guarantee of success. While the economy keeps evolving into the viability kernel it is possible for the authority to keep alive the system even if nothing ensures that it will find the appropriate values of the control.

According to the graph, below (above) the managed equilibrium locus, a cumulative process of growth leads the economy toward its higher (lower) sustainable frontier n (0) along the curve $L(H)$ γ rising (decreasing) at its maximum velocity such that the economy keeps being viable. The viability kernel displays all the couples (rate of growth of capital, γ) for which there exists at least one solution for maintaining the economy in a sustainable situation.

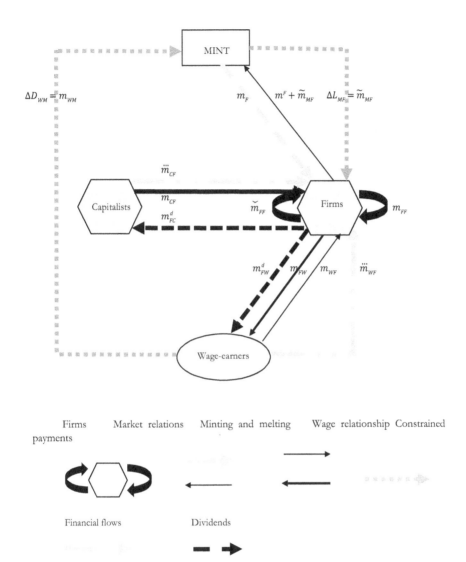

Figure 7.2 Global circulation in a capitalist economy

Outside the viability kernel nothing can be done except radically changing the rules of the game.

More than a technical innovation in the tools of economic dynamics, the viability approach obliges us to change our minds and our views about economic regulation.

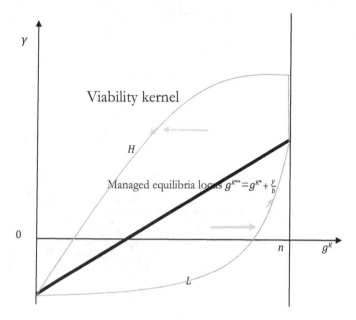

Figure 7.3 Graph viability kernel

From entrepreneur economy to finance

So far we have limited our description to a market economy in which a hierarchical relation between entrepreneurs and wage-earners deeply modifies the properties generally attributed to exchange relations. Now we introduce two forms of rights to profits, *i.e.* to forms of property over firms. One is that of entrepreneurs, assumed to be non-marketable, while the other, marketable, is that of a special group of owners, the capitalists. In order to complete our presentation of an entrepreneur economy, we will briefly sketch a description of a capitalist economy. However, we do not intend to present a fully-fledged theory of capitalism. We will limit ourselves to showing how it is possible to give a self-contained description of a capitalist economy relying exclusively on monetary magnitudes and exhibiting some properties which are out of reach of mainstream economic theory. We are just aiming at extending a little bit further what has been said until now. So far, Kalecki's principle and involuntary unemployment steady-states or equilibria rely on the specificity of a wage relationship as compared with exchange. Viability theory could be applied to dynamics since effective out-of-equilibrium situations could be dealt with. Now we intend to take into consideration not only new flows-of-funds (payment of dividends by firms to capitalists) but also the balance-sheets. This implies to introduce real and financial assets and to make precise the ownership of capital. A huge accumulation of real and financial assets is characteristic of capitalism. Even if it is possible to get the important properties above without assuming assets (assuming circulating capital is sufficient), it is necessary to integrate them in a basic description of a capitalist economy.

Real and financial assets

Entrepreneurs are not merely independent producers of a pure market economy producing without the help of other people. They produce openly, not to be recognized as individuals only but as profit-earners. Production in a pure market economy is the only means to get one's own preferred commodities, and production in a market economy with wage-earners is the only means to become richer, that is, to increase one's own wealth by profits.[2]

When firms are owned by entrepreneurs only, they get all the profits realized during the accounting period. Property rights may take also the convenient form of marketable equities, each equity giving the right to get a proportional amount of profit. For the sake of clarity and simplicity we will assume (a) that entrepreneurs' rights of property over the firms are not marketable while equities may be bought and sold in financial markets and (b) that equities owners form a special group called *capitalists*.

Definition 3

Capitalists own a fraction of the firms but they do not run any activity; equities are their exclusive titles to get part of the total profit.

The rationale for the existence of financial markets may be summed up by the word "liquidity" but, at a deeper level, it is the specific logic of production in an entrepreneur economy which matters.

In a pure market economy each individual may be said to maximize his own activity (total amount of receipts under a payment constraint). By contrast, in a market economy with a wage relationship, another rationality prevails. Entrepreneurs are supposed to search for a maximum of profit given the total capital of the enterprises they run. In principle every entrepreneur is eligible for the same rate of profit. Entrepreneurs are not chasing after some specified commodities, as it is the case for an independent producer in a pure market economy, but only after the greater amount of profit. Profit is compared to the amount of wealth (potentially source of new means of payment) which may be engaged. The rate of profit, the ratio of profit to total capital, is the strategic variable. The right to get the profit is what matters. That right is attached to the ownership of firms.

Hypothesis 5 (active individuals own the firms they run) now has to be relaxed.

Hypothesis 6

Firms are owned by entrepreneurs and by capitalists who hold equities giving a right to dividends

The way commodities and assets are evaluated differs in a market and in a capitalist economy.[3] Following the logic of capital, any economic object is valued according to the amount of future profit one expects from it. Commodities have been defined supra. Assets will be defined now. Assets are durable commodities. An apparent difficulty is that assets and commodities are not evaluated with the same accuracy.

The fact that evaluation of assets in balance-sheets, either real or financial, is arbitrary by contrast with that of flows-of-funds accounts seems a striking difficulty to overcome. Flows of payment are effective. Transfers of monetary units are performed and well attested, giving a high credibility and objectivity to accrual accounts. By contrast, assets displayed in balance-sheets are priced according to conventional rules, all subject to a strong and decisive objection. This is true of the two alternative basic rules: historical cost and "marked to market". Evaluating assets at their historical cost is hardly justifiable: such an evaluation has no clear relation to amounts of units of account the holder of these assets may hope to get from their sale in the market (when they are marketable). Choosing "marked to market" instead is no more convincing. That last evaluation reflects what may be observed in the market but not what the sale of the assets would yield to their owners: selling all these assets would probably produce a deep variation of their prices and would bring a market evaluation very different from the value observed prior to the sale. Moreover a fraction of the assets are not marketable. There is no theoretical solution to that problem and we must accept that accounting conventions are part of our economic reality as we have noticed in our introduction to a monetary analysis.[4]

Two further problems are (a) to define assets without any reference to physical properties of commodities and (b) to distinguish between real and financial assets. While commodities are defined by the expenses of the individual who produces them, assets are defined by the present value of the future net flows they are expected to yield to their owner until their maturity. A general expression for an asset observed at $t = 0$ is: $y \dfrac{1 - \left(\dfrac{1}{1+r}\right)^t}{I}$ if y is the constant (to keep the story simple) amount of net future flow per period, (t) is the number of periods and i the rate of interest used as a rate of actualization.

An asset is said to be a *real asset* if the expected future flow is a net profit ($y = \pi$). At $t = 0$, a real asset is $\pi \dfrac{1 - \left(\dfrac{1}{1+i}\right)^t}{i}$. If $t = 1$ we have a circulating capital $\dfrac{\pi}{1+i}$; if $t \to \infty$ a real asset is described by: $\dfrac{\pi}{i}$. Real assets are assumed not to be marketable (no second-hand markets). As a consequence (t) is the number of periods a firm has to hold the real assets whose value are written in the balance-sheet, the accrual accounts recording only successive amortization, not sales. If a real asset is produced by firm h, its amount being m_h, $\dfrac{\pi_k}{1+i}$ is the relevant definition for an individual k who desired to buy it as circulating

capital and $\pi \dfrac{1-\left(\dfrac{1}{1+i}\right)^t}{i}$ if it is as a real asset. To take this into account, we have to make our definition more precise: if individual k is concerned, the circulating capital (input) is $\dfrac{\pi_k}{1+i}$, and the flow of payment which corresponds to the purchase of $\dfrac{\pi_k}{1+i}$ by k to h is: m_{kh}; for real assets in general we have respec-

tively $\pi_k \dfrac{1-\left(\dfrac{1}{1+i}\right)^t}{i}$ and $\check{m}_{kh}$. At equilibrium (a special case indeed), the usual

equality holds: $\displaystyle\sum_k \pi_{kh} \dfrac{1-\left(\dfrac{1}{1+i}\right)^t}{i} = \overset{\text{``demand''}}{\sum_k \check{m}_{kh}} = \overset{\text{``supply''}}{\widetilde{m}_h}$, with π_{kh} being the profit

expected by k and i is equal to the marginal efficiency (or internal) rate of

return of capital h. $\displaystyle\sum_k \pi_{kh} \dfrac{1-\left(\dfrac{1}{1+i}\right)^t}{i}$ is the total flow of payment for acquiring

the real asset produced by h (its "demand"),m_h being its quantity (its "supply"). For the sake of simplicity we will assume that $t \to \infty$ so that a real asset is $\dfrac{\pi_{kh}}{i}$. Total real assets are $K = \displaystyle\sum_h \dfrac{\pi_h}{i}$.

An asset is said to be a *financial asset* if the expected future flow is made of interests or dividends ($y = q_C\pi$) plus the expected future price (financial assets are assumed to be marketable). The quantity of \$ representing a financial asset is: $E(t) = \dfrac{q_C\pi + E^e(t+1)}{1+i}$ where $E^e(t+1)$ is the expected future price. Financial assets are liquid: they may be bought and sold at any time (no constraint on t by contrast with real assets). Therefore it would be useful to distinguish between newly issued financial assets from existing assets whose dividend or interest payment is due by firm to a capitalist different from the initial buyer. Operations on existing financial assets do not affect their total quantity by contrast with those on newly issued financial assets. But we will not enter in these subtleties far beyond the modesty of our purpose.

Real and financial are the components of capital. Opposing real and financial assets is reminiscent of Keynes and the difference he emphasized on enterprise and casino.

An actualized version of the minting process is in order.

The minting process

The mere possibility to pay back interest has raised many controversies among some partisans of a monetary analysis: how is it possible to pay back to the bank more than the quantity of money issued? This seems to contradict the idea of decentralization which implies, as seen above, that current payments are not financed by current receipts. But this is not the case! Interest earned by the banks are spent exactly as other types of income are, providing the additional receipts that allows people to pay the interest. There is no mystery, no enigma here! Observing that a given quantity of money available during a period (between minting and melting) may finance a greater (lesser) amount of transfers is nothing but observing a velocity of circulation higher (lower) than one!

If for the sake of simplicity we assume that velocity of circulation of money when used between individuals is equal to one, the overall velocity of circulation of money is, if m_{MF} is the amount of expenditures of the Mint (banks included) to firms (and m_{FM}^d the amount of dividend (or interests) paid by the firms to the Mint): $\dfrac{\mu + m_{FM}^d}{\mu} = \dfrac{\mu + m_{MF}}{\mu}$. When entrepreneurs and wage-earners are distinct, the means of payment are issued through credits. Legal money is now issued by banks working under the control of a monetary authority. By contrast with a pure market economy, means of payment are issued by a monetization of *capital*.[5] Minting modifies the total amount of means of payment by contrast with operations which take place between individuals which alter their distribution only.

The minting process in a capitalist economy is well documented. It may be useful to refer, among others, to what may be found in the *Quarterly Bulletin of the Bank of England* (2014 Q1) under the title "Money Creation in the modern economy".

> In the modern economy, most money takes the form of bank deposits. But how those bank deposits are created is often misunderstood: the principal way is through commercial banks making loans. Whenever a bank makes a loan, it simultaneously creates a matching deposit in the borrower's bank account, thereby creating new money.

The reality of how money is created today differs from the description found in some economics textbooks:

- Rather than banks receiving deposits when households save and then lending them out, bank lending creates deposits.
- In normal times, the central bank does not fix the amount of money in circulation, nor is central bank money 'multiplied up' into more loans and deposits.

Although commercial banks create money through lending, they cannot do so freely without limit. Banks are limited in how much they can lend if they are to remain profitable in a competitive banking system. Prudential regulation also acts as a constraint on banks' activities in order to maintain the resilience of the financial system. And the households and companies who receive the money created by new lending may take actions that affect the stock of money – they could quickly 'destroy' money by using it to repay their existing debt, for instance.

(p. 14)

We completely endorse that expert description of the modern minting process. We would like to complete it by linking it with the more general view about means of payment issuance presented above in Chapter Five. Transformation of wealth into means of payment (minting) and of means of payment into wealth (melting) is what takes place continuously in decentralized economies. In pure market economies (Chapter 6) wealth was assimilated to "gold" as the symbol of commodities whose monetization gives birth to legal money. In a capitalist economy, wealth takes the form of capital, *i.e.* of assets. The minting process, as described by the quotation above, makes it very clear as soon as credit is distinguished from financial operations and loans from financial assets.

In modern systems grounded on banks, the minting support is no longer gold but capital. A commercial bank convinced at period (0) that an individual will pay back $\dfrac{x}{i}\left(1-\left(\dfrac{1}{1+i}\right)^{t}\right)$ dollars at period (t), recognizes that this individual holds, at least, a capital of x dollars, the present value of $\dfrac{x}{i}\left(1-\left(\dfrac{1}{1+i}\right)^{t}\right)$ being x. Consequently, the bank is ready to lend him/her x dollars, *i.e.* "to coin" a fraction of his/her capital which amounts to x dollars. Banks proceed to that "coinage" under the supervision of an institution (the central bank) endowed with last lender capacity.

The asset which is the counterpart of the means of payment is not of type $E(t)=\dfrac{q_{C}\pi+E^{e}(t+1)}{1+i}$, which would assume that it is marketable. Capital, as a minting basis, is no more marketable than coined gold. The holder of legal coins must melt them in order to get back the gold they contain, the holder (commercial banks) of IOUs of borrowers (monetized capital) have to securitize them in order to sell them in the market. In both cases, institutional rules (legal price of gold) or entities (central bank fixing a "legal" rate of interest) prevent means of payment issuance from being a private affair. Minting is neither an exchange nor a purchase/sale. Means of payment cancellation requires either melting of legal coins or reimbursement of bank loans ("melting" of capital).

There are some evident differences between "gold" and "capital" as minting supports. The former is tangible, while the latter is volatile since it relies on private agreements under the control of a monetary authority. The markets for gold and for capital do not work along the same lines. But important as these differences may appear they do not prevent us from treating these two minting processes as two versions of a unitary theory of payment systems.

In a credit system demand deposits ("coined capital") circulate through checks or transfers. Checks and other instruments are means of payment, demand deposits are a fraction of capital coined as means of payment (acknowledged by the banks). At the end of the period, individuals pay back their credits cancelling the corresponding demand deposits ("melting" down the checks). Imbalances are settled by constrained financial operations (transfers of capital under diverse forms: new debts, LBO, mergers and acquisitions, etc.). New balance-sheets appear.

Firms are all eligible for the minting process. For the sake of clarity they are distinguished according to the type of operations they are dedicated to: production and real assets for the firms and financial assets for the capitalists. Of course such a distinction does not make sense from a realist point of view. But we are trying to provide less a realistic description of what happens in the "real word" than a conceptual framework to make the real world intelligible. What matters is the theoretical relevance of monetary analysis and not the particularities of an empirical description of real economies. Intelligibility is favoured at the expenses of realism.

A brief description of a simplified capitalist economy

"Simplified" here means that capitalists are treated as non-active individuals (they are not eligible for the minting process) and consequently have no more initiatives than wage-earners. What makes them differ from the latter is that their receipts from the firms are not costs since they are not necessary for the activity of the firms.

The description below is also a simplified one for obvious reasons. Our purpose is more illustrative than explicative. We intend mainly, at a first step, to extend Kalecki's principle to an economy where dividends are distributed and to give an example of viability approach applied to balance-sheets rather than to flows-of-funds as done above.

The following assumptions will help to maintain our story within reasonable limits.

1. Firms manage real assets (K) and pay dividends (respectively m_{FC}^d and m_{HW}^d) to the equities holders, capitalists (E_{CF}) and wage-earners (E_{WF}); capitalists and wage-earners buy new equities out of their saving, respectively $\ddot{m}_{CF}$ and $\ddot{m}_{WF}$

2. Wage-earners' unexpected saving is ΔD_{WM} by contrast with their normal saving $\ddot{m}_{WF}$

3. The Mint lends to firms as a counterpart of variation of wage-earners' balances ($\Delta L_{MF} = \Delta D_{WM} = \tilde{m}_{MF}$)

4. Loans by the Mint to the firms signal the possibly cumulated amount of (effective) disequilibria; they are constrained operations

5. The Mint do not get interests (no consumption, no saving) in order to avoid confusion between the minting process and the fact that the Mint is made of banks which get incomes and spend it

6. Capitalists and wage-earners have the same saving behaviour: $s_W = s_C = s$

Simple as it is the description below, however, differs from the current ones (and even sophisticated). Not only minting and melting are made explicit and the wage relationship is treated on a specific footing (wage-earners do not perform and do not need any constrained operation), but the economy is by no means supposed to be at equilibrium. Equilibrium is no longer a necessary condition for knowing the effective amounts of wealth. The fact that constrained operations are made explicit (even if they boil down in that simplified version to loans by the Mint as a lender of last resort) gives a sense to the dynamics of that economy. Starting from balance-sheets dressed at the beginning of the period (they are forward-looking), the diverse groups of individuals carry out their voluntary operations (described in the flows-of-funds accounts, in the payment matrix and represented in scheme of circulation). Coordination *a posteriori* makes appear the necessity of constrained operations which modify the relative position of these groups (backward-looking balance-sheets).

What has happened during the period prompts a change in the expectations and, at the very same point of time, forward-looking balance-sheets will be dressed again. They may reveal a more or less sharp gap depending on the reactions of entrepreneurs.

Here are the balance-sheets of our group of individuals at the beginning of a period:

Assets	Mint (Central bank *plus* banks)	Liabilities
L_{MF}	Loans	
	Demand deposits	D_{WM}
	Net Value	0

Assets	Firms	Liabilities
K	Real assets	
	Equities	$E_{CF} + E_{WF}$
	Loans	L_{MF}
	Net Value	NV_F

Assets	Capitalists	Liabilities
E_{CF}	Equities	
	Net Value	NV_C

Assets	Wage-earners	Liabilities
D_{WM}	Demand deposits	
E_{WF}	Equities	
	Net Value	NV_W

Figure 7.4 Balance-sheets beginning

The flows-of-funds diagram 3 describes the flows of payments of that economy.

These flows will bring about the following backward-looking balance-sheets.

On the basis of the above (simplified) description of a capitalist economy, two issues may be dealt with: Is Kalecki's principle still valid when the profits are partly or entirely distributed to capitalists? Is a dynamics of stocks analogous to a dynamics of flows?

Extension of Kalecki's principle to an economy with capitalists

It is true that Keynes's widow's cruse and Kalecki's principle are counterintuitive. They are not conceivable by mainstream theory based on interdependence

Table 7.2 Payment matrix in a capitalist economy

	Minting	I	...	H	...	Firms (total)	I	...	J	Capitalists (total)	Wage-earners	Total
Minting	0	$m_{MI} = \Delta L_{MI}$	...	$m_{MH} = \Delta L_{MH}$	...	m_{MF} $\tilde{m}_{MF} = \Delta L_{MF}$	0	...	0	0	0	$m_M + \tilde{m}_{MF}$
I	m_{MI}	0	...	m_{IH} $\check{m}_{IH}$	...	m_I $\check{m}_I$	m^d_{II}	...	m^d_{IJ}	m^d_I	m^d_{IW} m_{IW}	m_I
...	...	...	...	...	...	...	...	...	...	...	...	...
H	m_{HM}	m_{HI}	...	0	...	m_H $\check{m}_H$	m^d_{HI}	...	m^d_{HJ}	m^d_H	m^d_{HW} m_{HW}	m_H
Firms (total)	m^F	m_{FI}	...	m_{FH}	...	m_{FF} $\check{m}_{FF}$	m^d_{FI}	...	m^d_{FJ}	m^d_{FC}	m^d_{FW} m_{FW}	m_F
I		m_{c1I} $\dddot{m}_{c1I}$	...	m_{c1H} $\dddot{m}_{c1H}$	...	m_{c1F} $\dddot{m}_{c1F}$	0	...	0	0	0	m_{c1F} $\dddot{m}_{c1F}$
...		...	...	...	...	...	...	...	...	...	...	...
J		m_{cjI} $\dddot{m}_{cjI}$	...	m_{cjH} $\dddot{m}_{cjH}$	...	m_{cjF} $\dddot{m}_{cjF}$	0	...	0	0	0	m_{cjF} $\dddot{m}_{cjF}$
Capitalists (total)	m_{CM}	m_{cI} $\dddot{m}_{cI}$	...	m_{cH} $\dddot{m}_{cH}$	...	m_{CF} $\dddot{m}_{CF}$	−	...	−	−	0	m_{CF} $\dddot{m}_{CF}$
Wage-earners	$\tilde{m}_{WM} = \Delta D_{WM}$	m_{WI} $\tilde{m}_{WFI}$	...	m_{WH} $\tilde{m}_{WFH}$	...	m_{WF} $\tilde{m}_{WF}$	0	...	0	0	0	m_W
Total	$m^M = m^F + \tilde{m}_{WM}$	m^I	...	m^H	...	$m^F + \tilde{m}_{MF}$	0	...	0	m^c	m^w	μ

Assets	Mint (Central bank *plus* banks)	Liabilities
$L_{MF} + \Delta L_{MF}$	Loans	
	Demand deposits	$D_{WM} + \Delta D_{WM}$
	Net Value	0

Assets	Firms	Liabilities
$K + \tilde{m}_{FF}$	Real assets	
	Equities	$E_{CF} + \ddot{m}_{CF} + E_{WC} + \ddot{m}_{WF}$
m^d_{FC} or m^d_{FW}	Loans	$L_{MF} + \Delta L_{MF}$
	Net Value	$NV_F + \Delta NV_F$

Assets	Capitalists	Liabilities
$E_{CF} + \ddot{m}_{CF}$	Equities	
	Net Value	$NV_C + \Delta NV_C$

Assets	Wage-earners	Liabilities
$D_{WM} + \Delta D_{WM}$	Demand deposits	
$E_{WF} + \ddot{m}_{WF}$	Equities	
	Net Value	$NV_W + \Delta NV_W$

Figure 7.5 Balance-sheets backwards looking

and exclusivity of equilibrium situations. A monetary analysis, however, easily hosts these principles which are grounded on the primacy of expenses, which, in turn, makes sense only because access to means of payment – the minting process – is at the core of the theory. Does the introduction of capitalists, who receive dividends paid by firms out of their profits, weaken these principles?

The answer is no. Quite the opposite! The mere fact that firms have to pay a fraction of their profits to the holders of equities who own part of the firms far from diminishing the global amount of profit increases it! This needs some comments and a formal presentation.

When dividends are distributed the profits of the firms are reduced by $m^d_{FC} + m^d_{FW}$ but their receipts are increased by $m_{CF} = (1 - s)m^d_{FC}$ spent by the

Table 7.3 Flows accounts

Payments	Mint (central bank plus banks)	Receipts
	Demand deposits	ΔD_{Wm}
ΔL_{MF}	Loans	
m_F	Minting=Voluntary expenses	
$(-\tilde{m}_{MF})$	Melting=Spontaneous receipts + balances settlement	$m^F\left(+\tilde{m}_{MF}\right)$

Payments	Firms	Receipts
m_{FF}	Intermediary consumption	m_{FF}
m_{FW}	Wages	
$m_{FC}^d + m_{FW}^d$	Distributed profit	
$\check{m}_{FF}$	Real assets	m_{FF}
	Consumption	$m_{WF} + m_{CF}$
	Financial assets (equities)	$\dddot{m}_{CF} + \dddot{m}_{WF}$
$\tilde{m}_F$ (positive balance z')	Balances settlement	$\tilde{m}_F$ (negative balance z')

Payments	Capitalists	Receipts
m_{CF}	Consumption	
	Distributed profit	m_{FC}^d
$\dddot{m}_{CF}$	Financial assets (equities)	

Payments	Wage-earners	Receipts
	Wages	m_{FW}
m_{WF}	Consumption	
	Dividends	m_{FW}^d
$\dddot{m}_{WF}$	Equities	
ΔD_{WM}	Deposits	

capitalists and an additional $\Delta m_{WF} = (1 - s)m_{FW}^d$ spent by wage-earners; besides, the profits of capitalists rise by m_{FC}^d.

If q_C (respectively q_W) is the fraction of capital owned by capitalists (respectively wage-earners):

$$\Delta^\pi = ((1 - s)(q_C + q_W)\pi \tag{7–17}$$

Table 7.4 Extension of Kalecki's principle to an economy with capitalists

Δ_F^π	$-m_{FC}^d - m_{FW}^d + m_{CF} + (1-s)m_{FW}^d$
Δ_C^π	m_{FC}^d
Δ_W^π	m_{FW}^d
Total $\Delta\pi$	$(1-s)\left(m_{FC}^d + m_{FW}^d\right)$

It is easy to check that

$$\frac{\Delta^\pi}{\pi} = \left((1-s)(q_C + q_W)\right) > 0 \qquad (7\text{–}18)$$

There is thus no mystery in the generalized Kalecki's principle. What entrepreneurs spend amongst them do not correspond to costs since these expenses are not wages and are receipts at the same time. What entrepreneurs pay to capitalists is not a cost either but a fraction of their profits. Part of these profits are consumed and give additional sales. To that extent, a distribution of profits tends to increase them. The same reasoning holds for wage-earners when it is about dividends but not about wages since wages are a pure cost.

Kalecki's principle extended, as Kalecki's principle itself, holds valid only for the firms taken as a whole. Obviously, for any firm considered in isolation, the distribution of a fraction of its profits do not change its global amount. But the economy has to be studied with all its inter-relations. The payment matrix is very useful to make understood this very basic point.

Let's see more formally what this is about.

To make the story simple we assume $\Delta L_{MF} = \Delta D_{WM} = \tilde{m}_{MF} = 0$ postponing the effective out-of-equilibrium situations to the study of dynamics.

Profits are equal to: total nonfinancial receipts *minus* total costs (for the firms as a whole, costs are nothing but wages and distribution of dividends). We have:

$$\pi_F = \check{m}_{FF} + m_{WF} + m_{CF} - m_{FW} - m_{FC}^d$$
$$\pi_C = m_{FC}^d$$
$$\pi_W = m_{FW}^d$$
$$\pi = \check{m}_{FF} - s(m_{FW} + m_{FW}^d) + (1-s)m_{FC}^d + m_{FW}^d \qquad (7\text{–}19)$$

Define total income y as

$$y \equiv \check{m}_{FF} + m_{WF} + m_{CF} = \underbrace{\check{m}_{FF}}_{investment} + \overbrace{(1-s)\left(m_{FW} + m_{FC}^d + m_{FW}^d\right)}^{consumption}$$

$$\overbrace{\check{m}_{FF} - sm_{HW} + (1-s)(m^d_{FC} + m^d_{HW})}^{profit} + \overbrace{m_{HW}}^{wages}$$

$$\underbrace{\check{m}_{FF}}_{investment} = \pi + s\overbrace{\left(m_{HW} + m^d_{FC} + m^d_{HW}\right)}^{saving} \tag{7-20}$$

Assume

$$m^d_{FC} = q_C\pi \text{ and } m^d_{HW} = q_W\pi \tag{7-21}$$

with q_C and q_W being respectively the fraction of total capital K owned by capitalists and the wage-earners.

Total profit may be rewritten as:

$$\pi = \check{m}_{FF} - sm_{HW} + \left((1-s)(q_C + q_W)\right)\pi \tag{7-22}$$

so that:

$$\pi = \frac{\check{m}_{FF} - sm_{HW}}{1 - \left((1-s)(q_C + q_W)\right)} \tag{7-23}$$

The global rate of profit is thus:

$$\frac{\pi}{K} = r = \frac{g_K}{1 - \left((1-s)(q_C + q_W)\right)} - \frac{(1-\alpha)s}{\alpha\left[1 - \left((1-s)(q_C + q_W)\right)\right]}r \to r = \eta g_K \tag{7-24}$$

with $\eta = \dfrac{\alpha}{\alpha\left[1 - \left((1-s)(q_C + q_W)\right)\right] + (1-\alpha)s} > \dfrac{\alpha}{\alpha + (1-\alpha)s}$ which is the slope of the relation between the rate of profit and the rate of growth of capital when there are entrepreneurs only and no capitalists.

The mere existence of a dividends distribution to a special group or class of capital owners – the capitalists – modifies the level of the global rate of profit. Kalecki's principle – a cornerstone of Keynes's economics – is now extended to encompass dividends.

Proposition 17

Entrepreneurs earn what they spend and what they distribute as dividends (less saving out of wages and dividends); capitalists and wage-earners spend what they earn

Figure 7.6 below shows how that extension of Kalecki's principle affects Harrod's razor-edge argument.

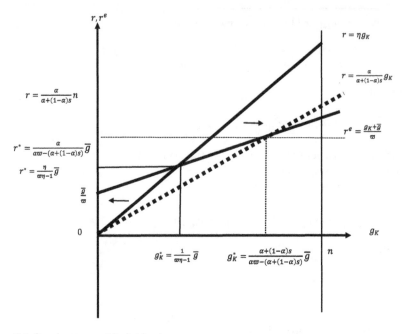

Figure 7.6 Steady-states with dividends

The extension of Kalecki's principle to an economy with capitalists, with $\eta > 1$:

1 modifies the zones from which explosive trajectories may start; it increases the zones of explosive expansions and decreases the zone of contractions.
2 reduces the equilibrium rate of profit and level of the steady-state rate of growth, as a consequence of the multiplicative effect of the distribution of dividends ($s < 1$).

Voluntary and constrained operations

In a decentralized economy, active individuals are supposed to spend according to their desires and expectations (under the constraint of the minting process) – an assumption less demanding and rewarding than the usual utility maximization program! – which does mean that payees always accept these payments. This is obvious in the case of purchases/sales where payments are nothing but the usual consequence of a contract between the buyer and the seller. This holds also for wage payments even if mutual agreements are the effect of a *sui generis* relation due to unequal spaces of available strategies. When it comes to real and financial assets, the assumption above is less obvious. We will admit, however, for the sake of simplicity that assets are issued or created on demand so that payees' acceptation of payments is trivial.

As we have already noted, from the fact that payments are voluntary and accepted it does not follow that voluntary payments m_h are equal to the receipts m^h. Decentralization is responsible for inequalities to be the general case for any individual even if, at the level of the economy, total receipts are identically equal to total receipts.

Mediation of money, another term for decentralization in our societies, does not allow active individuals to master *ex ante* their budgetary constraint but obliges them to respect it *ex post*. An entrepreneur experiencing a deficit at the end of the period (market) may incur bankruptcy if he/she cannot pay back the bank or any of his/her mature debt. He/she can square his/her accounts only if some excess individual is willing to lend what is necessary to cover the deficit or if the bank accepts to report that debt to next period. Note that only active individuals – independent producers or firms – are concerned by bankruptcy. Wage-earners are not submitted to that commercial law.

Squaring of accounts leads to unexpected and constrained operations. That does not mean that active individuals do not agree to realize them; they may opt for bankruptcy and disappear. In order to avoid the spiny problem of bankruptcy, we have assumed that no firm or independent producer will choose bankruptcy, which amounts to only dealing with viable economies. (Hypothesis 1, Chapter 5)

However it is still necessary to distinguish the squaring operations from the voluntary ones which is why we will call them constrained to make it clear that they are performed as an alternative to economic death. What has been said above (Chapter 5) about such operations in pure market economies holds valid here with a qualification. Means of payment being issued by means of capital minting, their cancellation is also realized by transfers of capital (the minting basis), that is by a restructuration of capital at the end of the period. Loans of excess to deficit agents perform transfers of capital between them, transfers which are observed in the balance-sheets dressed at the closure of the period. These operations take place in the markets for financial assets, either directly from lenders to borrowers or with an intermediation of banks and specialized institutions. The complexity of financial operations is such that they cannot be detailed in a simple table. They will appear there as a variation of wealth $\Delta\omega_h$ so that $\sum_h \Delta\omega_h \equiv 0$.

Variations of wealth are the straightforward consequences of the settlement of balances (or the postponement of it). It is a source of great astonishment to realize that mainstream economic theory, in accordance with the real analysis, leaves absolutely no room for that aspect of economic life which is, however, recognized as primal in official reports on the world economy (IMF, OECD or BIS reports, for example). The reason for that incredible failure is simple: it is entirely the unavoidable consequence of the exclusive attention to equilibrium situations. By contrast, the so-called mercantilist tradition of the balance of accounts, as well as the neo-mercantilist flavour of official reports, give a large attention to these phenomena. From a purely theoretical point of view, Steuart's *Inquiry* appears as the outstanding reference.

In the simplified description of a capitalist economy given above, the only constrained operation is carried out by the Mint intervening as a lender of last resort. The Mint lends to the firms the "excess saving" of wage-earners who have unexpectedly increased their deposits (see Schema 6.3 Global money circulation in an entrepreneur economy). This creates a stock-disequilibrium dynamics.

A brief inquiry into stock-disequilibrium dynamics: viability once again

Instead of focusing on the gap between current expected receipts and effective expenditures, or between $g_k K$ and g_K, we will take into consideration how unexpected and *cumulated* deficits (or surplus) bring about not only flows disequilibria but also permanent situations of balance-sheets distortion.[6]

For the sake of simplicity, rewrite the condition of investment financing as:

$$\overbrace{\lambda y + \pi}^{\text{total saving}} = \overbrace{\check{m}_{FF}}^{\text{investment}} \tag{7-25}$$

where $(\lambda y = s\left(m_{BW} + m_{FC}^d + m_{BW}^d\right) = \lambda\left((1-\alpha)s + q_C + q_W\right)$ (see 7–20). The new expression for the equilibrium rate of growth is $g_K^* = \left(\dfrac{\lambda}{\alpha}+1\right)r$.

Introducing an out-of-equilibrium situation means, according to assumptions above:

$$\overbrace{\Delta L}^{\substack{\text{constrained} \\ \text{operation}}} + \lambda y + \pi = \check{m}_{FF} \tag{7-26}$$

Let $Z(t)$ be the cumulated gap between receipts and expenses or, which amounts to the same thing, the amount of *constrained* indebtedness (and accumulation) and define $Z'(t) = -\Delta L$. A positive $Z'(t)$ means that total voluntary saving $\lambda y + \pi$ is greater than voluntary investment. Firms' indebtedness involuntarily increases or, in other terms, firms' accumulation of capital is too low as compared to voluntary saving:

$$Z'(t) = \lambda y + \pi - \check{m}_{FF} \rightarrow \frac{Z'}{K}(t) = \frac{\lambda}{v} + r - g_K(t) \tag{7-27}$$

When effective saving exceeds investment (resp. investment exceeds saving), entrepreneurs experience unexpected losses (resp. windfall profits). What matters here is not only that, in conformity with Kalecki's principle, realized differ from expected profits (flows), but the consequence on the evolution of wealth (stocks).

Let define $z(t) = \dfrac{Z(t)}{K(t)}$. We have $z'(t) = \dfrac{Z'}{K}(t) - \dfrac{K'}{K}(t)\dfrac{Z}{K}(t)$. Finally:

$$z'(t) = g_K^* - g_K(t)\big(1 + z(t)\big) \tag{7-28}$$

Let's now assume that the rate of growth of capital decided by entrepreneurs depends not only on the animal spirits tempered by exogenous public investment as above (7–9), replaced here by the rate of interest (reflecting the crowding-out effect), but also on the gap observed between actual and desired wealth, that is:

$$g_K(t) = \varpi r^e - \lambda i - bz(t) = G\big(i(t)\big) - bz(t) \tag{7-29}$$

where b is the intensity of reaction to involuntary level of debt.

An excess of g_K over $\dfrac{\lambda}{\nu} + r$ creates a motive for an acceleration of accumulation but here what counts is not the flows but the stocks.

Combining the two equations leads to the following differential equation:

$$z'(t) = bz^2(t) + \big(b - G\big(i(t)\big)\big)z(t) + \big(g_K^* - G\big(i(t)\big)\big) \tag{7-30}$$

Solutions are:

$$z_1, z_2 = \frac{-\big(b - G(i)\big) \mp \sqrt[2]{\big(b - G(i)\big)^2 + 4b\big(G(i) - g_K^*\big)}}{2b} \tag{7-31}$$

If $\big(b - G(i)\big)^2 + 4b\big(G(i) - g_K^*\big) \geq 0$, which implies $g_K^* \leq \dfrac{\big(b + G(i)\big)^2}{4b}$, solutions are real numbers. Maximum g_K^* shows off if strict equality $g_K^* = \dfrac{\big(b + G(i)\big)^2}{4b}$ occurs. In this case, $z_1 = z_2 = \dfrac{G(i) - b}{2b}$.

It is interesting to study the influence of the choice of the parameter g_K^* (i being constant) on the position of the equilibria and on the monotonicity of z. For fixed z, the parameter providing the equilibrium solution is given by:

$$g_K^*(z) = -bz^2(t) - \big(b - G\big(i(t)\big)\big)z(t) + G\big(i(t)\big) \tag{7-32}$$

This function defines a parabola dividing the $z - g$-plane into two monotonic zones: below the parabola, $z'(t)$ is negative and above $z'(t)$ is positive (see Figure 7.7 Parabola).

The relative position of the curve $g_K^*(z)$ depends uniquely on $G(i)$ and b. When animal spirits are strong enough as compared with b, the parabola's maximum is at the right of the vertical axis $z = 0$ (in this example, g_K^* is at its maximum for $z = \dfrac{G(i) - b}{2b} > 0$, while balance-sheet equilibrium corresponds to a higher debt than expected. It stands to the left in the opposite case. In both cases, full equilibrium does not correspond to g_K^*. In other words, full equilibrium and full-employment ($g_{max} = n$) do not coincide except for $G(i) = b$ which corresponds to $z1 = z2 = 0$.

Below (above) the parabola, forces moving z are left-(right-)oriented. This means that all the points of the left (right) part of the curve form the locus of stable (unstable) equilibria.

As done above it is worth completing this preliminary observations with a viability study.

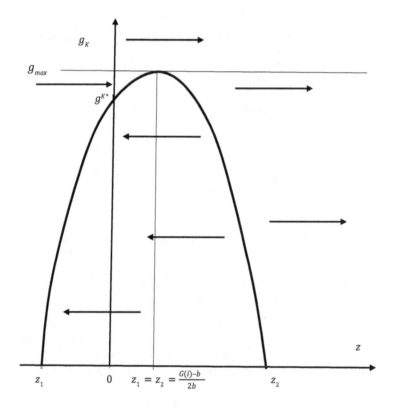

Graph

Figure 7.7 Parabola

We have seen in Chapters 5 and 6 that viability theory deals with dynamics in a way completely different from the view mostly adopted in economics. Some reasons have been invoked supra in favour of a change of perspective.

An additional reason to adopt a viability point of view is to be found in the special character of economic regulation. In the great tradition of political economy, the adjustment of some variables to disequilibria plays a prominent role. The so-called "law of supply and demand" states that prices react in a determined direction in response to a difference between supply and demand in the market: the price of a particular commodity is assumed to vary according to the sign of the excess demand of this commodity. Another famous law of adjustment concerns the variation of the quantity in reaction to the profitability of its production. For instance, in Walras's theory of production, the quantity varies according to the sign of the profit (sales minus costs). In our model, two variables are candidates to play this role: i and g_K. System (7–30) generates trajectories depending on i and g_K. It would seem natural to assume that g_K changes according to the sign of $z(t)$ as it is generally done. Despite the respectability of the tradition, we follow another track, the one we have adopted above when Harrod's razor-edge argument has been dealt with. Instead of reasoning with a law of adjustment *a priori* given, we fix limits to the speed of variation of the controls but *the sign of variation is not preassigned*. These limits are more or less narrow, depending on the flexibility of the system. Intuitively, to more flexible economies correspond wider viability domains or viability kernels. Thus, g_K supposed to vary within certain limits but without any *a priori* law of variation.[7]

Keeping our basic equation, we take g_K as the control over $z(t)$: entrepreneurs modify the rate of growth of capital accumulation taking in consideration the level of $z(t)$. The deviation to normal values of z must not exceed some determinate levels $\underline{z} \leq z(t) \leq \overline{z}$, otherwise the viability of economy would be put into question. We had some limits to the speed of adjustment: $-u \leq g_K'(t) \leq u$. These limits indicate the degree of flexibility of the economy, while the rate of growth of capital is constrained to remain in the interval: $\underline{g} \leq g_K \leq \overline{g}$ which defines the *constraint set*.

We consider thus the two dimensional subsystem:

$$z'(t) = bz^2(t) + \left(b - G\big(i(t)\big)\right) z(t) + \left(g_K^\star - G\big(i(t)\big)\right) \tag{7–33}$$
$$-u \leq g_K'(t) \leq u$$

with $\underline{g} \leq g_K \leq \overline{g}$ and $\underline{z} \leq z(t) \leq \overline{z}$.

One can show that for this type of control system, the viability kernel is limited by two trajectories starting on the respective intersection points of the equilibrium parabola and the constraint set defined by $\underline{g} \leq g^K \leq \overline{g}$ and $\underline{z} \leq z(t) \leq \overline{z}$ such that g_K increases or decreases maximally (u and $-u$ respectively).

The viability kernel is as follows for $i = 0.05$ (see Aubin, 1997, p. 56). It can be shown that the viability kernel size varies inversely with the level of the rate of interest (see Cartelier & Müllers, p. 13).

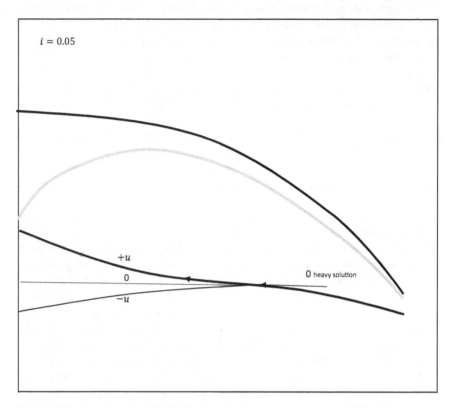

Figure 7.8 Viability kernel, the parabola curve and an example of heavy solution

As the viability approach radically differs from the usual dynamic analysis, it is worth commenting on these results a little bit.

The frontiers of the viability kernel show the extreme viability situations, from the point of view of involuntary indebtedness. The viability kernel is the set of all the rates of growth of capital, for which it makes sense to search for an appropriate regulation. The form of these frontiers is easy to interpret. Keeping in mind that the left part of the parabola is the locus of stable equilibria, it is understandable that the frontiers are downward sloping: it is *a priori* easier to keep the economy working in the constrained set (the whole figure) when its situation is in the left part than when it is in the right one: the size of the viability kernel is the graphic expression of that.

Keeping the rate of growth of capital constant (heavy solution) leads to the disappearance of the economy as indicated by the arrow. But it is not possible to find out a rule of regulation which would guarantee the sustainability of the economy. The economic conditions for the existence of such rules are difficult to establish even if mathematically speaking something may be said about it (see Aubin, Bayen & Saint-Pierre). This remark leads to considering somewhat critically the pretension of economists to confidently rely on some providential rules to dispense with discretionary interventions.

In the developments above we have considered that constrained operations are limited to additional loans covered by demand deposits held by wage-earners. A further step is possible by distinguishing two types of general squaring of accounts, one taking place without any intervention of the Mint, the other, just examined, with banks or a Central bank making sure that appropriate loans are effective.

The Mint may not intervene if wage-earners choose additional subscription to equities issued by firms to cover their deficit. In this case $\Delta D_W = 0$.

In order to deal with this case we need to add an equation to our model. Let be

$$D_W(t) = (1 - \mu i)(E_W(t)) \tag{7-34}$$

where $E_W(t)$ is, in this simple framework, the amount of debt equity of firms. The current increase of firms' debt is equal to the saving of wage-earners:

$$E_W'(t) = (1 - \alpha)sY(t) \tag{7-35}$$

Let's define $d \equiv \dfrac{D_W}{K}$; we have $d'(t) = \dfrac{D'K - K'D}{K^2} = \dfrac{D'}{K} - dg_K$; after some elementary manipulations we get:

$$d'(t) = (1 - \mu i(t))\frac{(1 - \alpha)s}{v} - (G\left[i(t) + \frac{\mu i'(t)}{1 - \mu i(t)}\right]d(t) + \mu d(t)z(t) \tag{7-36}$$

Condition $d'(t) = 0$ means a squaring of accounts without any intervention of the Mint. It is not without interest to combine equations (7–32) and (7–38) and to complete the study of the system.

Figure 7.9 below shows the locus of $z'(t) = 0$ and $d'(t) = 0$ in the (z,i) plane: Equilibrium e_1 is globally stable while e_2 is not. The curve shows the equilibrium locus without any intervention of the Mint. Below the curve firms are obliged to ask for constrained loans to the Mint, either to the banks or, if banks do not agree, to the central bank as a lender of last resort.

In the same way as above, it is possible to complete the analysis by resorting to viability method. It is possible to show how the viability kernel evolves for different levels of the rate of interest. High levels of the rate of interest reduce the size of the viability kernel, which means a higher instability and fragility of the economy (see Cartelier & Müllers, p. 12).

So far we have resorted only to a fraction of our framework. It would be desirable to broaden our analysis and to extend it to an economy where capitalists are eligible for the minting process on the same footing as entrepreneurs.

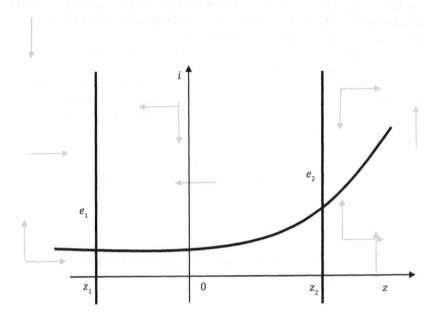

Figure 7.9 Locus z' = 0

This would be necessary in order to make intelligible the stylized facts typical of the last thirty years, namely the evolution of the financial ratios and the distribution of global profit between financial (capitalists) and non-financial (firms) agents.

We will not, however, try to do it, leaving this task to more skilled young colleagues. We will content ourselves with the main object of this essay: to plead for a revival of the monetary analysis as the best thing an economist can do in the particular intellectual context we experience today. Saying that such a position is not common among economists opposed to the mainstream is an understatement. Most of them search for a solution out of economics with the hope that other "social sciences" will welcome their strong dissent from economics. There is, however, an alternative. Since mainstream economics pervades most of our social representations, it would be better not to flee but to confront it on its proper ground. Bringing back the tradition of monetary analysis is what this essay proposes. Not only for the sake of economic theory itself but also because a monetary analysis allows conceiving an interesting and original relation of economics with other social disciplines. Far from being a new cloth for an imperialism of economics, reviving a monetary analysis may help us think anew about the way we consider our societies. A short conclusion is devoted to that perspective.

Appendix: Sraffa's system as a partial metaphor of monetary analysis[8]

Let's start from an observed economy as social accounting (FOF) allows doing it. Only current flows of payments from one account to another are to be seen. Some accounts are titled enterprises, others wage-earners and entrepreneurs under a common denomination of households. This is what social objectivity (by contrast with a so-called physical objectivity) is about.

The idea is to show that it is quite possible to derive from part of these data a Sraffian system of price determination exhibiting all the features of part I of *Production of Commodities by Means of Commodities* (PCMC hereafter), except rent. As a consequence the Sraffian system appears as it is, a partial metaphor of a monetary analysis. Partial is a way of saying not that Neoricardian value theory is parsimonious in the use of basic data but rather that such parsimony is regrettable since it prevents giving an account of out-of-equilibrium situations.

Consider an economy described by the flows of payment ($) observed during a given period. Whenever two quantities of $ are written in a cell, the first one comes from enterprises' accounts, the second one from entrepreneurs' accounts:

$$M_c = \begin{pmatrix} 0 & 50+30 & 40+60 & 120 & 300 \\ 30+50 & 0 & 50+30 & 240 & 400 \\ 50+30 & 30+50 & 0 & 40 & 200 \\ 140 & 240 & 20 & 400 & - \\ 300 & 400 & 200 & - & 900 \end{pmatrix}$$

Information brought up by that matrix is the following:

- There are three entrepreneurs and enterprises indexed 1, 2, and 3 the activity of which is respectively $300, $400 and $200 respectively.
- The rate of profit[9] is uniform over the economy: $r_1 = \frac{90}{90} = r_2 = \frac{80}{80} = r_3 = \frac{80}{80} = 1$.

The first step of the translation is to use only the first three rows and, in these rows, only the first three data, which gives:

$$M_S = \begin{pmatrix} 0 & 50 & 40 & 120 & 300 \\ 30 & 0 & 50 & 240 & 400 \\ 50 & 30 & 0 & 40 & 200 \end{pmatrix}$$

The second step is to introduce an assumption about physical commodities showing the specialization chosen by entrepreneurs:

1   → corn whose quantities are expressed in quarters (q)
2   → iron whose quantities are expressed in tons (t)
3   → petroleum whose quantities are expressed in barrels (b)

The third step is to interpret the quantities of $ as products of quantities of commodities by their prices in $ ($ per q, $ per t and $ per b):

$$
M_S = \begin{pmatrix}
0 & p_2 q_{21}^t & p_3 q_{31}^b & t_1 w_1 & p_1 q_1^q \\
 & 50 & 40 & 120 & 300 \\
p_1 q_{12}^q & 0 & p_3 q_{32}^b & t_2 w_2 & p_2 q_2^t \\
30 & & 50 & 240 & 400 \\
p_1 q_{13}^q & p_2 q_{23}^t & 0 & t_3 w_3 & p_3 q_3^b \\
50 & 30 & & 40 & 200
\end{pmatrix}
$$

with q_{ij}^g as the quantity of commodity i expressed in g used in order to produce q_j^h of commodity j expressed in h.

The fourth step is to change units in the following way: one Sraffa-unit of corn is $Srq = q_1^q$, one Sraffa-unit of iron is $Srt = q_2^t$ and one Sraffa-unit of petroleum is $Srb = q_3^b$, which is tantamount to taking produced quantities as physical units.

Quantities of waged labour are expressed in taking total labour as a unit, a procedure adopted by Ricardo. They are reckoned so: $l_1 = \frac{t_1 w_1}{W}$, $l_2 = \frac{t_2 w_2}{W} = \frac{3}{5}$ and $l_3 = \frac{t_3 w_3}{W} = \frac{1}{10}$ with $\Sigma l_i = 1$ and $\Sigma t_i w_i = W = 400$, which implies an average wage equal to $w = 400$.

The change of units allows doing the fifth step which consists in describing the technique used:

$$
\begin{pmatrix}
0 & a_{21}^t & a_{31}^b \\
 & \frac{1}{8} & \frac{1}{5} \\
a_{12}^q & 0 & a_{32}^b \\
\frac{1}{10} & & \frac{1}{4} \\
a_{13}^q & a_{23}^t & 0 \\
\frac{5}{30} & \frac{3}{40} &
\end{pmatrix}
\oplus
\begin{pmatrix}
l_1 \\ \frac{3}{10} \\ l_2 \\ \frac{3}{5} \\ l_3 \\ \frac{1}{10}
\end{pmatrix}
\Rightarrow
\begin{pmatrix}
1^q & 0 & 0 \\
0 & 1^t & 0 \\
0 & 0 & 1^b
\end{pmatrix}
$$

with a_{ij}^g as the quantity of commodity i expressed in Sraffa-units g necessary to produce one Sraffa-unit of commodity j.

The last step which completes the metaphor is to calculate the net income in view of normalizing the system. Net product S is:

$$
s' = \begin{pmatrix} 1^q - a_{12}^q - a_{13}^q & 1^t - a_{21}^t - a_{23}^t & 1^b - a_{13}^b - a_{31}^b \\ \left(\frac{11}{15}\right)^q & \left(\frac{4}{5}\right)^t & \left(\frac{11}{20}\right)^b \end{pmatrix}
$$

So that net income is $s'p = y$

Sraffa's system, with its normalization, is then:

$$(1+r)(\tfrac{1}{8}p_2 + \tfrac{1}{5}p_3) + \tfrac{3}{10}w = p_1$$
$$(1+r)(\tfrac{1}{10}p_1 + \tfrac{1}{4}p_3) + \tfrac{3}{5}w = p_2$$
$$(1+r)(\tfrac{5}{30}p_1 + \tfrac{3}{40}p_2) + \tfrac{1}{10}w = p_3$$
$$\tfrac{11}{15}p_1 + \tfrac{4}{5}p_2 + \tfrac{11}{20}p_3 = 1$$

Matrix M_S shows that net income in dollars is \$650, \$400 going to wages. Average wage w expressed in net income is $w = \frac{8}{13}$. Sraffa's system with $w = \frac{8}{13}$ gives: $r = 1.0$, $p_1 = 0.46154$, $p_2 = 0.61538$ and $p_3 = 0.30769$.

Adopting a dollar expression, with $y = 650$ and $w = 400$ gives $r = 1.0$, $p_1 = 300$ $p_2 = 400$ and $p_3 = 200$, *i.e.* those values which are immediately given by matrix M_C our starting point.

Notes

1 See J. P. Aubin (1997, p. 47)
2 Marx makes this point perfectly clear when he opposes C-M-C and M-C-M', even if his formula is not correct either.
3 Here is the origin of the so-called "transformation problem" which has produced more heat than light in Marxian economics. That question concerns not the origin of profit but the distinction between two types of economies.
4 Mainstream economists may say that there is no point here since, at full equilibrium, forward and backward evaluations are identical. But such situations are special cases in our economies and hence in our approach.
5 In Chapter 5 we have already introduced credit without making explicit the conditions for the existence of capital. We took for granted that even in a pure market economy interest exists as well as commercial capital. We reason now in an economy where a generalization of a wage relationship makes capital the common form of wealth.
6 These pages draw on Cartelier & Müllers (1994).
7 This does not mean we must renounce the very notion of a law of adjustment. We may hope to derive one from the study of the viability, which is far better than to postulate one beforehand. A more explicit formulation is given in Cartelier &Müllers.
8 A systematic presentation of translation of Sraffa equations into monetary approach is given in Benetti, Bidard, Klimovsky & Rebeyrol, (2012)] and Benetti, Klimovsky & Rebeyrol (2014)
9 Following Sraffa, wages are kept out of advanced capital.

Conclusion

Before putting an end to this essay a brief recapitulation of its main results is in order, at least for trying to convince the reader that it was worth writing it.

In the first part we have developed an *internal critique* of mainstream theories of money. We believe that a theory should not be criticized because its propositions seem unrealistic or seem methodologically ill-founded but mainly because they leave open a logical gap between what was intended and what is eventually obtained – it is the case when a theory of a market economy cannot account for what is unanimously considered as its main properties – market sanctions – or because they hold only in a too restricted domain. We have shown that the central notion of mainstream theory of money, fiat money, is more an obstacle than a help in dealing with the realization of desired transactions. In the same spirit, Kocherlakota's main assertion – money is memory – is valid only in a very extreme limit case (when the quantity of money is constant over time). In spite of its sophisticated models and of the cleverness of some of its tenets, the mainstream theory of money does not do the job its diverse authors have assigned to it. The micro-foundation of money theory emerges as an illusion and as a failure when it is examined from the point of view of mainstream theory itself. The roots of that failure are deep and not easy to identify.

Our working hypothesis is that these roots are nothing but the general spirit which pervades mainstream theory. This global attitude is analytically expressed by the fundamental postulates on which mainstream theory relies. Consequently we have searched for alternative postulates. At this point the basic opposition Schumpeter made in his *History of Economic Analysis* between Real and Monetary Analysis is very helpful. A rehabilitation of the old tradition of monetary analysis – historically prior to real analysis – could lead us out of the woods. This is what the second part of the essay is about.

Some advances of the present essay

Several points are to be mentioned.

Legal money

On the basis of three fundamental postulates (Chapter 4), the logical necessity of a "legal money" is demonstrated (Chapter 5, Proposition 2). We can prove the existence of what mainstream economists incorrectly think to have micro-founded – in fact they have presupposed it – "fiat money" as a non-privately produced intermediary of exchange. The by-product of the proof of existence of a legal money is a clear criterion for distinguishing "money" from "credit". Legal money is any concrete means of payment putting an end to a transaction in the market and leaving individuals free of any obligation to each other while credit is any means of payment keeping individuals in relation to each other until credit is settled by legal money. Note that this criterion is by no means an empirical but a theoretical one. This allows *hic et nunc* to deal with very various concrete situations. Many confusions are therefore avoided as the one regularly committed by monetarists and tenets of quantitative theory of money who aggregate several means of exchange to get a quantity M made of qualitatively different things, some being endogenous, others being assumed exogenous.

Out-of-equilibrium situations

Another important difference with real analysis is the ability of monetary analysis to study effective out-of-equilibrium situations. Common sense (and possibly mainstream economists when out of their models) attributes to the market the merits of sanctioning the "bad" economic decisions and rewarding the "good" ones. Such a reasonable intuition has no room in mainstream theory since equilibrium conditions are an ingredient of all the models and participate in the determination of the variables. Nothing out of equilibrium can be dealt with. "Bad" or "good" refer only to a ranking of equilibria according to welfare. A monetary analysis being grounded on a minting process (Chapter 4, definition 1) introduces a distinction between voluntary expenses (in mainstream terms: individual optimal decisions) and constrained operations (active) individuals do in order to avoid bankruptcy (no equivalent is to be found in the mainstream since some instantaneous and providential coordination device making decisions mutually compatible is supposed at work . . .). "Market sanctions" are at the centre of monetary analysis.

That a monetary analysis is capable of dealing with an *ex post* mode of coordination has two decisive advantages besides that one of giving a relevant description of what is going on in the market; this gives a sense to

- the difference between possession – a *de facto* observation – and property or ownership – a *de jure* consequence of market validation; some property rights in our societies have their origin in the working of the market, others not (a not uninteresting remark when relations between economics and other social disciplines – law, for instance – are about).

- an original and new method of dynamics: the viability approach; this mathematical tool is not yet much in use; of the two main reasons which make that method not common amongst economists, one will probably soon disappear (very demanding in calculation) and the other will hopefully be less present (economists' attachment to asymptotic properties of their models in relation with a more or less conscious philosophical stance which may be summed up by "social contract theory").

Involuntary unemployment equilibria and foundations for Keynes's economics

Finally, the most obvious advance in this essay is to have made clear the origin of Keynes's and Harrod's conjectures about the existence of involuntary unemployment equilibria (or steady-states) in a competitive economy with flexible prices and wages. In Chapter 6 we have explained why the current interpretations of that result as a consequence of an insufficient global demand are misleading. In spite of Keynes's insistence on his refusal of the "second Classical postulate" as a *necessary condition* of his conjecture, his followers and commentators have preferred to emphasize a too low level of demand, which is only an additional condition, relevant only when the first is met. ISLM and Clower's 1965 article reproduce Keynes's result but without showing what is at their root. In refusing the "second Classical postulate" Keynes denied that wage-earners may be treated on the same footing as entrepreneurs. Basically, Keynes's position is that equilibrium makes sense for the entrepreneurs only, not for the wage-earners. This is crystal-clear in the *Treatise* where profit is the sole income for which a "normal" level is defined (any deviation is the spring of dynamics); this is true also in *General Theory* where only the expenses of entrepreneurs give the move to the whole circuit. To put it in a nutshell, Keynes's and Harrod's conjectures rely on a radical difference in the status of entrepreneurs and wage-earners.

But that very difference is denied by mainstream economists who are ready to accept many asymmetries between entrepreneurs and wage-earners but only if they keep Walras's law valid. This is precisely what is at stake with the refusal of the "second Classical postulate", as we have shown in Chapter 6! Walras's law – the sum of the budgetary constraints over all the economy is identically zero – requires that all individuals had the same type of budgetary constraints. It is why a generalization of Clower 1965's argument to all agents, as done in fix-price models, fails to prove Keynes's conjecture. In our monetary analysis wage-earners are not eligible for the minting process; consequently they have a different budgetary constraint. The sum of all the budgetary constraints (wage-earners' included) gives now a Restricted Walras's law leaving the "market for labour" outside, to use mainstream terms. Nothing prevents involuntary unemployment from being effective. It will be the case when effective demand is less than a full-equilibrium level. When Full Walras's law prevails, a low level of effective demand brings about a disequilibrium in two markets at least: an excess-supply in the "labour market" and an excess-demand in the market for commodity. No involuntary unemployment equilibrium shows up! In the terms of our monetary analysis: wage-earners are not subject to constrained operations settling their accounts; the level of their expenses are just constrained by the level of entrepreneurs' activity. No market procedure may allow wage-earners to reveal a possible frustration. Unemployment benefits which follow a non-market logic may give information on it.

Not being aware of the source of Keynes's conjecture many followers and commentators, attached to treat entrepreneurs and wage-earners on a same footing, have attributed low-employment equilibria to rigidities of prices, wages or rates of interest. They have confused under-employment equilibria — which are not a surprising result for mainstream economists when rigidities are present! — and involuntary unemployment equilibria which have no room in the mainstream. That confusion has ideological and doctrinal consequences: in the former case it is sensible to plea for restoring a market free of any friction (a "more market" attitude) while in the second the market has to be supplemented by other means of regulation (a non-market attitude).

A more lucid concern about the theoretical foundations of Keynes's and Harrod's conjectures leads to stressing the strategic importance of a coherent theory of the wage relationship. In another essay (Cartelier, 2016) we have shown that neither mainstream nor Neoricardian theory account for the main "stylized fact" of the wage relationship, *i.e.* the monetary subordination inside the firms co-existing with an equal political status as citizen outside the firms. Neoricardians tend to treat wages "on the same footing as the fuel for the engines or the feed for the cattle" (Sraffa, p. 9) which means that wage-earners are some kind of machinery or slaves used in production non-susceptible to be citizens outside production. For mainstream economists the symmetric failure occurs: wage-earners are nothing but some kind of independent producers producing labour instead of producing corn or iron. By contrast a monetary analysis accounts for the "stylized fact" unravelling the difference between exchange and wage relationship by resorting to the different forms of money circulation which describe them.

In this sense we may claim that the three main aforementioned results exclusively belong to a monetary analysis. They are well-founded only in the framework shaped by our three postulates. Being aware of the strategic importance of the specific status of wage-earners and of Keynes's implicit monetary analysis may have prevented Keynesian and non-orthodox economists from leaving Keynes's economics to be reduced to a special case of mainstream economics, what is commonly admitted and taught in academic circles. But the prospects for a change of attitude are poor. Economists, be they orthodox or self-claimed heterodox, nowadays show little concern for theory, neither for a deep critique of the last advances of the mainstream nor for an alternative economic analysis. Empirical studies, econometrics and expertise are preferred to abstract thinking. In that context, non-orthodox economists have left the battlefield of economic theory for the exploration of other social disciplines, as sociology, psychology, history or anthropology. Another strategy is available. Ironically it relies on a narrow conception of economic relations – reduced to payments and debt settlements – but, as we try to show now, it opens a new type of relations between economics and other social disciplines.

Economics and the plurality of social disciplines: a suggested interpretation

In what follows we would like to explain why working along a monetary analysis may help to reevaluate the relations between economics and the "social sciences". Consider the example of "money" as a social fact.

It could be tempting to search for a general theory which would take seriously Mauss's idea that money is a *"fait social total"* (total social reality). In that direction a serious problem is to be overcome: which are the very precise questions to elucidate? It is not so easy to raise what may be called "good questions". A "good question" must satisfy two criteria: (a) relevance given the general scope of the theory and (b) the possibility of checking arguments and propositions for their consistency and internal logic. To take an example, "what is the essence of money?" is a "good question" only if its meaning is made precise and if the necessary set of assumptions is made explicit (one has at least to distinguish between what is taken for granted – postulates and hypotheses – and what is to be explained – propositions). Mainstream economic theory of money passes the second criterion well but not the first one. Note that it is because it satisfies the second that it is possible to show that it does not meet the first!

Many general theories of money are too loose to be able to pass the test so that it is difficult to evaluate their relevance. It is hard to see which precise common elements may account for the existence of money in societies as different as market and non-market ones. How is it possible to assess the relevance of such general statements as "money is debt", "money is power" or "money is an emanation of the state" when "debt", "power" and "State" are not well-defined or well-understood? If not, interesting as they may be, those statements cannot claim to be theories but only general intuitions or opinions.

If too general statements about money are not suitable for a test of relevance and consistency, empirical studies full of enumerations of observed means of payments and other data without reference to clear-cut notions are not very helpful either. An intermediate level of abstraction is not easy to define; it is even not sure that such a search would make sense.

A different attitude may be suggested. Instead of chasing for a right answer to "what is money?" it seems better to consider the social relations in which money enters. This amounts to inquiring into a set of social relations sharing a common characteristic, to be carried out by means of money. The question (hopefully a "good one") is whether the fact that money is the common medium of communication used in these relations may or may not be sufficient to consider them as belonging to a unique and well-defined social domain. In this essay we answer "yes"! The domain may be dubbed "economics". The delimitation of this field is the founding act of a monetary analysis, in the same manner that the idea that economic relations occur in a commodity-space is the founding act of a real analysis.

As money matters as the criterion of distinction between economic and non-economic relations, the connexion between economics and other fields is clearly conceived which cannot be the case with a real approach. In modern real analysis, *i.e.* mainstream theory, the distinction between economics and non-economics is not related to money, not to commodity-space either, but to rationality which has nothing to do with the most basic postulates. From the start we get a good signal: economics defined according to a monetary analysis is clearly distinct from other fields whereas this is not the case with mainstream. By an apparent paradox, a monetary analysis, self-contained as it is, meets most of the basic points made by non-economists such as Simmel or Luhmann on the subject. The whole story is, however, more complex as we shall see.

Money mediation as a self-referential system amongst others

Money is a name for the rules of the market game. As such money relations are autonomous and self-contained. No rationality foreign to the money mediation pervades them. But that feature paradoxically enough signs their incompleteness. Let us try to clarify this point.

Under the influence of mainstream economics – even for the uninitiated, which just goes to show how complete and overwhelming their influence really is – production and consumption activities are presented as having a finality external to themselves: personal utility and/or social happiness. They make sense for the society as a whole. Accordingly, although specific, economic activity like others (politics, family or religion) may be directly related to the whole of society. Its rationality is general and common to all activities. As a consequence it is legitimate to inquire into the efficiency of economic activity and to compare it to others (is it better to work or to enjoy family life? is market equilibrium socially optimal?). The so-called "imperialism of economic rationality" may find here some justification.

In contrast with mainstream economics, our alternative description of economic relations does not consider anything beyond them. No general category such as individual utility or collective welfare or human happiness is to be found here. Payments, which are the very substance of economic relations, are related to other payments and that is all. Payments are the cause of other payments and the outcome of all payments considered together is the individual's capacity to keep paying. Although it is possible to make commodities enter the picture and to speak about prices (to allow some comparison with mainstream economics for instance) it is by no means a necessity. Prices are nothing but the consequence of payments and no value theory is needed. The monetary analysis is self-sufficient. It supports itself without the help of any general concept or category. Such an observation has been made by Luhmann:

> An understanding of economy starting from payments as fundamental operations is capable of dealing with all basic concepts of economic theory – e.g. production, exchange, distribution, capital, labour – as derivatives.
>
> (Luhmann, 1984, p. 313)

In Luhmann's terms, the economic system, i.e. our payment matrix, is an *autopoietic* system. *Autopoiesis* refers to

> systems that reproduce all the elementary components out of which they arise by means of a network of these elements themselves and in this way distinguish themselves from an environment.
>
> (Luhmann, 1989, p. 143)

But why would such an apparently self-contained description of economics manifest a radical incompleteness? Why can the self-referential (autopoietic) system of payments not be the whole of society? Luhmann gives a simple and deep answer: the most characteristic feature of society is complexity. Complexity means here something precise and distinctive. By complex Luhmann denotes systems lacking the capacity to completely observe themselves, *i.e.* to be a unique self-referential system. As a consequence some kind of selectivity occurs which reduces complexity by the constitution of a diversity of systems less complex than their environment. These systems are plural but each of them is nevertheless self-referential. The mere fact that economic activity may take the form of an autopoietic system reveals the outstanding feature of modern society, its complexity. Luhmann names "ex-differenciation" (*Ausdifferenzierung*) the fact that society represents itself as a frictional co-existence of distinct autopoietic systems (law, payments, politics, religion, etc.). Partial systems (specially the economic one) play a preeminent role according to Luhmann.

> Partial autopoietic systems of society may exist, as is the case in economics. We presume that such systems gain some special pre-eminence in society precisely because their self-closure allows them to escape most influences from their social environment. Autopoiesis of such partial systems is related to the ex-differenciation of specific media of communication and relies on it.
>
> (Luhmann, 1984, p. 311)

For Luhmann, money is the medium of communication particular to economics and the basis for its autopoietic character.

Production and consumption activities do not form autonomous systems in every kind of society. When subsistence is the main incentive such activities are not considered as being specific. There is no reason to justify them in a special way, no need to express them by means of sophisticated mediations. Identifying their rationality is not a problem. When money is generalized, production and consumption require some justification and some rationalization. Resorting to that special medium is inexorably accompanied by a specialization of agents. The latter acquire an autonomy since the logic of their actions is not straightforward and immediate. Money supplies the necessary mediation. Payment is the social expression of these operations. But as such money is incomplete as compared with language. As Ganssmann ably remarks

> whereas language may be used to explain why it is used, even if it is a delicate task and if it implies some circularity, it is not possible to do so with money.
>
> (Ganssmann, 2001, p. 151)

The self-referential logic of the economic system reveals by itself its own incompleteness, as money does compared to language. In other words, the fact that economic activities are exclusively justified in economic terms signals their incompleteness. Simmel put that idea in a felicitous phrase:

> money (. . .) makes possible relationships between people but leaves them personally undisturbed.
>
> (Simmel, 1990, p. 303)

Although totally independent of Luhmann's thought, the alternative economic theory suggested above is very close to it.[1] Let us try some kind of comparison or translation between the two analyses. According to Luhmann three features characterize an autopoietic system: code, closure/openness and observation.

The code (binary) here is having access to the minting process/not having access to the minting process. The minting rule is in the monetary analysis what code is for Luhmann. Economic relations (*i.e.* a matrix of payments) concern only those people able to benefit from a transformation of wealth into payments near the Mint, *i.e.* people able to communicate.

Closure/openness finds an equivalent in the balances settlement which closes the period in determining individual wealth and opens the next period once the agents' solvency has been checked, a necessary condition for people to belong to the payment network. Here is a straightforward application of Luhmann's principle:

> conditions of reproduction are taken from the code of the medium itself.
>
> (Luhmann, 1984, p. 320)

Closure/openness has something to do also with the possible relations between different systems. The point is whether an operation realized by means of a given code may or may not have some meaning according to another code. The fact that some payments may have a special meaning in politics (taxes, bribes, etc.) does not affect in principle the rules of the payment system. This does not mean it is not relevant to inquire into the political signification of payments but rather that such an inquiry is interesting only if the logics ruling the different systems are made explicit. In short, a phrase like "money is power" is deprived of any precise signification unless economics and politics are represented as two distinct autopoietic systems.[2]

Observation is the most difficult point. Eva Knodt, in her introduction to *Social Systems* (Luhmann, 1995), sums it up:

> Whatever is observed is observed by an observer who cuts up reality in a certain way in order to make it observable.

The possibility of observation is part of what is observed. The question is not so much

> how a system may reproduce itself without an environment?' than the following: 'what type of operation may allow a system to become a self-reproducing system resorting only to self-generated information and to become able to distinguish its internal needs from what are perceived as environmental problems.
>
> (Luhmann, 1995, p. 75)

In our alternative analysis, accounting or payment registration is the device by which economic reality is observed and attested. Accounts are periodically settled and closed; members of the system are publicly informed about their individual wealth. The economic reality is in that sense a pure product of accounting. As such, it is part of the self-referential system. Accounting has a performative property. Of course, the environment, what is outside the economic system, may be more or less strongly influenced by that self-observation. But it seems important to emphasize the radical break between what a system of accounts reveals and its external effects. The platitude about the gap between "the logic of profit" and "the human and social values" is symptomatic of that break. It clearly shows (a) that there is a system of observation capable of working without any reference external to it, (b) that another system of observation may deliver different points of view and (c) that no meta-system exists which may encompass and conciliate the two. As Luhmann once wrote:

> The distinction between self- and external reference necessarily is an internal one.
>
> (Luhmann, 1995, p. 76)

"Economic reality" is nothing but what a self-referential system of payments allows us to observe. This holds true not because payments would give an image of something real existing independently of it (the economy?) but, on the contrary, because there is nothing economic except payments. Or, to be less provocative, because payments and accounting rules determine the outcomes of the game and because, quite obviously, people participating in the game are essentially interested in its result. Being profitable or solvent matters, being socially benevolent or being clever does not. A comparison may help. It is sometimes said about a football match that "the score does not reflect what happened in the field". It is nevertheless the score which determines the winner and the loser. It is the score alone which matters according to the rules of football. The possible pleasure of players and spectators is meaningless from this point of view. The very "substance of the match" is put aside, "undisturbed" just as individual persons are in money relations, according to Simmel.

Self-referential systems and complexity

Economic reality is sometimes at stake when people contest its possible external consequences: underemployment, environmental problems, negative moral consequences such as greed or envy, etc. Some people strive to resist it in the name of other realities or other values (solidarity, universality, etc.). Other people perceive it as the true social reality and deny the importance of other considerations (economic growth first). Here is obviously a major philosophical and social problem. Clearly, repeated invocations to make economic relations subject to superior values are as much protestations against an alienation to economics as the very sign of a monetary autopoiesis. They denote less a variable combination between sub-systems à la Parsons than the complexity of our society (à la Luhmann) responsible for problems whose solutions require compromises and new objects à la Boltanski & Thévenot (1991).

If complexity is the essential feature of modern society, a plurality of specific social sciences (law, management, economics, politics, etc.) does not come as a surprise. It is a necessary feature of a society whose members cannot perceive it but as a frictional coexistence of self-referential systems. A multiplicity of (scientific) points of view is not contingent. Some social scientists regret it as being an obstacle to a clear vision of society. What may be an obstacle is rather refusing to admit that the plurality of social sciences is part of the object to be studied. A unique and general social science is probably a utopia. It would misapprehend its object. The plurality of disciplines is thus an inescapable state of affairs. We must work with it rather than against it. But neither can we content ourselves with the present state of the so-called "social sciences" nor with that of "economics". Is not the very idea of "social sciences" a little puzzling? Is not the belief in a possible scientific knowledge of our society a very characteristic of our society, unheard of in others? If so, complexity would be an interesting concept to understand. A founding myth of our society is that it stands by itself as the result of an agreement between free individuals (social contract) looking for their own interest (utility, security, etc.). For each of us, our society is an autonomous and objective entity as external as Nature. A scientific and objective knowledge is thus possible. Discovering the objective laws ruling its working and evolution would allow us to master it. Social sciences derive from and enforce the myth of autonomy of modern society.

A critique of social sciences in general and of economics in particular should probably be the first step in any attempt to understand what kind of society we are living in. Each of these so-called "social sciences" has to be scrutinized and questioned, especially economics due to its particular nature.

On the scale of what needs to be done, the strategy suggested in this essay may seem ridiculously modest but at the same time, fairly realistic. It may be considered modest because it explicitly limits its domain of validity to economics, taking for granted its self-referential character, and realistic because it takes in account that such a restriction is part of the object it is trying to elucidate. The complexity of our society, in the sense intended by Luhmann, casts some doubt over our capacity to attain the objectives traditionally assigned to the social sciences. But at the same time it supplies some reasons to embark upon a critique of them, long after Marx.

Notes

1 The tradition of the monetary approach is as old as political economy. The modern version we have suggested (with Carlo Benetti) in 1980 owes nothing to Luhmann (we had not yet encountered any of his works at that time). The convergence comes for us as a surprise and as an interesting signal.
2 Smith's critique to Hobbes's "Wealth is Power" in the *Wealth of Nations* may be understood along this line of reasoning.

References

Aglietta, Michel & Orléan, André, (1982), *La violence de la monnaie*, PUF, Paris.

Aglietta, Michel & Orléan, André, (2002), *La monnaie entre violence et confiance*, Odile Jacob, Paris.

Amir, R., Sahi, S., Shubik, M. & Yao, S., (1987), "A Strategic Market Game with Complete Markets", in *CFDP 813R, Cowles Foundation*, Yale University Press, New Haven, CT.

Araujo, Luis & Camargo, Braz, (2015), "Limited Monitoring and the Essentiality of Money", *Journal of Mathematical Economics*, 58, May, 32–37.

Araujo, Luis & Guimaraes, Bernardo, (2014), "Coordination in the Use of Money", *Journal of Monetary Economics*, 64, May, 38–47.

Aubin, Jean-Pierre, (1997), *Dynamic Economic Theory: A Viability Approach*, Springer Verlag, Berlin.

Aubin, Jean-Pierre, Bayen, Alexandre & Saint-Pierre, Patrick, (2011), *Viability Theory, New Directions*, Springer, Heidelberg.

Aydinonat, Emrah, (2011), "Explaining the Origin of Money, Interdisciplinary Perspectives", in *New Approaches to Monetary Theory*, edited by H. Ganssmann, Routledge, London, pp. 46–66.

Benetti, Carlo, (1985), "Economie monétaire et économie de troc: la question de l'unité de compte commune", *Economie appliquée*, 1.

Benetti, Carlo, (1996), "The Ambiguity of the Notion of General Equilibrium with a Zero-Price for Money", in *Money in Motion*, edited by G. Deleplace & E. Nell, MacMillan, London, pp. 365–376.

Benetti, Carlo, Bidard, Christian, Klimovsky, Edith & Rebeyrol, Antoine, (2012), "Reproduction and Temporary Disequilibrium: A Classical Approach", *Metroeconomica*, 63 (4), 614–633.

Benetti, Carlo & Cartelier, Jean, (1980), *Marchands, salariat et capitalistes*, Maspéro, Paris, p. 207.

Benetti, Carlo & Cartelier, Jean, (1987), "Monnaie, valeur et propriété privée", *Revue économique*, 38 (6), 1157–1170.

Benetti, Carlo & Cartelier, Jean, (1999), "Market and Division of Labour: A Critical Reformulation of Marx's View", *Rivista di Politica Economica*, April–May, 119–139.

Benetti, Carlo & Cartelier, Jean, (2001), "Money and Price Theory", *International Journal of Applied Economics and Econometrics*, 9 (2), 203–223.

Benetti, Carlo, Klimovsky, Edith & Rebeyrol, Antoine, (2014), "Monetary and Physical Observable Magnitudes in Sraffa's System", mimeo.

Bezemer, Dirk, (2009), "Banks as Social Accountants: Credit and Crisis through an Accounting Lens", *MPRA Paper No. 15766* (http://mpra.ub.uni-muenchen.de/15766/).

Binmore, Ken, (2005), *Natural Justice*, Oxford University Press, Oxford.

Boltanski, Luc & Thévenot, Laurent, (1991), *De la justification*, Gallimard, Paris.

Bridel, Pascal, (1997), *Money and General Equilibrium Theory*, Edward Elgar, Cheltenham.

Cantillon, Richard, [1755], (1955), *Essai sur la nature du commerce en général*, INED, Paris.

Cartelier, Jean, (1991) "Marx's theory of value, exchange and surplus value: a suggested interpretation", *Cambridge Journal of Economics*, 15 (3), 257–270.

Cartelier, Jean, (1996), "Chômage involontaire d'équilibre et asymétrie entre salariés et non-salariés", *Revue économique*, 47 (3), 655–665.

Cartelier, Jean, (2004), "Budgetary Constraints, Stocks and Flows in a Monetary Economy: Keynes's Economics Once More", in *Money, Credit and the Role of the State*, edited by R. Arena, Asgate, Aldershot.

Cartelier, Jean, (2007a), "The Hypostasis of Money: An Economic Point of View", *Cambridge Journal of Economics*, 31 (2), 217–233.

Cartelier, Jean, (2007b), "Money and Markets as Twin Concepts?", in *Money and Markets, a Doctrinal Approach*, edited by A. Giacomin & M. C. Marcuzzo, Routledge, Abingdon, UK, pp. 79–95.

Cartelier, Jean, (2010), "Money Is the Scribe of a Market Economy", in *Money and Calculation*, edited by M. Amato, L. Doria & L. Fantacci, Palgrave Macmillan, pp. 16–33.

Cartelier, Jean, (2011), "Money and Sovereignty, a Comparison between Hobbes and Modern Money Theory", in *New Approaches to Monetary Economics and Theory*, edited by H. Ganssmann, Routledge, London.

Cartelier, Jean, (2014a), "Endogenous Money in an Elementary Search Model: Intrinsic Properties versus Bootstrap", in *Economics and Other Branches: In the Shade of the Oak Tree*, edited by R. Baranzini & F. Allisson, Pickering & Chatoo.

Cartelier, Jean, (2014b), "The Positive Surplus Hypothesis: Social versus Physical Objectivity", in *Towards a New Understanding of Sraffa: Insights from Archival Research*, edited by R. Bellofiore & S. Carter, MacMillan.

Cartelier, Jean, (2016), *L'intrus et l'absent, Essai sur le travail et le salariat dans la théorie économique*, Presses de l'Université Paris-Ouest.

Cartelier, Jean & Müllers, Katarina, (1994), "Viability in a Keynesian Model: A Preliminary Approach", *IIASA Working Papers*.

Cartelier, Jean & Saint-Pierre, Patrick, (2012), "A Viability Model for a Monetary Economy", *Communication to the Conference "Around Viability Boundaries"*, December 12–14, Paris, UPMC, Marie Curie Actions & C&O.

Caverzasi, Eugenio & Godin, Antoine, (2013), "Stock-Flow Consistent Modeling through the Ages", *University of Pavia, Pavia, Working Paper No. 745*.

Clower, Robert W., [1965], (1984), "The Keynesian Counter-Revolution: A Theoretical Appraisal", reprint in *Money and Markets, Essays by Robert Clower*, edited by D. A. Walker, Cambridge University Press, Cambridge.

Clower, Robert W., [1967], (1984), "A Reconsideration of the Micro-Foundations of Monetary Theory", reprint in *Money and Markets, Essays by Robert W. Clower*, edited by D. A. Walker, Cambridge University Press, Cambridge.

Cohen, J., (1972), "Copeland's Moneyflows after Twenty-Five Years: A Survey", *Journal of Economic Literature*, 10 (1), 1–25.

Copeland, M. A., (1949), "Social Accounting for Moneyflows", *The Accounting Review*, 24 (3), 254–264.

Debreu, Gérard, (1959), *Theory of Value: An Axiomatic Analysis of Economic Equilibrium*, Cowles Foundation, monograph 17, Yale University Press, New Haven, CT.

Debreu, Gérard, (1974), "Excess Demand Functions", *Journal of Mathematical Economics*, 1, 15–21.

Deleplace, Ghislain, (1996), "Does Circulation Need a Monetary Standard", in *Money in Motion: The Post Keynesian and Circulation Approaches*, edited by G. Deleplace & E. Nell, MacMillan, London, pp. 305–329.

Deleplace, Ghislain, (2017), *Ricardo on Money: A Reappraisal*, Routledge, Abingdon, UK, p. 417.

Drèze, Jacques & Polemarchakis, Herakles, (2000), *Monetary Equilibria*, CORE, Louvain-la_Neuve.

Gale, Douglas, (1982), *Money: In Equilibrium*, Cambridge University Press, Cambridge.

Ganssmann, Heiner, (2001), "La monnaie comme fait social", *Sciences de la Société*, (52), 137–157.

Geneakoplos, John, (1987), "Overlapping Generations Model of General Equilibrium", in *The New Palgrave*, edited by J. Eatwell, M. Milgate & P. Newman, MacMillan.

Glustoff, Errol, (1968), "On the Existence of a Keynesian Equilibrium", *Review of Economic Studies*, 327–334.

Godley & Lavoie, Marc, (2007), *Monetary Economics: An Integrated Approach to Credit, Money, Income, Production and Wealth*, Palgrave Macmillan, p. 530.

Graeber, David, (2011), *Debt, the First 5000 Years*, Melville House, London.

Grandmont, Jean-Michel, (1983), *Money and Value*, Cambridge University Press, Cambridge.

Gurley & Shaw, (1960), *Money in a Theory of Finance*, Brookings Institution, p. 385.

Hahn, Frank, (1965), "On Some Problems of Proving the Existence of an Equilibrium in a Monetary Economy", in *Monetary Theory*, edited by R. W. Clower, Penguin Modern Economics, 1969.

Hahn, Frank. (1971), "Equilibrium with Transaction Costs", *Econometrica*, 39, 417–439.

Hawtrey, Reginald G., (1919), *Currency and Credit*, Longmans, Green and Co, London, p. 393.

Hayek, Friedrich, [1931], (1967), *Prices and Production*, Augustus Kelley.

Hellwig, Martin, (1993), "The Challenge of Monetary Theory", *European Economic Review*, 37, 215–242.

Hicks, John, (1937), "Mr. Keynes and the 'Classics' a Suggested Interpretation", *Econometrica*, 5 (2).

Hume, David, (1970), "Of Money", in *Writings on Economics*, edited by E. Rotwein, The University of Wisconsin Press, Madison.

Iwai, Katsuhito, (1988), "The Evolution of Money: A Search-Theoretic Foundation of Monetary Economics", *University of Pennsylvania CARESS Working Paper No. 88–03*.

Jacob, C., (1972), "Copeland's Moneyflows after Twenty-Five Years: A Survey", *Journal of Economic Literature*, 10 (1), 1–25.

Jacques, Jean-François & Rebeyrol, Antoine, (2009), "Primitive Accumulation, Growth and the Genesis of Social Classes", *Metroeconomica*, 2.

Jones, R. A., (1976), "The Origin and Development of Media of Exchange", *Journal of Political Economy*, 84, 757–775.

Keynes, John Maynard, [1930], (1973), "A Treatise on Money", in *The Collected Writings of John Maynard Keynes*, (volumes 5, and 6), MacMillan, St Martin Press.

Keynes, John Maynard, [1936], (1973), "The General Theory of Employment, Interest and Money", in *The Collected Writings of John Maynard Keynes*, (volume 7), MacMillan, St Martin Press.

Kiyotaki, Nobuhiro & Wright, Randall, (1993), "A Search-Theoretic Approach to Monetary Economics", *The American Review*, 83 (1), 63–77.

Kocherlakota, Narayama R., (1998), "Money Is Memory", *Journal of Economic Theory*, 81, 232–251.

Kocherlakota, Narayama R. & Wallace, Neil, (1998), "Incomplete Record-Keeping and Optimal Payment Arrangements", *Journal of Economic Theory*, 81, 272–289.

Lagos, R. & Wright, R., (2005), "A Unified Framework for Monetary Theory and Policy Analysis", *Journal of Political Economy*, 113, 463–484.

Lakomski-Laguerre, Odile, (2002), *Les institutions monétaires du capitalisme*, L'Harmattan, Paris, p. 365.

Lavoie, Marc, (2014), *Post-Keynesian Economics: New Foundations*, Elgar, Cheltenham.

Law, John, (1934), "Money and Trade in Oeuvres complètes", ed. by P. Harsin, (3 vol.), Sirey, Paris, [1705].

Luhmann, Niklas, (1984), "Die Wirtschaft der Gesellschaft als autopoietisches System", *Zeitschrift für Soziologie*, 13 (4), Oktober, 308–327.

Luhmann, Niklas, (1989), *Ecological Communication*, University of Chicago Press, Chicago.

Luhmann, Niklas, (1995), *Social Systems*, Stanford University Press, Stanford.

Mantel, R., (1974), "Homothetic Preferences and Community Excess Demand Functions", *Journal of Economic Theory*, 7, 197–201.

Marx, Karl, [1867], (1976), *Capital*, Penguin Books, London.

Matsuyama, Kiminori, (2006), "The Lawrence R. Klein Lecture: Emergent Class Structure", *International Economic Review*, 47 (2), 327–360.

Mehrling, Perry, (2011), *The New Lombard Street, How the Fed Became the Dealer of Last Resort*, Princeton University Press, Princeton, NJ, p. 174.

Menger, Carl, (1892), "On the Origin of Money", *Economic Journal*, 2, reprint in (R. M. Starr ed.), *General Equilibrium Models of Monetary Economies*, Academic Press, 1989.

Morishima, Michio, (1992), *Capital & Credit*, Cambridge University Press, Cambridge.

Mun, Thomas, [1664], (1895), *England's Treasure by Forraign Trade*, MacMillan and Co, New York.

Niehans, Jürgen, (1978), *The Theory of Money*, John Hopkins University Press, Baltimore.

North, Dudley, [1691], (1907), *Discourses upon Trade: Principally Directed to the Cases of the Interest, Coinage, Clipping, Increase of Money*, J. Hollander, Baltimore.

Oresme, Nicolas, (1990), *Traité monétaire, Treatise on money (1355)*, Édition trilingue juxtaposée Latinus-Français-English, Editions Cujas, Paris.

Ostroy, J. M. & Starr, R. M., (1974), "Money and the Decentralization of Exchange", *Econometrica*, 42 (6), 1093–1113, reprint in *General Equilibrium Models of Monetary Economies*, edited by R. M. Starr, Academic Press, London, 1989, pp. 131–169.

Patinkin, Don, (1965), *Money, Interest and Prices*, (2nd edition), MIT Press, Cambridge, MA, p. 640.

Patinkin, Don, (1987), "Walras's Law", in *General Equilibrium: The New Palgrave*, edited by J. Eatwell, M. Milgate & P. Newman, MacMillan.

Piccione, Michele & Rubinstein, Ariel, (2007), "Equilibrium in the Jungle", *Economic Journal*, 117, July, 883–896.

Rebeyrol, Antoine, (1999), *La pensée économique de Walras*, Dunod, Paris.

Rupert, Peter, Schindler, Martin, Shevchenko, Andreï & Wright, Randall, (2000), "The Search-Theoretic Approach to Monetary Economics: A Primer", *Economic Review*, 36 (4), 10–28.

Saari, D. & Simon, C., (1978), "Effective Price Mechanisms", *Econometrica*, 53, 1117–1131.

Sahi, S. & Yao, S., (1989), "The Non-Cooperative Equilibria of a Trading Economy with Complete Markets and Consistent Prices", *Journal of Mathematical Economics*, 18, 325–346.

Schumpeter, Joseph A., (1954), *History of Economic Analysis*, edited from manuscript by E. B. Schumpeter, Oxford University Press, New York.

Schumpeter, Joseph A., (1970), *Das Wesen des Geldes*, edited and introduction by F. K. Mann, Vandenhoeck & Ruprecht, Goettingen.

Seabright, Paul, (2006), "The Evolution of Fairness Norms: An Essay on Ken Binmore's Natural Justice", *Politics, Philosophy & Economics*, 2 (5–1), 33–50.

Shapley, L. S. & Shubik, M., (1977), "Trade Using One Commodity as a Means of Payment", *Journal of Political Economy*, 85, 937–968.

Shi, Shouyong, (2006), "Viewpoint: A Micro-Foundation of Monetary Economics", *Canadian Journal of Economics*, 39 (3), 643–688.

Simmel, Georg, [1907], (1990), *The Philosophy of Money*, (2nd edition), Routledge, London.

Smith, Adam, [1776], (1996), *An Inquiry into the Nature and Causes of the Wealth of Nations: The Glasgow Edition of the Works and Correspondence of Adam Smith*, (volumes 1 and 2), Clarendon Press, Oxford.

Sonnenschein, Hugo, (1972), "Market Excess Demand Functions", *Econometrica*, 40, 549–563.

Sorin, Sylvain, (1996), "Strategic Market Games with Exchange Rates", *Journal of Economic Theory*, 69, 431–446.

Starr, Ross, (2011), *General Equilibrium Theory: An Introduction*, Cambridge University Press, Cambridge.

Steuart, James, [1767], (2015), *An Inquiry into the Principles of Political Economy*, (2 volumes), Liguori Editore, Napoli.

Trejos, A. & Wright, Randall, (1995), "Search, Bargaining, Money and Prices", *Journal of Political Economy*, 103, 118–141.

Tsiang, S. C., (1966), "Walras' Law, Say's Law, and Liquidity Preference in General Equilibrium Analysis", *International Economic Review*, 7, 329–345, reprint in *Finance Constraints and the Theory of Money*, edited by M. Kohn, pp. 133–151.

Ulgen, Faruk, (ed.) (1996), *New Contributions to Monetary Analysis, the Foundations of an Alternative Economic Paradigm*, Routledge, Abingdon Oxon, p. 259.

Veendorp, (1970), "General Equilibrium Theory for a Barter Economy", *Western Economic Journal*, 8, March, 1–23.

Wallace, Neil, (2001), "Whither Monetary Economics?", *International Economic Review*, 42 (4), 847–869.

Walras, Léon, [1874], (1988), *Eléments d'économie politique pure, Oeuvres économiques complètes d'Auguste et Léon Walras*, (volume 8), Economica, Paris.

Werner, Richard, (2014), "How Do Banks Create Money, and Why Can Other Firms Not Do the Same? An Explanation for the Coexistence of Lending and Deposit-Taking", *International Review of Financial Analysis*, 36, 71–77.

Wicksell, Knut, (1935), *Lectures on Political Economy*, (2 volumes), George Routledge, London.

Williamson, Steve & Wright, Randall, (1994), "Barter and Monetary Exchange under Private Information", *American Economic Review*, 84, 104–123.

Index

Page numbers in *italic* indicate a figure and page numbers in **bold** indicate a table on the corresponding page.